Thomas Collyns Simon

The Mission and Martyrdom of St. Peter

Did St. Peter ever leave the East?

Thomas Collyns Simon

The Mission and Martyrdom of St. Peter
Did St. Peter ever leave the East?

ISBN/EAN: 9783741166327

Manufactured in Europe, USA, Canada, Australia, Japa

Cover: Foto ©Andreas Hilbeck / pixelio.de

Manufactured and distributed by brebook publishing software (www.brebook.com)

Thomas Collyns Simon

The Mission and Martyrdom of St. Peter

THE

MISSION AND MARTYRDOM

OF

ST. PETER:

OR,

DID ST. PETER EVER LEAVE THE EAST?

"They (the alleged passages) speak for themselves in a way which *those who are sincere* in their inquiries after religious truth cannot possibly mistake; *those who are not sincere*, it would be hopeless to attempt to convince."

FATHER McCORRY (*in his Tract upon this subject*, p. 11).

THE

MISSION AND MARTYRDOM OF ST. PETER:

OR,

DID ST. PETER EVER LEAVE THE EAST?

CONTAINING

THE ORIGINAL TEXT OF ALL THE PASSAGES IN ANCIENT
WRITERS SUPPOSED TO IMPLY A JOURNEY
INTO EUROPE,

WITH

Translations and Roman-catholic Comments;

SHOWING

THAT THERE IS NOT THE LEAST SIGN IN ANTIQUITY OF THE ALLEGED FACT,
NOR EVEN OF THERE HAVING BEEN A TRADITION TO THAT EFFECT.

SECOND EDITION, WITH CORRECTIONS AND ADDITIONS.

BY

THOMAS COLLYNS SIMON,

AUTHOR OF "THE NATURE AND ELEMENTS OF THE EXTERNAL WORLD,"
"SCIENTIFIC CERTAINTIES IN PLANETARY LIFE," "ANSWER TO ESSAYS AND REVIEWS,"
ETC. ETC.

LONDON:
RIVINGTONS, WATERLOO PLACE.
MDCCCLXII.

LONDON:
SAVILL AND EDWARDS, PRINTERS, CHANDOS STREET,
COVENT GARDEN.

PREFACE

TO THE SECOND EDITION.

During the controversy publicly carried on by Cardinal Wiseman in 1850-1, as to the Pagan inscription believed to exist concealed on the chair in which St. Peter is said to have sat, and which is now to be seen in St. Peter's church at Rome, I sent the following letter to the *Times*, which was immediately inserted:—

"To the Editor of the Times.

"Sir,—You are far from being mistaken when you say, in your leading article of Friday last, that we have no reasonable historical proof of Peter's having ever been at Rome at all, and you will render signal service to truth and to that great question now pending between Englishmen and Rome, if you invite Dr. Wiseman to state in your columns what evidence he has to produce upon this point. He will hardly, I think, make use even of Hegesippus for this purpose; but whether he does or not, I challenge him to analysis before the British public of whatever evidence he may think proper to adduce upon this, which he admits to be 'a vital and important point' of the Romish Faith. In this matter also, however, it is but too probable that he will refuse to take the cover off the chair.

"I am, Sir,
          "Your obedient Servant,
"Jan. 11th, 1851."   "Historicus.

A few days afterwards that letter appeared in the *Times*, to which so much prominence is here given, signed "*Truth*," and with indications sufficient to satisfy any one acquainted with Dr. Wiseman's writings, that this letter was written by him. (See copy, p. 302.) No scholar was deceived by its assertions. The utter worthlessness of almost every testimony therein adduced had been fully shown in my letter to the Editor of the *Times*, inserted a week or two previously in reply to Bishop Pearson's collection of testimonies, which a correspondent of that Journal had put forward as conclusive. But as many of those who take an interest in this question are unacquainted with the documents and passages referred to on these occasions, the present work was then written, in order to enable every person for himself to sift the merits of all such statements as those contained in Dr. Wiseman's letter.

No Roman Catholic has disputed anything contained in this work since it first appeared nine years ago. Any such objection should have had, and shall always have, my best attention.

The errors now corrected were wholly unconnected with the argument. They were against myself only, and, however purely accidental, cannot, I fear, fail to have misled some of my readers as to the amount of information and care employed in the production of the work.

The additions consist mainly of a Synoptical Table of Contents, and of some notes to illustrate my own opinion now given respecting the sense of the "pergit" and the "mittitur" in the statement that Jerome attributes to Eusebius about "The Fiery Chariot" in the 2nd year of Claudius.

It is evident that whether the Second Epistle of Peter be held authentic or not, the argument here drawn from it is of equal force; for in the one case we have Peter's own statement as to where his death was likely to take place; in the other the general belief of the early Church as to where it really had taken place.

I may be permitted here again to remind the Roman Catholics of this country that Baratier, the German lad whose Collection of testimony Cardinal Wiseman urges so strongly upon their attention as well as upon ours, wrote this college exercise in Latin when he was but 16 or 17 years old, dying at 19. The Cardinal calls him a divine, and acknowledges that his collection contains all the proof that the subject admits of. It only differs, however, from other similar documents, in asserting everything with extraordinary vehemence, and in adducing every testimony on the subject—ten in number—which the Roman Catholics themselves acknowledge to be spurious;—so much so, that, as I have elsewhere said, the reader will see much reason to suspect that the publication was intended as a jest (see pp. 51, 53, 59, 79, 120, of this work), and will not be unlikely to ask why the Roman Catholics of this country should be dealt with as a more ignorant people than those of Spain, France, Austria, or Italy.

From the following pages, it will be seen that all that

this writer, or any educated Roman Catholic, tries now-a-days to make out, is that the isolated conjecture of Eusebius nearly 300 years after the event, to the effect that the martyrdom might not have taken place at Babylon as the skeleton had just been found at Rome, was really not a conjecture of Eusebius, although he thus expresses it, but an historical fact universally attested.

This point, the Roman Catholic divines tell us, is the real question upon the solution of which our sole hope of pleasing God depends. This point, every statesman must see, may sooner or later be found to be one of vast political importance.

T. C. S.

The following *Errata*, and perhaps a few others, still remain:—

Page 20, line 22, *for* συνειρασιτι, *read* συνειρασατι.
„ 55, „ 14, *for* he states, *read* it is stated.
„ 71, „ 12, *for* . The, *read* ; the.
„ 96, „ 3, *for* memoriæ, *read* memoria.
„ 118, „ 33, *for* beoome, *read* became.
„ 149, „ 9, *for* ποκεν *read* ποκεν, .
„ 198, „ 14, *for* additions, *read* editions.
„ 248, „ 15, *for* on, *read* no.

CONTENTS.

	PAGE
INTRODUCTION, 1—18.	
The object in publishing this investigation	1
The statement in question first alleged as a fact by the Church of Rome at the Reformation	5
Method of this work	6
Eighteen causes why the statement was supposed true	7
Many enlightened Roman Catholics acknowledged its groundlessness from the first	9
Charles de Moulin	10
Father Leland (see also 189)	ib.
Marsile de Padua (see also 189)	ib.
Father Caron (see also 188)	11
Father Hardouin (see also 188)	ib.
All who withdrew from the Church of Rome acknowledged the story to be groundless	12
Bower	ib.
Scaliger	13
Calvin	ib.
All Protestant scholars (except Bishop Pearson) report its groundlessness	14
Adam Clarke	ib.
Dr. Kitto	14
Baronius first endeavours to prove the story (see also 291).	ib.
Bellarmine (see also 293)	15
Father Feuardent (see also 296)	ib.
Henry de Valois (Valesius—see also 297)	ib.
Bishop Pearson (see also 207)	ib.
The Lactantian MS. of 1678 (see also 173, &c.)	16
The young Baratier (see also 300)	16
Cardinal Wiseman (the Correspondent in the *Times* of Jan. 16, 1851; see also 302)	17

CONTENTS.

	PAGE
Father M'Corry, likewise in 1851 (see also 306)	
Former works showing the fallacy of the notion have defeated their own object	17

THE ORIGINAL TEXT OF ALL THE ALLEGED TESTIMONIES ARRANGED IN CHRONOLOGICAL ORDER 19-28

PART I.—ALLEGED ANTENICENE RECORDS.
First Century.

The Book called "Peter's Proclamation" (nothing on the subject)	29
Mentioned by Clement of Alexandria, Origen, Lactantius and Eusebius (see also 135, 160)	ib.
Linus (spurious writings)	31
Anacletus, (ditto)	32
Clemens Romanus (Peter's death at Babylon)	33
(This Clemens came to Rome from Asia, where he had been a long time with Peter, and where he probably remained till after the latter's death at Babylon: see p. 55.)	
Where Paul's death and Peter's are mentioned together, only Paul's is ever said to have occurred in Europe, the locality of Peter's being known from Scripture (see also 115, 149)	34
Our Lord's indication of Peter's crucifixion with his head downwards	36
Our Lord's indication of the Jews as Peter's persecutors	37
Our Lord's indication of Babylon as Peter's place of residence (see also 179)	38
Babylon wholly dependent on the Roman Government at the time of Peter's death there	39
The two great political factions then at Babylon	40
Nero's persecution of the Christian Church at Babylon	42
Babylon's population then nearly half a million, and half of these Jews	45
Three centuries later the whole population were Jews	ib.

Second Century.

Ignatius (Peter's proclamation to the Romans, at Jerusalem in person, and by writings at Rome)	45

CONTENTS.

	PAGE
"Peter and Paul," a patristic formula from the earliest period to denote all the original apostles of the Jews and of the Gentiles	46
Papias (nothing on the subject)	47
Mark wrote in Egypt after leaving Babylon (see also 80, 83, 197, 246)	48
The *on-dit* about Rome being called Babylon not sanctioned by Papias nor by any one of the Fathers (see also 169)	49
Not believed by the more enlightened of the Roman Catholic Clergy and Commentators (see also 188)	50
Heracleon (nothing to that effect)	51
Recognitions, (nothing to that effect)	52
Peter sends twelve missionaries to Rome instead of going there himself	ib.
The Clementina (epitome of the recognitions)	53
Rejected by all Roman Catholics	54
The Apostolic Constitutions (nothing to that effect)	55
Linus was ordained first Bishop of Rome by Paul and not by Peter	56
Dionysius Corinthius (Peter's being put to death about the same time, at Babylon, as Paul was at Rome; and Peter's having founded the Church of Corinth as well as that of Rome)	ib.
Hegesippus (spurious writings)	57
Victor (ditto)	59
Irenæus, (Peter's having founded the Roman Church)	60
All the first Churches founded from Jerusalem	61
Gregory of Nissa shows Peter did not leave the East	66
His statement that the Roman Church was founded at Jerusalem	ib.
Irenæus's similar statement that the Church of Rome was founded by Peter's words at Jerusalem	ib.
Jerome says that Peter founded the Church of Babylon at the same time	67
St. Athanasius shows how the Roman Church was founded	ib
St. Chrysostom repeats this, and says the same of the Church at Babylon	ib.
His statement that the Church of England was founded by St. Peter at the same time and in the same manner as that of Rome (see also the same statement in Arnobius, 128)	68

CONTENTS.

	PAGE
How Baronius considered the first Churches were founded by Peter	68
And that to found a Church did not imply the presence of the founder	69
The Roman clergy generally think the same	71
Irenæus himself thought it (three proofs)	ib.
Evangelizing a Church	73
A flourishing Church at Rome under Tiberius	ib.
St. Peter's relations to the different Churches	74
Father Parsonius proves St. Peter to have been in Canterbury	75
Lucianus Charinus (nothing)	79

Third Century.

Clemens Alexandrinus (Peter's book at Rome called "The Preaching")	80
Mark's Gospel written in Egypt at the request of Peter's hearers at Jerusalem, who were natives of different cities (see also 47, 197, 246)	80-83
Peter's proclamation of the Gospel at Rome was not in person	81
Caius (Peter's Tomb at Rome)	84
All the Apostles had the τρόπαια (i. e. emblems of victory), or insignia of martyrdom at Rome	85
And are enrolled in the Roman martyrologies	ib.
Stephen's τρόπαια in Italy at Ancona from the very first, although he never was in Europe	87
Peter and all the Apostles had τρόπαια and a μαρτύριον at Constantinople	ib.
Ignatius, though he died at Rome, had his at Antioch	91
Baronius admits that Peter's bones at Rome are no proof of his having died there	ib.
St. Peter's τρόπαια and "remains" at Canterbury in former days, no proof of his having been there	92
St. Mark has τρόπαια at Venice, and even his bones are there, though he died at Alexandria, and never had been in Venice	94
St. Hippolytus ("Peter's Chair")	97
Carthage was "Peter's Chair"	98
Canterbury was "Peter's Chair"	ib.
Alexandria was "Peter's Chair," &c.	ib.

CONTENTS.   xi

	PAGE
The Anonymous Author in Eusebius, v. 28. ("Third or fourth bishop from Peter's time")	98
The Roman Catholics admit that Eusebius did not think Peter was Bishop of Rome	99
Several "Bishops of Rome" never even saw Rome	100
Sextus Julius Africanus (nothing)	
Tertullian ("Peter died in the Christian Church, and baptized in the Gentile rivers")	101
His language vehement and figurative	102
What is meant by Peter's "baptizing in the Tiber"	ib.
St. John was living at Ephesus when he was banished to Patmos, and it was to Ephesus that he returned from banishment	105
St. John's "immersion in the flaming oil"	107
When Paul's death and Peter's are mentioned together, only Paul's is said to have occurred at Rome, the place of Peter's being shown in Scripture (see also 34, 149)	115
St. Cyprian ("Peter's Chair;" see also 97, 227, 249)	116
Every local Bishop has "Peter's Chair," according to the Roman-catholic clergy and all the Fathers	117
No wooden chair at Rome that St. Peter sat in	118
St. Firmilian ("Peter's succession")	128
Every local bishop had "Peter's succession"	ib.
St. Stephen (nothing)	122
Origen (nothing)	123
Valesius, Delarue, and Baronius upon the alleged passage	ib.

Fourth Century.

Petrus Alexandrinus (spurious writings)	125
Arnobius ("The Fiery Chariot," see also 223, 224, 247, 258)	127
The Fiery Chariot was in the reign of Tiberius	128
The Fiery Chariot was an allegory according to Justin Martyr's writings, Irenæus's, Tertullian's, &c.	131
Lactantius. (The book called κηρυγμα Πετρου; see also 29, 160)	135
The spurious MS. on the "Deaths of the Persecutors"	137
Father Le Nourry, Palma, Stephen Baluze, &c, on the subject	ib.

End of the alleged Antenicene Records.

PART II.

Eusebius, a bishop of Palestine in the fourth century, conjectures (and is the only one who does so) that Peter may have been taken from Babylon to Italy to have been put to death, as some relics of his were said to be in his martyr's tomb at Rome, which conjecture is not alluded to again by any one for three hundred years, when Isidore, an obscure Latin writer in Spain, supposes Eusebius to have stated it as a fact (see p. 269)	144
Cardinal Bellarmine acknowledges the insufficient grounds on which the conjecture of Eusebius rests	146
Where Peter's death and Paul's are mentioned together by any ancient writer, only Paul's is said to have occurred at Rome, the locality of Peter's death being a tradition from Scripture (see also 34, 115)	149
The time of Peter's death at Babylon about the same as Paul's at Rome	150
A martyrium—what it was	ib.
Peter's relics—what, and where supposed to be	153
The five other passages of Eusebius say nothing about Peter's having ever left Asia	158
Eusebius, 2—14. (Peter's κηρυγμα at Rome; see also 29, 135)	160
The Roman clergy acknowledge that Peter could not have left the East in the reign of Claudius	161
Neither Eusebius, nor Jerome, nor any one of the Fathers, says he did so (see also 244, and Addenda)	163
Bishop Pearson and young Baratier acknowledge that there is not the slightest trace in antiquity of his having done so, but the clearest proof of the contrary	166
Eusebius, 2, 15. (The on-dit about Babylon meaning Rome in 1 Peter)	167
Eusebius says he does not believe it	ib.
What sort of Jews had this on-dit among them	168
Papias does not sanction it, or even allude to it . . .	169
Nor does Jerome or any one of the Fathers (see also 67 and 246)	ib.
Yet Jerome, misunderstanding the Greek words, imputed this belief to Eusebius.	ib.
The Eastern commentators all understand "Babylon" to mean Babylon in 1 Peter	170

CONTENTS.

	PAGE
St. John does not call Rome " Babylon" in the Apocalypse, but always " Babylon the Great"	171
Millions of Jews always in and around Babylon in Peter's time, as the metropolis of the Dispersion (see also 45)	173
Only about 8000 in Rome, the Gentile capital; sometimes none at all in it	174
Nearly 50,000 Jews had been massacred at Seleucia about twenty years before Peter's time	175
Constant intercourse between Jerusalem and Babylon in Peter's time (see also 186)	177
Babylon was four times nearer to Jerusalem than Rome was, and the facilities of travelling very great	ib.
Babylon, the head quarters of the Lost Sheep of the House of Israel (see also 173)	179
The city existed in Peter's days the same as ever (see also 45)	181
The two factions there (see also 41)	187
Many of the most enlightened of the Roman clergy acknowledge that "Babylon" does not mean Rome in 1 Peter	188
Any who thought it did, thought so from supposing that the Fathers thought so	ib.
All the educated Roman clergy are agreed that 1 Peter was written under Claudius in A.D. 45, and therefore not from Rome	191
Baronius and others who thought that "Babylon" there meant Rome, acknowledge that Babylon was the more likely place for Peter to have gone to	ib.
All Protestant scholars, even Bishop Pearson and young Baratier, admit that the Scripture statement is the true one, and to be preferred to the *on-dit* of the fourth century	ib.
The reason the Roman Catholics sanctioned the *on-dit*	194
Import of the παρα in παρεπιδημοι in 1 Peter i. 1	ib.
Babylonia, the parent country of the Jewish nation	ib.
The flourishing Christian Church at Babylon in Peter's days, described by the Roman-catholic writers	195
Babylon was Parthian to A.D. 229; and afterwards Persian	ib.
Eusebius (ib.) (Mark's Gospel; see also 47, 83, 80, 246)	196
The mistake respecting the commencement of the chapter i. 15 in Eusebius	198

xiv   CONTENTS.

	PAGE
Eusebius, 3, 4. ("The bishops after Peter's time;" see also 98)	199
The Roman Catholic Archbishop De Marca on this passage	ib.
Cardinal Bellarmine	200
Six further considerations	ib.
Eusebius (2, 17) only mentions a saying that Philo was at Rome in the reign of Claudius, and thence communicated with Peter, who was then still at Jerusalem. (See also 161, &c.)	207
Eusebius's Chronicon. No such work extant, either in the original Greek, or in Latin Translation. (See also the article, Jerome, p. 239, &c.)	210
Scaliger's account of what he himself drew up under this name in Greek	214
Jerome's account of what he drew up under this name in Latin	215
Account given of it by the Roman clergy	216
Scaliger, on Jerome's knowledge of Greek	ib.
Even Scaliger's Greek Chronicon does not contain the alleged statement	ib.

PART III.—ALLEGED POSTNICENE RECORDS.

Julian the Apostate (Peter's relics carried about from city to city)	219
Eutropius (Peter's death at Babylon in Nero's persecution)	220
Anastasius (Peter's share in the words, "You must bear witness of me at Rome")	
Philastrius (The Fiery Chariot; see also 127, 159, 247, 258)	222
St. Cyril (ditto)	224
St. Ambrose (spurious writings and interpolation)	225
St. Optatus ("sitting in a chair;" see also 97, 116, 249)	227

Fifth Century.

The Old Roman Calendar published by Bucherius and Henschenius ("Bishop of Rome")	229
Peter's Roman Episcopate began immediately after the Ascension, under Tiberius	ib.
It ended when Paul and Linus went to Rome, about twenty-five years after it began	ib.

CONTENTS.

	PAGE
About twelve years afterwards Peter died at Babylon, and Paul at Rome	229
Peter's Episcopate general, and never confined to any one city	231
A third of it was over at Rome before the reign of Claudius	ib.
Epiphanius (repeats the old Roman Calendar)	232
The first of the Fathers who calls Peter "Bishop," but considered him a universal one, and Bishop of Rome, though at Jerusalem	235
Theodoret and St. Augustine say he was bishop of all cities, and not of one only	ib.
Prudentius (Peter's relics at Rome)	236
Chrysostom (Peter's tomb at Constantinople and Rome)	238
Jerome (translations of Eusebius, 2, 14)	239
His original works say that Peter lived at Babylon (see also 67, 170)	242
No writer holding this, thinks he ever left the East	ib.
Jerome's original works say nothing about Peter's having left the East *at any time*	ib.
The two translations of the passage in Eusebius (2, 14) about the reign of Claudius	243
Express neither the opinion of St. Jerome nor of Eusebius	ib.
The facts and principles that illustrate them (see also ADDENDA, at the end of the volume)	244
The mistranslation of Eusebius (2, 15) about 1 Peter (see also 49, 167)	246
Jerome's passage about Mark's Gospel	ib.
Sulpitius Severus (Peter's general Episcopate. The Fiery Chariot. Nero's persecution at Babylon)	ib.
St. Augustine (The supposed Relics at Rome—"Peter's chair")	248
The doubt always existing about Peter's relics at Rome	ib.
The Fisherman's tomb at Rome as at Constantinople	249
Paulinus of Nola (Peter's tomb at Rome and supposed relics there)	250
Cyril Alexandrinus (nothing)	251
Sozomen ("Peter's Chair")	ib.
Orosius (misapprehension of Eusebius)	252
His want of information and ignorance of Greek	253
Palladius (Nero's persecution in the East)	255
Petrus Chrysologus (nothing)	ib.
Theodoret (Peter's tomb and the Fiery Chariot)	256
St. Leo (Peter's tomb at Rome)	259

CONTENTS.

	PAGE
St. Prosper (spurious writings)	260
St. Maximus of Turin (ditto)	261

Sixth Century.

Elpis of Messina (nothing)	265
Arator (Nero's persecution in the East)	ib.
Gregory of Tours (ditto)	266

Seventh Century.

St. Gregory the Great (" Peter's Chair")	267
St. Isidore (the conjecture of Eusebius and Jerome's translation from Euseb. 2, 14)	268
The Golden Legend of the Learned Dogs, and the Fiery Chariot	270

End of the alleged Postnicene Records.

APPENDIX.

Collection of Evidences	by	Cardinal Baronius	291
"	"	Cardinal Bellarmine	293
"	"	Father Feuardent	296
"	"	Henry de Valois (*Lat.* Valesius)	297
"	"	Bishop Pearson	ib.
"	"	The young Baratier	300
"	"	The Correspondent in the *Times* (Cardinal Wiseman)	302
"	"	Father M'Corry	306

ADDENDA.

Notes on Jerome's alleged misinterpretations of Eusebius 2, 14 . . . 311

NOTICE

BY

THE REV. ALEXANDER M'CAUL, D.D.

PROFESSOR OF DIVINITY IN KING'S COLLEGE, LONDON,
PREBENDARY OF ST. PAUL'S,
AUTHOR OF "THE OLD PATHS," "THE MESSIAHSHIP OF JESUS,"
ETC. ETC.

HAVING been permitted to read the proof-sheets of Mr. Simon's Work, I have great pleasure in stating my opinion that it is a most useful review of an interesting topic of the Controversy with Rome, clear and intelligible to the general reader as to the controversialist; and that its value is enhanced by the fact that Mr. Simon is a layman, who justly feels that the controversy is at least as important to the laity as to the clergy. The plan pursued of going through all the supposed testimonies, one by one, is very satisfactory and instructive.

ALEX. M'CAUL.

Rectory, London Bridge,
Aug. 2, 1852.

NOTICE

BY

THE REV. JOHN CUMMING, D.D.

AUTHOR OF
"FORESHADOWS," "APOCALYPTIC SKETCHES," ETC.

—

I HAVE read several sheets of this work, by the kind permission of the Author, as they passed through the press. I am strongly persuaded it is one of the most able and searching investigations of the subject of Peter's relation to the Church of Rome, and alleged presence in the city of Rome, that have yet appeared. I do not agree with all the reflections of the learned Author, especially those in his Introduction; but the main object of the Treatise is discussed with a patient and exact research that renders his Work of no common value.

JOHN CUMMING.

THE

MISSION AND MARTYRDOM

OF

ST. PETER.

INTRODUCTION.

1. *Objects &c. of the Work.*—At a period when the Ecclesiastical History of the First Ages attracts more than ordinary attention, it is hoped that an attempt to rescue from uncertainty and misrepresentation some important particulars respecting the life and death of the Apostle Peter, as these are indicated in the Holy Scriptures, will not be without interest to the reading public; especially as misconceptions, and consequent mis-statements respecting these particulars, and respecting what the Fathers say about them, have been lately put forward as the basis of an Italian supremacy in this country.

It would be an erroneous and most unjust view of the intention of these pages to suppose that they have been written in hostility to the Roman Catholics of Great Britain and Ireland, and to the peaceful existence of their church among us. The exact contrary of this is the truth. One of my main objects in their publication is, to place that large and important class of the community upon an easier and happier, because *truer*, footing than they are on at present, with regard to the other divisions of the Christian Church that subsist around them; and thereby to augment as much as possible, that religious liberty which they even now enjoy to a greater extent among us than we ourselves are allowed to enjoy at Rome.

The shortest and easiest mode of effecting this is to show (since it can be shown) that the Roman-catholic church in our islands, although entitled to its freedom and to its clergy, to its buildings and to its ordinances —as fully entitled to these by our glorious laws, as even the church of England herself is,—cannot with anything like historical or even traditional warrant, be used as an instrument for the temporal aggrandizement of the church that is at Rome, or of the continental sovereign that is at the head of it. I do not say one word against the ordinances of the Roman-catholic church, from the first to the last page of what I have written. I only seek to show the members of it in Great Britain and Ireland, that they are wholly independent of the head of the same church in Italy: that St. Peter did nothing whatever,—nor, until the Reformation, was ever thought to have done anything for the Roman-catholic church in Italy that he did not equally do for the Roman-catholic church in Ireland and Great Britain; and that it is fully competent to the different communities of this church in every country in the world to elect their own head and to order their own affairs, without depending for these matters upon the will of any one country or sovereign which happens to profess the same religion as themselves. I only seek to show that the efforts made by an Italian sovereign to place himself at the head of all the Roman-catholic communities in Christendom, and most of all at the head of that in these islands, have no foundation in history; and that the story of the thirteenth century, upon which his agents still ground his claim, was never until now put forward in England as a true story, having been merely composed for popular amusement, by the same Roman-catholic archbishop of that period as wrote the other similar story of St. George and the Dragon. The native independence then of the Roman-catholic church in these islands, is one of the main objects of these pages. In them I have done no more than set forth the historical, or as it is now-a-days termed, the traditional truth connected with that proposition; the inference from that truth being too easy to require any elucidation. I write, therefore, in defence of religious liberty in the largest sense of the expression—the religious liberty of the whole world—of Roman Catholics as well as of Protestants,—not only as far as this concerns the building of a church within the walls of a city, or the assembling of a congregation by the tolling of a bell, or the permission to possess whatever religious books may be deemed necessary,—matters now so intolerantly obstructed in some of the most prominent Roman-catholic states of Europe,—but also with regard to the creation, if necessary, of such ecclesiastical titles as shall avoid all confusion with the titles of other churches, with regard to the free right of each community to elect its own head, and with regard to whatever other means may be considered essential to the due exercise of their religion by the Roman Catholics of these realms. I may, however, be permitted to say that I am one of those who look forward to the time when it shall please the Dispenser of all good to enlighten our fellow countrymen as to the great fact that His word, however interpreted, is infinitely more precious than the word of its interpreters, and when we shall be thus enabled to congratulate both them and ourselves upon their happy, though long delayed, return into the bosom of His church.

And the other object of the present publication, although more strictly connected with the Protestant church wherever it exists, will be found to be equally exempt from hostility to the religious liberty of the Roman Catholic. That object presents itself in the obvious check which the facts here, for the first time made known, will naturally exercise upon the importance attached by some of our Protestant clergy to the doctrines derivable from the church that is at Rome, and to the ecclesiastical surveillance of the sovereign who is at the head of it. It cannot be denied that the very general though mistaken notion about one of our Lord's first twelve apostles having superintended in person the proceedings of that church, and about a distinct expression or act on his part, authorizing this surveillance, has led many a conscientious Protestant, who was at first shocked at its innovations, to palliate them afterwards, and even finally to approve of them. When, however, it is now seen that that apostle's personal relations with the Italian church were but the same (in all respects exactly the same) as they were, for instance, with the church of England—that he never was in either of the countries, and that he never was bishop in or had his Chair in either church in any other than the vague and figurative sense in which these expressions are employed by the Fathers respecting his relation to all the local churches in the world—when this, I say, is clearly seen, we have good grounds to hope that the words of Scripture will again resume, upon the minds of all our clergy, the same unresisted influence which they happily possessed until the learning and conscientiousness of our universities had been cheated of their birthright by a delusion into which we have seen that the learned and the conscientious were but too liable to fall. To disperse this delusion then, where it has gathered, and to guard against it more effectually where it has not, is the other of the two main objects which have induced me to undertake this analysis, the accuracy of which, fortunately for truth, none can from their education better estimate than this very section of those in whose interests it has been undertaken.

All the present pretensions of the Roman clergy

respecting the superiority of their church, will be found to resolve themselves into the single proposition that on some occasion or other St. Peter left the East. This is the pivot of the whole theory. Whether he was five-and-twenty years in Europe, or only a few days before his death, is looked upon by them as of little moment. The question is, Was he there at all? Now, it will be seen not only that this is not matter of history, but, what is still more remarkable, that there never was even a tradition to this effect; a fact which must astonish all who are aware of the confidence with which the Roman clergy have expressed themselves upon the subject. It will be seen that when, in the fourth century, a bishop of Rome professed to have just discovered the relics of St. Peter in the catacombs, it was then first conjectured by a Greek writer who had never been at Rome, that the apostle might perhaps have been put to death there. It will also be seen that words supposed to contain a statement of his having left the East a good many years before his crucifixion at Babylon occur, for the first time, in the fifth century, in a Latin translation from the same Greek writer; it being well known that this Greek writer never made such a statement, and admitted by all the Roman Catholic scholars that these words either do not contain any such statement, or are not to be depended on if they do. It will be seen that neither the conjecture nor the translation was ever afterwards alluded to at all, by more than about one writer out of every two or three hundred who wrote upon ecclesiastical matters, and that there was never any other statement on the subject until the Reformation; for that as to the story called the "Golden Legend," invented in the 13th century, about the Learned Dogs and the Flying Chariot, the scene of which is laid in Europe, and in which St. Peter and his daughter are two of the principal characters introduced, every one was aware from the first that this was a mere invention, like the other "Golden Legend" about St. George and the Dragon, composed at the same time and by the same writer; nor was there ever any one found until the period of the Reformation, and scarcely any one even since then, to defend these stories as statements of authentic facts, until this was attempted last year, for the first time, in two English publications. The evidence I have to offer on all these points is such as no Roman Catholic will refuse. I produce the original Greek or Latin text of all the authentic passages that have ever been adduced, accepting as authentic all such as have been ascertained to be so by the learned in communion with the church of Rome, and I show that such language was never understood by the Roman clergy to admit of the sense attempted now-a-days to be forced upon it by a few of them, in defence of the great ecclesiastical hypothesis under consideration. Unlike my predecessors, therefore, on this subject, who have all confined themselves to the historical inconsistencies of the hypothesis, and to the incompetency of the ancient writers supposed to have entertained it, I deal merely with the alleged interpretation of the Greek and Latin texts referred to in these writers; and of course, where necessary, with the alleged existence of such texts at all. In all cases I cite no other authorities respecting these texts, except the Roman clergy themselves, and such as they have thought proper to cite or to refer us to. So overwhelmingly evident, nevertheless, is the point to be established, that if it were not for the existence in our metropolis of an abundant library, accessible to everybody, and supplied with attentive and intelligent attendants, I should have seen little use in putting forward a mass of evidence so diametrically opposed to what is now the general impression in England—so diametrically opposed, I may add, even to what my own impression was until my suspicions were excited by some remarkable expedients to which the two Roman-catholic writers of last year upon this subject had recourse. At the library of the British Museum, however, every statement that I have made may be strictly tested.

But, it will naturally be asked, how has it happened that so many people of all persuasions since the Reformation, should have been deceived by the propagators of the story into the belief that there did exist the tradition in former times? An abundance of circumstances explains this. I shall here indicate a few of the more prominent of these; but the share that each has had in the result can only be appreciated by those who are at the pains of going thoroughly into the whole subject. 1. The existence at Rome of a book called "Peter's Preaching," during the apostle's lifetime. 2. The mistranslation of Greek words and passages by some modern, and even by one or two ancient Latin writers. 3. Spurious mediæval writings, supposed for centuries to be authentic. 4. Peter's name alone being frequently used in the Fathers to represent all our Lord's twelve apostles. 5. The Fathers frequently combining Peter's name, on this account, with that of Paul, who was known to have been at Rome, and to have been put to death there. 6. Peter's death at Babylon having taken place during Nero's persecution of the Christians in the East, and his being therefore said to have been "put to death by Nero." 7. Peter's death at Babylon having occurred about the same time as Paul's at Rome. 8. Peter's being spoken of as having founded all the churches while he was at Jerusalem, and that of Rome among the rest. 9. Its being supposed that the Fathers describe Mark's Gospel as composed at Rome, and under Peter's superintendence. 10. Its being supposed that the Fathers, or some of them, or, at least, one of them, understood "Babylon," in 1 Peter, to mean Rome. 11. Its being supposed that Babylon scarcely existed in Peter's time, and was a great deal farther from Jerusalem than Antioch. 12. Peter's relics and tombs at Rome being more frequently mentioned in the Latin writers than his relics and tombs in other cities. 13. The practice in the Fathers of dating the episcopal successions in the different churches from the apostles. 14. Peter's being mentioned in the Fathers as bishop of all the Christian cities, and therefore frequently by the Latin Fathers as bishop of Rome. 15. His chair being said to be in all the local Christian churches, and therefore, by Latin writers, in that at Rome. 16. Its being supposed that the Fathers, or some of them, thought St. John had been at Rome, and that, therefore, a passage in one of them which might be understood as stating this both of John and Peter, is to be so understood. 17. Its being supposed that the scene of the Golden Legend about the Learned Dogs and the Fiery Chariot being laid at Rome was authorized by the Fathers. 18. The manifest historical inconsistency of the alleged facts respecting the mission and martyrdom of this apostle, has contributed greatly to their being now regarded as traditional. For the establishment of this inconsistency at the period of the Reformation was allowed to supersede all inquiry as to the reality of the traditional character ascribed to them; and the assertions of Cardinal Baronius, Cardinal Bellarmine, and the rest, upon this latter point, have been, therefore, ever since allowed to remain in full possession of the public mind.

I am conscious that what is here written will be found to labour under a defect of style generally looked upon as inexcusable; viz., it contains frequent repetitions. This defect it is hoped that the reader will on this occasion tolerate. Those who are acquainted with the peculiar mode of arguing adopted by the Roman clergy, will recognise the necessity of it. Those who are not, will experience no disadvantage from it, except the addition of perhaps some half dozen pages to the book, which will be more than made amends for by the circumstance that each Part, and, to a great extent, each Section, being thereby rendered independent of the other, the book will be more available as one of reference.

I have here only to add, that as one of my objects— hopeless and distant though it may seem to some—in publishing this analysis is to alleviate, in the shortest and surest way in which this is possible, the unhappy position in which the pretensions of a foreign prince have lately placed my Roman-catholic fellow-countrymen, and to arouse them for this purpose to a sense of their own ecclesiastical independence, so am I most anxious to disclaim anything like controversial animosity (if my expressions should on any occasion seem to indicate a feeling of this kind) towards such of their clergy as have written in opposition to the important truth that I now seek to illustrate. So far am I, in fact, from any feeling of this kind, that I think, on the contrary, we have all reason to feel indebted to these gentlemen, especially to the two of last year, for the pains they have been at to explain, as much as they have done, the grounds of the extraordinary pretensions in question; and let us hope that they and others will not be deterred by the difficulty of the undertaking, but that if they still retain the opinions they have expressed, they will see the necessity of further explanations, in proportion as the public has been unable to appreciate those which have been already laid before it; or the necessity, at least, of revising their statements, and letting Englishmen know what it is that, on this subject, Englishmen are now expected to believe.

2. *Past and Present State of the Inquiry.*—A Roman-

catholic correspondent in the *Times* of January 16th, 1851, to whom we shall frequently have occasion to allude, seems to be under an impression that none but a few "weak Protestants" ever asserted that there was no proof—either history or tradition—of St. Peter's having left the East. That writer will find upon inquiry, that he has been totally misinformed. This assertion not only is not confined to "weak" Protestants, but has been honestly and openly made by some of the most esteemed and stoutest-hearted of the Roman Catholics themselves. Charles Du Moulin, for instance, the great ecclesiastical lawyer (A.D. 1566), whom Father Calmet speaks of as a steadfast Roman Catholic, and than whom no writer ever enjoyed a higher reputation for learning and intelligence, has unequivocally stated it as his opinion that there never was even a vague tradition among the ancients about Peter's having left the East, and that one might very well be a Roman Catholic without thinking that there was. In one passage he writes thus: "Even when after the breaking up of the empire, the bishops of Rome began to extend their authority over other churches, they never alleged or put forward this story of Peter's being at Rome, and of his primacy devolving in succession upon them, which they would not have omitted to do, if there had been any such thing to put forward; a clear proof that there was not; the story, I suppose, not having been yet invented." (Jamais n'alleguerent et ne mirent en avant ladite fable du siege St. Pierre à Rome et du Primat d'iceluy à eux successivement devolu, ce qu'ils n'eussent pas obmis, s'il en eust esté aucune chose; claire demonstrance qu'il n'en estoit rien, dit que ladite fable n'avoit encore esté controuvée. *Vol.* iv. *p.* 460.) Father Leland, the celebrated English antiquarian (A.D. 1552), and Marsilius, a distinguished

Italian writer (A.D. 1324), both of whom Father Calmet also mentions as members of his church, were equally positive upon this point. Father Caron, an Irish Franciscan of the highest eminence, (A.D. 1666), took the same view of the matter; as did also Father Hardouin, a French Jesuit (A.D. 1729), likewise in very high repute at Rome. "We Roman Catholics hold," says Father Hardouin, "that at least Peter's head was brought to Rome after his crucifixion, and that it ought to be duly worshipped there; but that the pope is Christ's substitute (vicarius) and Peter's successor, is clear enough without our being bound to suppose that Peter himself ever came to Rome." But it is unnecessary to enumerate individual cases. Several elaborate works, not intended for Protestants, have been written for the last three or four hundred years, by Roman-catholics of great distinction, to assign reasons for thinking that St. Peter must have left the East—in short, during all that time scarcely a work of any kind came out by a Roman Catholic holding this view, that did not contain some little sketch of the controversy. Does not this of itself show to what an extent educated Roman Catholics must from the first have disbelieved, and must even still disbelieve, the story? Is it to be supposed for an instant that all this labour would have been bestowed upon an assertion which no one but a Protestant had expressed a doubt about, and no one but a Protestant was at all likely to experience any difficulty in believing? Nor is that all. It is a remarkable fact that not one of all those who have left the church of Rome (and many of them have been men of the greatest learning) has hesitated to assure us that they never could see the slightest reason for supposing that the great Apostle of the Circumcision had left the East. What stronger proofs can we require of what Roman

Catholics think upon this subject? And as to the "weak Protestants," who are supposed to have been "almost" as incredulous in this matter as educated Roman Catholics, the writer alluded to is quite as much mistaken. Mr. Bower, for instance, who wrote the "Lives of the Popes," is represented by him as one of the weak Protestants who "almost" denied this story. But this is not a fair statement of Mr. Bower's case. He did not almost deny it. This gentleman, who was a convert from the Roman persuasion, did, as I have just said Saumaise, Spanheim, Bishop Bale, Luther, Calvin, Scaliger, and so many other men of the most energetic minds, felt it incumbent upon them to do after they had changed their opinion respecting the Christian purity of that church—he declared, in the most emphatic manner, that there was not, and that he had never been able to discover (even while he was a Roman Catholic), the slightest pretext for such a supposition. "In this controversy," says Bower, in one place, "the silence of St. Paul in particular, if duly attended to, must be thought by every unbiassed man a far more convincing proof of St. Peter's not having been at Rome, than all the authorities that have been yet alleged are of his having been there." I give Mr. Bower's own words to show how little reliance can be placed upon the statements in the letter published in the *Times*, that I have alluded to, most of which the correspondent seems to have transcribed second-hand from other writers, though not always, as here, acknowledging that he does so. Father M'Corry, of Scotland, in the other statement published last year upon this subject, seems also to have taken everything at second-hand from others, for there is scarcely any one of his statements that is not contrary to fact. One or two instances may be given here; others will be found in the course of these pages. He says (p. 21 of the tract called "Was St.

Peter ever at Rome?") that Scaliger expresses his "amazement that this great leading fact of church history should be matter of litigation." Whereas Scaliger's amazement seems to have been all the other way. "That this false interpretation cannot stand," says he, speaking of the Roman clergy thinking Babylon meant Rome in 1 Peter, "I have clearly shown in the third book of the Canons, at the twelfth epoch; and assuredly they have no other argument in support of Peter's alleged journey except that which they think they have in this Epistle." (Thesaurus Temporum, p. 424.) And again, this very learned and stout-hearted man declares—"As to Peter's having gone to Rome, and having been put to death there, there is no person with the least education that could believe such a story." (Nam de ejus Romani adventu et supremo capitis supplicio ibidem, nemo qui paulo humanior fuerit, credere posset.—*Scaliger's Notes on the New Testament.*) Father M'Corry also (p. 22) describes Calvin as saying that he could not "withstand" the evidence of Peter's having died in Italy; whereas what Calvin says is (after mentioning that some writers agreed in supposing it), "I am not now raising the question as to whether he may have died there, since these writers suppose he did (propter hunc scriptorum consensum, non pugno quin illic mortuus fuerit); but I positively deny that he was bishop there."—*Instit.* iv. 6. And again, still more distinctly, in his commentary on 2 Peter i. 14: "But how with this intimation of his approaching end at Babylon, could Peter have been put to death at Rome? Unless we suppose that he could fly, it is manifestly certain that he did not die in Italy." (Certe nisi maria et terras momento transvolaverit, procul ab Italiâ mortuum esse constat.) Adam Clarke was another of these "weak" Protestants. With all his learning and all his research, he could see no pretext for supposing that the apostle had ever left the East. "I am of opinion," says this profound scholar, "that St. Peter did not write from Rome—that he was neither bishop of Rome nor martyred at Rome—in a word, that he never was at Rome." Dr. Kitto is another. "There is no sufficient reason," (says he, in his Encyclopædia of Biblical Literature), "for believing that Peter was ever even so much as within the walls of Rome." Father Feuardent (A.D. 1610) seems to think that there were a great many Protestants in this predicament in his day, but attributes it rather to hardihood that to weakness. "I cannot but wonder," exclaims the indignant priest, "at the abandoned impudence (profligatam impudentiam) with which Valesius (not Henry de Valois, the commentator on Eusebius), Illyricus, Functius, Gallatius and others who have left our church, dare to prate (audeant blatterare) about Peter's never having been at Rome." "Several Protestants," says Father Tillemont (A.D. 1698), "have lately maintained that Peter could never have been in Italy." "The majority of Protestants," says the Bibliographie Universelle, a work under the sanction of the Roman clergy, and largely contributed to by many of them — "the majority of Protestants (la plupart des Protestans) reject this supposition." (Art. Bauldri.)

The first systematic attempt of any note which seems to have been made to remove the doubts and convictions entertained upon this point by the educated classes of the Roman communion was that of Cardinal Baronius (A.D. 1607), who, seeing the arguments vanishing in the hands of his predecessors, thought to secure something by making a grasp at everything. So, to the utter astonishment of all the world, he took his stand upon two supposed mistranslations of Greek text, by a Latin writer in the 5th century, and sought to make it appear not only that the apostle had not been put to death at Babylon (where Peter himself tells us that his martyrdom was impending), but that Europe was the head-quarters of the mission entrusted to him by our Lord, and that he occupied it as such five-and-twenty-years, *i.e.* more than twice as long as he did Jerusalem. Almost immediately the Roman clergy of all grades refused to countenance such a proposition. Cardinal Bellarmine (A.D. 1621), from whom we have the next collection of what were supposed to be testimonies respecting Peter's having left the East, says nothing about the alleged residence of five-and-twenty years in Europe, and wisely premises that, even if it could not be proved by history or tradition, that the apostle ever left the East, it was nevertheless very clear that he had been Bishop of Rome as well as of all the other churches of Christendom, and that this ought to be sufficient for the Roman Catholic supremacy anywhere. Two briefer collections of these supposed testimonies appeared soon afterwards;—one by Father Feuardent, the celebrated Franciscan orator already alluded to,—the other by Henry de Valois (Valesius A.D. 1676), the still more celebrated Roman-catholic editor of Eusebius,—in which collections these two eminent men, eminent alike for their zeal and for their learning, confine themselves, unlike the two cardinals, to Antenicene writers only, as the sole true ground of tradition in such matters. These writers also, it is almost needless to say, abandoned, as untenable, the grand point of Baronius, that Europe had been Peter's head-quarters for five-and-twenty years, and contented themselves with merely making out as good a case as possible for the supposition that he died here. The next collection of supposed testimonies to which we are referred is that by Bishop Pearson (A.D. 1686), in which the bishop utterly denies that there was ever the least pretext for the hypothesis about the five-and-twenty years, and only tried to show that the apostle might not have died in the East, for which purpose, however, he considers that the Antenicene evidence of Feuardent and Valesius was insufficient. About this period of the controversy a singular occurrence took place. A Roman-catholic antiquarian, on the continent, found in Colbert's library a little MS. which was firmly believed by him and everybody else to be of very high historical character, and in which it was plainly stated that the apostle really had come into Europe. So much satisfaction did this statement occasion, that the Roman-catholic clergy hesitated not to join the antiquarian in acknowledging that this, after all, was the only direct and substantial testimony there was upon the subject. Within about thirty years afterwards, however, it was discovered by themselves that there had been a mistake made about the MS., and that it was not authentic! The names, dates, and other circumstances connected with this event, are given here in the section on Lactantius, whose work it was supposed to have been. Since the confusion of opinions consequent upon this discovery no writers of any note have meddled with the question. Mr. Barntier, indeed, (A.D. 1740), a talented young German, who was about nineteen years old when he died, and was not aware that the Lactantian MS. was unauthentic, wrote in a tone of great confidence upon the subject, and is considered by the Roman clergy, apparently on this sole account, as a very valuable auxiliary. He denounces, of course, the old supposition about the five-and-twenty years, adding, that the learned of all parties had long since proved it to be absurd, and does little else in reality than refer to, and repeat the collection of supposed testimonies that was made by the Bishop of Chester. We now come to the two most recent collections that have appeared. One is that of the Correspondent in the

Times, already alluded to, contained in a letter addressed to the Editor, and signed " Truth." The other is that of Father M'Corry of Scotland, in his tract, entitled " Was St. Peter ever at Rome?" in which he admits that the affirmative of this question has been very extensively denied, and that it requires proof, and professes to give the strongest points that he could find in the writings of four other parties, viz., Noel Alexander (a Doctor of the Sorbonne), Father Foggini, Father Dollinger, and Father Palma, which dispenses with any separate reference to these writers here. Incredible as it may appear, both the recent writers now indicated seek to revive in England the old theory of Baronius, about the Five-and-Twenty years, that had been rejected at Rome from its first promulgation, literally centuries ago! as well as Jacques de Voragine's Golden Legend, about the Learned Dogs and the Fiery Chariot at Rome! In addition to which remarkable points, Father M'Corry is led by his authorities to repeat, without examination, all the old mis-statements about the city of Babylon, mentioned in Peter's First Epistle; while the Correspondent in the *Times* professes not to be aware that the Lactantian MS. was discovered, and that too by his own church, to be a forgery. In other respects they merely repeat the usual references, which, as it will be seen, are precisely similar to those by which some of the Roman clergy have tried to prove that Peter was at Canterbury. In order that the reader may be able to see the utmost that was ever attempted to be adduced from antiquity, he will find appended to this work the *eight* foregoing statements, viz., that of Baronius, Bellarmine, Feuardent, Valesius, Bishop Pearson, and Baratier, together with the Roman-catholic Letter that appeared in the *Times*, and the twelve supposed testimonies translated in Father M'Corry's Tract.

As to the other side of the question, the fallacy of supposing that Peter ever left the East has from the first been felt rather than proved. Father Foggini, indeed, mentions that our proposition has been always more or less asserted in books ever since the 14th century, *i. e.* since the Roman clergy, in order to protect themselves against the Reformers, began first to assert the contrary. Father Mamachi (A.D. 1792) makes a similar statement, enumerating upwards of a dozen writers on this other side of the question. Owing, however, to one grand defect common to them all, the exertions of these writers have not been attended with that success which we might have expected from the labours of such men. Instead of examining the passages adduced by the opposite party, these controversialists many of them men of learning and ability unsurpassed (among whom we may reckon Calvin, Saumaise, Spanheim, and Scaliger), contented themselves with merely denying the accuracy of those Fathers who either wrote or were supposed to have written these passages, and with indicating the glaring historical inconsistency of the statement supposed to be contained in them; thus rather confirming the evil than removing it; for these men of world-wide fame thereby seemed to give their high sanction to the mistaken interpretation of some of these passages, and to the mistaken authenticity of others. What they have omitted to do is what is now done.

A LIST

OF

All the Writers and of all the Greek and Latin Passages that have ever been alleged as testimony of St. Peter's having left the East.

CHRONOLOGICALLY ARRANGED.

First Century.

THE BOOK CALLED THE Κηρυγμα Πετρου. A.D. 45.
LINUS. A.D. 70.
ANACLETUS. A.D. 91.
CLEMENS ROMANUS. A.D. 100.

Αλλ' ινα των αρχαιων υποδειγματων παυσωμεθα, ελθωμεν επι τους εγγιστα γενομενους Αθλητας, λαβωμεν της γενεας ημων τα γενναια υποδειγματα δια ζηλον και φθονον εκκλησιας, λαβωμεν προ οφθαλμων ημων τους αγαθους αποστολους. Ὁ Πετρος δια ζηλον αδικον ουκ ενα ουδε δυο αλλα πλειονας υπηνεγκεν πονους και ουτω μαρτυρησας επορευθη εις τον οφειλομενον τοπον της δοξης. Δια ζηλον και ὁ Παυλος υπομονης βραβειον υπεσχεν, επτακις δεσμα φορησας, φυγαδευθεις, λιθασθεις, κηρυξ γενομενος εν τε τῃ ανατολη και εν τῃ δυσει το γενναιον της πιστεως αυτου κλεος ελαβεν, δικαιοσυνην διδαξας όλον τον κοσμον, και επι το τερμα της δυσεως ελθων, μαρτυρησας επι των ηγουμενων, οὑτως απηλλαγη του κοσμου και εις τον άγιον τοπον επορευθη υπομονης γενομενος μεγιστος υπογραμμος.—*Epist. ad Corinth.* c. 5.

Second Century.

IGNATIUS. A.D. 107.

Ουχ ὡς Πετρος και Παυλος διατασσομαι ὑμιν. Εκεινοι αποστολοι, εγω κατακριτος· εκεινοι ελευθεροι, εγω δε μεχρι του δουλος· αλλ' εαν παθω, απελευθερος Ιησου, και αναστησομαι εν αυτῳ ελευθερος.—*Epist. ad Rom.* c. 4.

PAPIAS. A.D. 110.

Και τουθ' ὁ πρεσβυτερος ελεγε. Μαρκος μεν ἑρμηνευτης Πετρου γενομενος, ὁσα εμνημονευσεν ακριβως εγραψεν, ου μεντοι ταξει τα ὑπο του

Χριστον η λεχθεντα η πραχθεντα. Ουτι γαρ ηκουσι τον Κυριου ουτι
παρηκολουθησεν αυτῳ· υστερον δε, ὡς εφην, Πετρῳ ὃς προς τας χρειας
εποιειτο τας διδασκαλιας, αλλ' ουχ ὥσπερ συνταξιν των κυριακων ποιουμενος
λογων· ὥστε ουδεν ημαρτε Μαρκος ουτως ενια γραψας ὡς απεμνημονευσεν,
Ἑνος γαρ εποιησατο προνοιαν, του μηδεν ὧν ηκουσι παραλιπειν η ψευσασθαι
τι εν αυτοις. Ταυτα μεν ουν ιστορηται τῳ Παπιᾳ περι του Μαρκου.—*Apud.
Euseb*. 3, 39.

HERACLEON. A.D. 126.
THE RECOGNITIONS.
THE CLEMENTINA.
THE APOSTOLIC CONSTITUTIONS.

The heading of the chapter is: Τινας πεμποντες εχειροτονησαν οἱ
ἁγιοι Αποστολοι. *The chapter then proceeds thus:* Περι δε των ὑφ'
ἡμων χειροτονηθεντων επισκοπων εν τῃ ζωῃ τῃ ἡμετερᾳ, γνωριζομεν ὑμιν
ὅτι εισιν οὑτοι· .... Αντιοχειας δε Ευοδιος μεν ὑπ' εμου Πετρου, Ιγνατιος
δε ὑπο Παυλου..... Της δε Ρωμαιων εκκλησιας Λινος μεν ὁ Κλαυδιας
πρωτος, ὑπο Παυλου, Κλημης δε μετα τον Λινου θανατον, ὑπ' εμου Πετρου,
δευτερος, εχειροτονηται..... οὑτοι οἱ ὑφ' ἡμων επιστευθεντες τας εν
Κυριῳ παροικιας.—*lib. c.* 40.

DIONYSIUS CORINTHUS. A.D. 170.

Ταυτα και ὑμεις δια της τοσαυτης νουθεσιας την απο Πετρου και Παυλου
φυτειαν γενηθεισαν Ρωμαιων τε και Κορινθιων συνεκερασατε, και γαρ
ἀμφω και εις την ἡμετεραν Κορινθον φυτευσαντες ἡμας, ὁμοιως δε και εις
την Ιταλιαν, ὁμοσε διδαξαντες, εμαρτυρησαν κατα τον αυτον καιρον.—
Extract preserved in Euseb. 2, 25, *from a letter addressed to the Romans.*

HEGESIPPUS. A.D. 180.
VICTOR. A.D. 200.
IRENÆUS. A.D. 200.

Ὁ μεν δη Ματθαιος εν τοις Ἑβραιοις τῃ ιδιᾳ διαλεκτῳ αυτων επι γραφην
εξηνεγκεν ευαγγελιον, του Πετρου και Παυλου εν Ρωμῃ ευαγγελιζομενων
και θεμελιουντων την εκκλησιαν. Μετα δε την τουτων εξοδον, Μαρκος
ὁ μαθητης και ἑρμηνευτης Πετρου και αυτος τα ὑπο Πετρου κηρυσσομενα
εγγραφως ἡμιν παραδεδωκεν.—*lib.* 3, *c.* 1.

Quoniam valde longum est in hoc tali volumine, omnium ecclesiarum
enumerare successionem, maximæ et antiquissimæ et omnibus cognitæ,
a gloriosissimis duobus Apostolis Paulo et Petro (*so in the Jesuit MS.
called Claromontano, and said by the Roman-catholics to be* "*optimæ
notæ codex; so also in the Vossian MS., called by the Roman-catholics,
"optimus" et "verissimus,"*) Romæ fundatæ et constitutæ ecclesiæ,
indicantes, &c.—*Chap.* 3. (*Greek lost.*)

Θεμιλιωσαντες ουν και οικοδομησαντες οι μακαριοι Αποστολοι την εκκλησιαν, Λινω την της επισκοπης λειτουργιαν ενεχειρισαν. Τουτου του Λινου Παυλος εν ταις προς Τιμοθεον επιστολαις μεμνηται. Διαδεχεται δε αυτον Ανεγκλητος. Μετα τουτον δε τριτω τοπω απο των Αποστολων την επισκοπην κληρουται Κλημης.—*ibidem.*

LUCIANUS CHARINUS. A.D. 200.

Third Century.

CLEMENS ALEXANDRINUS. A.D. 217.

Ανθις δ'εν τοις αυτοις ο Κλημης βιβλιοις περι της ταξεως των ευαγγελιων παραδοσιν των ανεκαθεν πρεσβυτερων τιθεται τουτον εχουσαν τον τροπον. Προγεγραφθαι ελεγετο των ευαγγελιων τα περιεχοντα τας γενεαλογιας· το δε κατα Μαρκον ταυτην εσχηκεναι την οικονομιαν. Του Πετρου δημοσια εν Ρωμη κηρυξαντος τον λογον, και Πνευματι το ευαγγελιον εξειποντος, τους παροντας πολλους οντας παρακαλεσαι τον Μαρκον ως αν ακολουθησαντα αυτω πορρωθεν και μεμνημενον των λεχθεντων αναγραψαι τα ειρημενα· ποιησαντα δε το ευαγγελιον, μεταδουναι τοις δεομενοις αυτου· Οπερ επιγνοντα τον Πετρον προτρεπτικως μητε κωλυσαι μητε προτρεψαι.—*Apud. Euseb.* 6, 14.

CAIUS. A.D. 218.

Και εκκλησιαστικος ανηρ, Γαϊος ονομα, κατα Ζεφυρινον Ρωμαιων γεγονως επισκοπον· ος δη Προκλω της κατα Φρυγας προισταμενω γνωμης εγγραφως διαλεχθεις, αυτα δη ταυτα περι των τοπων ενθα των ειρημενων Αποστολων τα ιερα σκηνωματα κατατεθειται, φησιν· Εγω δε τα τροπαια των αποστολων εχω δειξαι. Εαν γαρ θελησης απελθειν επι τον Βατικανον, η επι την οδον την Ωστιαν, ευρησεις τα τροπαια των ταυτην ιδρυσαμενων την εκκλησιαν. *Apud. Euseb.* 2, 25.

HIPPOLYTUS. A.D. 250.
AN ANONYMOUS AUTHOR. A.D. 250.

Φασι γαρ τους μεν προτερους απαντας και αυτους τους αποστολους παρειληφεναι τε και εξδεδαχεναι ταυτα α νυν ουτοι λεγουσι και τετηρησθαι την αληθειαν του κηρυγματος μεχρι των Βικτορος χρονων, ος ην τρισκαιδεκατος απο Πετρου, εν Ρωμη επισκοπος· απο δε του διαδοχου αυτου Ζεφυρινου παρακεχαραχθαι την αληθειαν.—*Apud. Euseb.* 5, 28.

SEXTUS JULIUS AFRICANUS. A.D. 250.
TERTULLIAN. A.D. 250.

Quam felix Ecclesia ("*ista quam*" is in no MS.), cui totam doctrinam apostoli cum sanguine suo profuderunt! Ubi Petrus passioni

Dominicae adaequatur; ubi Paulus Joannis exitu coronatur; ubi Apostolus Joannes (postquam in oleum igneum demersus nihil passus est) in insulam relegatur.—*De Praescript. c.* 36.

Nec quidquam refert inter eos quos Joannes in Jordane, et Petrus in Tiberi tinxit.—*De Baptis. c.* 4.

Vitas Caesarum legimus. Orientem fidem Romae primus Nero cruentavit. Tunc Petrus ab altero cingitur cum cruci astringitur. Tunc Paulus civitatis Romanae consequitur nativitatem, cum illic martyrii renascitur generositate.—*Scorpiacum, c.* 15.

Romani—quibus evangelium et Petrus et Paulus sanguine quoque suo signatum reliquerunt.—*Adversus Marcionem, c.* 6.

CYPRIAN. A.D. 250.

Factus est autem Cornelius Episcopus cum Fabiani locus, id est, cum locus Petri et gradus Cathedrae sacerdotalis vacaret.—*Epist.* 55, c. 6.

Roma—Cathedra Petri.—*Passim.*

FIRMILIAN. A.D. 250.

Atque ego in hac parte justo indignor ad hanc tam apertam et manifestam Stephani stultitiam quod qui sic de episcopatus sui loco gloriatur et se successionem Petri tenere contendit, super quam fundamenta ecclesiae collocata sunt, multas alias petras inducat et ecclesiarum multarum nova aedificia constituat. . . . . Stephanus qui per successionem Cathedram Petri habere se praedicat, nullo adversus haereticos zelo excitatur.—*Apud Cyprian. Epist.*

STEPHEN. A.D. 250.
ORIGEN. A.D. 254.

Fourth Century.

PETRUS ALEXANDRINUS. A.D. 311.
ARNOBIUS. A.D. 330.

Viderant enim cursum Simonis Magi et quadrigas igneas Petri ore difflatas et nominato Christo evanuisse. Viderant inquam fidentem diis falsis et ab iisdem metuentibus proditum, pondere praecipitatum suo, cruribus jaculisse praefractis. Post deinde perlatum Brundam crucistibus et pudore defessum, ex altissimi culminis se rursum praecipitasse fastigio. Quae omnia vos gesta neque scitis, neque scire voluistis, neque unquam vobis necessaria judicastis; ac dum vestris fiditis cordibus etc.—*Lib.* 2.

LACTANTIUS. A.D. 330.

Discipuli (Christi) vero per provincias dispersi, fundamenta Ecclesiae ubique posuerunt, facientes et ipsi in nomine Magistri Dei magna et pene incredibilia miracula; quia discedens instruxerat eos virtute ac potestate quâ posset novæ annuntiationis ratio fundari et confirmari: sed et futura aperuit illis omnia quæ Petrus et Paulus Romæ prædicaverunt, et ea Prædicatio, in memoriam scripta, permansit; in quâ cum multa alia mira, tum etiam hoc futurum esse dixerunt, ut post breve tempus immitteret Deus regem qui expugnaret Judæos et civitatem eorum solo adæquaret etc. . . . Itaque post illorum obitum cum eos Nero interemisset, Judæorum nomen et gentem Vespasianus extinxit sicitque omnia quæ illi futura prædixerant.—*Institut. lib.* 4, *c.* 21.

EUSEBIUS. A.D. 340.

(*Title of Chapter*—Περι του κατα Ρωμην Κηρυγματος Πετρου του Αποστολου) . . . . Επιβας δε (Ὁ μαγος) της Ρωμαιων πολεως, συναρομενης αυτῳ τα μεγαλα της εφεζομενουσης ενταυθα δυναμεως, εν ολιγῳ τοσουτον τα της επιχειρησεως ηνυστο ὡς και ανθρωπινος αναθεσει προς αυτων ἡρεϊ οἷα θεον τιμηθηναι. Ον μην εις μακρον αυτῳ ταυτα προυχωρει. Παραποδας γουν επι της αυτης Κλαυδιου βασιλειας, ἡ παναγαθος και φιλανθρωποτατη των Ὁλων προνοια τον καρτερον και μεγαν των Αποστολων τον αρετης ἑνεκα των λοιπων ἁπαντων προηγορον, Πετρον επι την Ρωμην ὡς επι τηλικουτον λυμαωνα βιου χειραγωγει, ὃς οἷα τις γενναιος Οιον στρατηγος ταις θειοις ὁπλοις φραξαμενος, την πολυτιμητον εμποριαν του νοητου φωτος εξ ανατολων τοις κατα δυσιν εκομιζεν,—φως αυτο και λογον ψυχων σωτηριον, το Κηρυγμα της των ουρανων βασιλειας ευαγγελιζομενος οὑτω δ᾽ ουν επιδημησαντος αυτοις του θειου λογου, ἡ μεν του Σιμωνος (του μαγου) απεσβη και παραχρημα συν και τῳ ανδρι κατελιλυτο δυναμις.—2.14.

(*Title of chapter*—Περι του κατα Μαρκον ευαγγελιου.) Τοσορδ᾽ επελαμψεν ταις των ακροατων του Πετρου διανοιαις ευσεβειας φεγγος ὡς μη τῇ εισαπαξ ισανως εχειν αρκεισθαι ακοῃ, μηδε τῃ αγραφῳ του θειου κηρυγματος διδασκαλιᾳ, παρακλησεσι δε παντοιαις Μαρκον, ὁν το ευαγγελιον φερεται ακολουθον οντα Πετρου λιπαρησαι, ὡς αν και δια γραφης ὑπομνημα της δια λογου παραδοθεισης αυτοις καταλειψοι διδασκαλιας, μη προτερον τε ανειναι, ἡ κατεργασασθαι τον ανδρα, και ταυτῃ αιτιους γενεσθαι της του λεγομενου κατα Μαρκον Ευαγγελιου γραφης. Γνοντα δε το πραχθεν φασι τον αποστολον, αποκαλυψαντος αυτῳ του πνευματος, ἡσθηναι τῃ των ανδρων προθυμιᾳ, κυρωσαι τε την γραφην εις εντευξιν ταις εκκλησιαις (Κλημης εν ἑκτῳ των ὑποτυπωσεων παρατεθειται την Ἱστοριαν, συνεπιμαρτυρει δ᾽ αυτῳ και ὁ Ἱεραπολιτης επισκοπος ονοματι Παπιας.) τον δε Μαρκον μνημονευειν τον Πετρον εν τῃ προτερᾳ επιστολῃ, ἡν και συνταξαι φασιν επ᾽ αυτης Ρωμης, σημαινειν τε τουτ᾽ αυτον, την πολιν τροπικωτερον Βαβυλωνα προσειποντα δια τουτων, Ασπαζεται ὑμας ἡ εν Βαβυλωνι συνεκλεκτη, και Μαρκος ὁ υἱος μου.—2.15.

Ὁν (Φιλωνα) και λογος εχει κατα Κλαυδιον επι της Ρωμης εις ὁμιλιαν

ελθειν Πετρω, τοις εκεισε τοτε κηρυττοντι. Και ουκ απεικος αν ιη τουτο
γε, επει και ο φαμεν αυτω συγγραμμα σαφως τους εις ετι νυν και εις ημας
τεφυλαγμενους της εκκλησιας περιεχει κανονας.—*Euseb.* 2.17.

Πετρος δε εν Ποντω και Γαλατια, και Βιθυνια, Καππαδοκια, τε και Ασια,
κεκηρυχεναι τοις εν διασπορα Ιουδαιοις εοικεν, ος και επι τελει εν Ρωμη
γενομενος ανεσκολοπισθη κατα κεφαλης, ουτως αυτος αξιωσας παθειν.—
Euseb. 3.1.

Λινος δε ου μεμνηται (Παυλος) συνοντος επι Ρωμης αυτω κατα την
δευτεραν προς Τιμοθεον επιστολην, πρωτος μετα Πετρον της Ρωμαιων
εκκλησιας την επισκοπην ηδη προτερον ειληφθεις εδηλωται. Αλλα και
ο Κλημης της Ρωμαιων και αυτος εκκλησιας τριτος επισκοπος καταστας
Παυλου συνεργος και συναθλητης γεγονεναι προς αυτου μαρτυρειται.—
Euseb. 3.4.

JULIAN THE APOSTATE.   A.D. 361.

Λειψανων δε οιμαι και τα μνηματα Πετρου και Παυλου, λαθρα μεν,
ακουων δε ομως αυτα περιφερομενα ("circumferri," *in Father Herved's Paris
edition,* 1604,—*alii,* "θεραπευομενα") πρωτος ετολμησεν ειπειν.—*Apud.
Cyril. Alexan. adv. Jul.* lib. 10.

EUTROPIUS.   Before A.D. 400.

Denique omnibus flagitiis suis etiam hoc addidit (Nero) quod Sanctos
Dei Apostolos Petrum Paulumque trucidavit.—*Lib.* 7.

ATHANASIUS.   A.D. 373.

Πετρος δε ο δια τον φοβον των Ιουδαιων κρυπτομενος, και Παυλος ο
αποστολος εν σπυριδι χαλασθεις και φυγων, ακουσαντες, εις Ρωμην δει
υμας μαρτυρησαι, ουκ ανεβαλοντο την αποδημιαν. Χαιροντες δε μαλλον
απηλθον, και ο μεν ως προς τους ιδιους σπευδων εγιννυτο σφαζομενος,
ο δε και παροντα τον καιρον ου κατεπτησεν αλλα και εκαυχητο λεγων.
Εγω γαρ ηδη σπενδομαι, και ο καιρος της αναλυσεως μου εφεστηκε.—
Apolog. de Fugâ suâ. c. 18.

PHILASTRIUS.   A.D. 380.

Qui (Magus) cum fugeret læsum Petrum de Hierosolymitanâ
civitate, Romamque veniret, cum læso Apostolo apud Neronem regem,
devictus undique oratione beati Apostoli atque percussus ab angelo,
sic meruit interire ut ejus magis evidens mendacium cunctis homini-
bus patefieret.—*c.* 29.

CYRIL OF JERUSALEM.   A.D. 386.

Παρατεινομενης δε της πληγης, αγαθων ξυνωρις διορθουται το πταισμα
Πετρος και Παυλος παραγενομενοι, οι της εκκλησιας προστατας· και επι-
διωκοντα τον νομιζομενον θεον Σιμωνα νεκρον ευθυς απεδειξαν. Επαγ-
γελλομενον γαρ του Σιμωνος μετεωριζεσθαι εις τους ουρανους και επ'

οχηματος δαιμονων επ'αιρος φερομενου, γονυ κλινοντες δι του Θεου δουλοι και την συμφωνιαν ενδειξαμενοι, ην ειπεν Ὁ Ιησους, κ. τ. λ. (Matt. xviii. 19, 20,) το της ὁμονοιας ξιλος δια της προσευχης νιμψαντες κατα του Μαγον κατιβαλον αυτον εις την γην. . . . . . . Ουτος πρωτος ὁ της κακιας δρακων.—*Catech.* 6.

AMBROSE. A.D. 397.
OPTATUS. Before A.D. 400.

Negare non potes scire te in urbe Româ Petro primo Cathedram Episcopalem esse collatam, in quâ sederit omnium Apostolorum Caput Petrus.—2.2.
Ergo Cathedram unicam sedit prior Petrus. Cui successit Linus. —2.3.

Fifth Century.

OLD ROMAN CALENDAR. After 400.
EPIPHANIUS. A.D. 403.

Εν Ρωμῃ γαρ (Επισκοποι) γεγονασι πρωτοι Πετρος και Παυλος, οἱ αποστολοι αυτοι και επισκοποι, ειτα Λινος, κ. τ. λ.—lib. i. *Hæres.* 27.
Ἡ των εν Ρωμῃ επισκοπων διαδοχη ταυτην εχει την ακολουθιαν, Πετρος και Παυλος, Λινος, κ. τ. λ.—*Ibid.*

PRUDENTIUS. A.D. 406.

Unus utramque dies, pleno tamen renovatus anno,
Vidit superbâ morte laureatum.
Scit Tiberina palus, flamine quæ lambitur propinquo,
Binis dicatum cespitem tropæis.
Et crucis et gladii testis, quibus irrigans easdem
Bis fluxit imber sanguinis per herbas.
  * * * *
Dividit ossa duûm Tibris.
        Peristeph. Hymn. 12.

Discede Jupiter,
Relinque Romam liberam plebemque jam Christi fuge.
Te Paulus hinc exterminat, te sanguis exturbat Petri,
Tibi id, quod ipse armaveras, factum Neronis officit.
       Hymn. de S. Laurentio.

CHRYSOSTOM. A.D. 407.
JEROME. A.D. 420.

Hujus (Claudii) anno secundo Petrus Apostolus quum primùm Antiochenam ecclesiam fundasset, Romam mittitur, ubi evangelium prædicans XXV annos ejusdem urbis episcopus perseverat.—*The Latin Chronicon, translated from Eusebius.*

Petrus, post episcopatum Antiochenæ ecclesiæ et prædicationem dispersionis eorum qui de circumcisione crediderunt in Ponto, Galatiâ, Cappadociâ, Asiâ, Bithyniâ, secundo Claudii anno ad expugnandum Simonem Magum Romam pergit, ibique viginti quinque annos cathedram Sacerdotalem tenuit usque ad ultimum annum Neronis, id est, decimum quartum, a quo suffixus cruci martyrio coronatus est.—*De Scriptoribus Ecclesiasticis, also translated from Eusebius.*

Marcus discipulus et interpres Petri, juxta quod Petrum referentem audierat, rogatus Romæ a fratribus, breve scripsit Evangelium; quod quum Petrus audiisset, probavit. Meminit hujus Marci et Petrus in Epistolâ primâ sub nomine Babylonis figuraliter Romam significans.— (1 Peter, v. 13.)—*Ibid.*

SULPITIUS. A.D. 430.

Namque eo tempore (in Nero's reign) divina apud urbem religio invaluerat, Petro ibi episcopatum gerente, et Paulo posteaquam ab injusto præsulis judicio Cæsarem appellaverat, Romam deducto. Ad quem tum audiendum plures conveniebant; qui veritate intellectâ, virtutibusque Apostolorum quas tum crebro ediderant, permoti, ad cultum Dei sese conferebant. Etenim tum illustris illa adversus Simonem Petri ac Pauli congressio fuit. Qui cum magicis artibus, ut se deum probaret, duobus suffultus demoniis evolasset, orationibus Apostolorum fugatis demonibus, delapsus in terram populo inspectante, disruptus est.—*Lib.* 2, c. 40.

Latis legibus religio vetabatur, palamque edictis propositis, Christianum esse non licebat. Tum Paulus ac Petrus capitis damnati; quorum uni cervix gladio desecta, Petrus in crucem sublatus est.— *Ibid.* c. 41.

AUGUSTINE. A.D. 430.

Cathedra tibi quid fecit ecclesiæ Romanæ in quâ Petrus sedit et in quâ hodie Anastasius sedet?—*Contra. lit. Petil. lib.* 2, c. 51.

Jacet Petri corpus Romæ, dicunt homines. Jacet Pauli corpus Romæ; Laurentii corpus Romæ; aliorum sanctorum martyrum corpora jacent Romæ, et misera est Roma! ... Tot strages mortis fiunt, ubi sunt memoriæ Apostolorum!—Quid dicis?—*Serm. in Natali Apostol.*

PAULINUS of Nola. A.D. 431.

    Ipsaque cœlestûm
  Sacris procerum monumentis Roma
  Petro Pauloque potens.
     Natal 3.

A LIST OF ALL THE WRITERS, ETC.   27

Cyril of Alexandria. A.D. 444.
Sozomen. A.D. 450.

Ολιγον δε χρονον Φιληκος επιβιωσαντος, μονος Λιβεριος της εκκλησιας (εν Ρωμη) προϊστατο. Ταυτη τη του Οσιου ξεοικησαντος, ωστε τον Πετρου θρονον μη αταξειν, ύπο ξυο ηγεμοσιν θυνομενον· ο διχονοιης συμβολον εστι, και εκκλησιαστικου θεσμου αλλοτριον.—*Hist.* iv. 14.

Orosius. A.D. 450.

Exordio regni ejus (Claudii) Petrus Apostolus . . . Romam venit, et salutarem cunctis credentibus fidem fideli verbo docuit, potentissimisque virtutibus adprobavit.—*Lib.* 7, c. 6.

Palladius. A.D. 450.

Νερωνος του βασιλεως—του κολασαντος τους αοιδιμους αποστολους Πετρον και Παυλον.—*De Brachmanibus.*

Petrus Chrysologus. A.D. 452.
Theodoret. A.D. 457.

Εχει δε και των κοινων πατερων και διδασκαλων της αληθειας Πετρου και Παυλου τας θηκας των πιστων τας ψυχας φωτιζουσας. 'Η δε πρεσματαρια τουτων και θεια ξυνωρις ανετειλε μεν εν τη εῳα και παντοσε τας ακτινας εξεπεμψεν· εν 'δε τη δυσει προθυμως εδεξατο τας του βιου δεσμας, εραειθεν νυν καταυγαζει την οικουμενην. 'Ουτοι μεν τον υμετερον περιφανεστατον απεφηναν θρονον. 'Ουτος των αγαθων των υμετερων ο κολοφων. 'Ο δ' εκεινων Θεος και νυν τον εκεινων ελαμπρυνε θρονον, την υμετεραν αγιωσυνην ιδρυσας εν τουτῳ, της ορθοδοξιας τας ακτινας αφιεισαν.—*Epist. ad Leonem.*

Leo. A.D. 461.

Hodierna festivitas, præter illam reverentiam, quam toto terrarum orbe promeruit, speciali et propriis nostræ urbis exultatione veneranda est, ut ubi præcipuorum Apostolorum glorificatus est exitus, ibi in die Martyrii eorum sit lætitiæ principatus.—*Serm.* 1 *de Natali Apost.*

Prosper. A.D. 463.
Maximus. A.D. 465.

Sixth Century.

Elpis. A.D. 520.

O felix Roma!—quæ tantorum principum,
Es purpurata pretioso sanguine,

Non laude tuâ, sed ipsorum meritis
Excellis omnem mundi pulchritudinem.
Hymn. de Apostolis.

ABATOR. A.D. 556.

Dignaque materies Petri Paulique coronæ
Cæsareas superare minas, et in arce tyranni
Pandere jura Poli, summumque in agone tribunal
Vincere, ne titulos parvus contingeret hostia.
Act. Apost. in fine.

GREGORY OF TOURS. A.D. 595.

Nero Petrum cruce, Paulum gladio jubet interfici.—*lib.* 1, *c.* 25.

Seventh Century.

GREGORY THE GREAT. A.D. 604.

Itaque cum multi sint Apostoli, pro ipso tamen principatu sola Apostolorum principis sedes in auctoritate convaluit, quæ in tribus locis unius est. Ipse enim sublimavit sedem in quâ etiam quiescere et præsentem vitam finire dignatus est. Ipse decoravit sedem, in quam Evangelistam discipulum misit. Ipse firmavit sedem in quâ septem annos quamvis discessurus sedit. Cum ergo unius atque una sit sedes, cui ex auctoritate divinâ tres nunc Episcopi præsident, quidquid ego de vobis boni audio, hoc mihi imputo, si quid de me boni credidit, hoc vestris meritis imputate, quia unum sumus, &c.—*lib.* 6, *Epist.* 40.

ISIDORE OF SPAIN. A.D. 636.

Septimo et tricesimo anno post passionem Domini a Nerone Cæsare in urbe Româ deorsum verso capite, ut ipse voluit, crucifixus est.—*In Vit. Petri.*

Thirteenth Century.

THE GOLDEN LEGEND. A.D. 1298.

PART I.

THE ANTENICENE RECORDS.

I.

The Κηρυγμα Πετρου, (A.D. 45,) called in English "Peter's Proclamation," "Preaching," or "Doctrine," and in Latin "Prædicatio Petri," "Doctrina Petri," &c., was a document which appeared against the Gnostic heresy among the Gentiles at Rome, before the siege of Jerusalem, and even as early as the reign of Claudius. It seems to have contained an account of the doctrines taught by Peter and the apostles in Judæa, with some of our Lord's predictions respecting the destruction of Jerusalem, and to have been looked upon by the earlier Fathers as really the production of St. Peter himself, or at least as having been authorized by him. Clement, the eminent bishop of Alexandria, in the beginning of the third century, quotes a good deal from it as such. Eusebius also considered it in the same light, although he says that the authenticity of the work extant under that name in his time was by no means universally acknowledged,—Origen having rejected it as spurious, and none of the quotations cited by the bishop of Alexandria being discoverable in it. The original authentic document was, he tells us, (*Hist.* 2, 14), sent to Rome by St. Peter himself, a little before he went to Babylon, for the purpose of counteracting the Gnostic heresy in that city, in the reign of Claudius; and this historian has written a whole chapter respecting its success there upon that occasion, with the title "On the Κηρυγμα Πετρου at Rome." Lactantius also bears witness that this work was sent to Rome prior to the destruction of Jerusalem, and, therefore, during the apostle's lifetime; that it contained our Lord's predictions relative to that event, and that it was the means adopted by the apostles (or, according to the usual expression, "by Peter and Paul") to announce these predictions in that city, in such a way that they might be afterwards seen to be such. (Ea Prædicatio, in memoriam scripta, permansit. *Lactantius, Institut.* 4, 21.) I draw attention to these particulars respecting the book called "Peter's Proclamation," because its name seems to have been one of the main sources of the modern error about Peter's having left the East. As to its supposed testimony, however, upon this subject, the book in question is not now extant, nor is there any extract from it in which it is pretended that there is the slightest allusion to anything of the kind. Baratier and Bishop Pearson, who alone cite it as authority in this case, admit that there is not, but think that it must have contained some such passage, as Lactantius seems to say so. But Lactantius says exactly the reverse. Lactantius says: "Christ disclosed some predictions to His disciples, of which the apostles made public proclamation at Rome; and that Proclamation (ea Prædicatio) being in writing, to perpetuate the predictions, was still extant after their fulfilment. IN THIS PROCLAMATION, among many other extraordinary things, THEY SAID (in quâ dixerunt) that Providence would soon send a king to exterminate the Jews," &c. (*Lact. Instit.* 4, 21.) Does not Lactantius here say as distinctly as he could well have said it, that it was not in person, but in the written document called "Peter's Proclamation" that the apostles publicly announced our Lord's predictions among the Gentiles at Rome upon the occasion alluded to? And does he not thereby corroborate the account given by Eusebius, that this document was sent to Rome by Peter, a little before the final departure of the apostles from Jerusalem? In all which, however, we have not a shadow of reason for supposing, either that "Peter's Proclamation" contained anything about Peter's being in Europe, or that Lactantius was under the impression that it did.

Some writers seem to have considered that "Paul's Proclamation" and "Peter's Proclamation" were two distinct works; others that Peter and Paul were the joint authors of the same work; and others, with more probability, that Paul's name became connected with a work exclusively under Peter's name, from a mistake on the part of Lactantius, who was a Latin writer, with regard to a Greek passage in Clemens Alexandrinus, by whom this work was so often quoted. That point, however, has nothing to do with the present question.

II.

ST. LINUS (A.D. 70) a bishop of Rome, is one of those upon whose testimony the Roman Catholics have been taught to believe that Peter was not put to death on the Euphrates, at the ancient Babylon, in the territory of the king of Parthia, where Peter himself says that he was living in expectation of his martyrdom in the reign of Nero, at the very time that he was writing his epistles to the other districts of the Dispersion. In the work attributed to this bishop on Peter's crucifixion, it is said that Peter was put to death by Agrippa, in a city where Agrippa was the governor, and that Nero was very much annoyed when he came to hear of the apostle's death, and sent Agrippa into retirement, where he died. The MSS. of this document are said to mention Rome and not Jerusalem as the scene of the story; but Agrippa was never governor of Rome. As, however, the work in question is confessedly a recent production, I need do no more than show that father Ceillier, and all the Roman clergy, now admit that it affords no indications of Peter's not having been put to death, as is intimated in the Scriptures, in Parthia,—that they consider it full of the absurdest fictions, and that St. Linus had nothing whatever to do with the composition of it.

Father Ceillier (vol. l. p. 490) says: "The work that we have in two books, under the name of St. Linus, is full of ridiculous fables, and is not even worth reading."

Father Tillemont, in his fifty-first article on St. Paul, says of this document—"It is one of the worst invented pieces that ever were written." Again, in his sixtieth note on St. Paul: "It signifies very little what this work asserts, or what it denies." And again, in his chapter on the first Popes: "This work is full of errors. Baronius maintains that it is a forgery, or at least very much corrupted, if it ever was authentic—and several other writers pronounce the same judgment."

Cardinal Bellarmine, in his Ecclesiastical Writers, says,—"We consider that Linus's writings are not extant, and that those which now pass under his name are forgeries."

The Dominican Fathers Richard and Giraud, in their Bibliothèque Sacrée, remark: "The two books which bear the name of Linus, about Peter's martyrdom, are forgeries, as well as being full of fictions and heresies."

As far, therefore, as Linus's testimony is concerned, there is no reason to suppose that Peter was not put to death at Babylon.

III.

ANACLETUS, (A.D. 91,) also a bishop of Rome, is another of those upon whose testimony the Roman Catholics have been taught to rely for the alleged fact that Peter left the lost sheep of the house of Israel to come and live in Europe. Three decretals (or papal briefs) have been attributed to Anacletus, the MSS. of which are said to contain words to this effect; but the recent origin of these documents has been for many years placed beyond all doubt, and the Roman clergy, without one exception, now admit that whatever they contain, they cannot any longer be considered as affording the alleged evidence, inasmuch as there is not the least pretext for supposing them to have been written by Anacletus.

Father Tillemont says,—"We have three decretals under the name of St. Anacletus. We do not examine them. All the learned are agreed now-a-days that these letters are frauds and forgeries, (faussés et supposées,) and that all the decretal letters attributed to the popes that lived prior to Pope Siricius (A.D. 385) are equally so."

Father Dupin, in his chapter on the false decretals, says: "The first epistle attributed to Pope Anacletus is evidently a forgery." (He here assigns eight grounds for this opinion.) "Nor is there less proof that the second letter attributed to Anacletus is an imposture also." (He here assigns five grounds.) "And, for the same reasons, we must pass the same judgment upon the third letter attributed to this pope."

The Dominican fathers, in their Bibliothèque Sacrée, say,—"All the decretals attributed to the popes who preceded Siricius are considered by the learned as forgeries."

It is unnecessary to multiply these quotations from the Roman-catholic authorities. They are all now agreed that Feuardent was wrong, and that Anacletus has not left one word to justify the supposition that the apostle Peter ever came to Europe.

IV.

CLEMENS ROMANUS (A.D. 100), another bishop of Rome, is supposed to have said that Peter did not undergo his martyrdom at Babylon, in Parthia; but it will be seen that he does not say so, and that he does not even say anything from which this could be inferred; but quite the reverse. His words addressed to the Corinthians are (after adverting to Moses and other pious persons mentioned in the Old Testament): "But to leave the examples of antiquity, and to come to the most modern, let us take the noble examples of our own times. Let us place before our eyes the good apostles. Peter, through unjust dislike, underwent not one or two, but many sufferings; and having undergone his martyrdom, he went to the place of glory that was due to him. Paul, also, having seven times worn chains and been hunted and stoned, received the prize of such endurance. For he was herald of the gospel in the West as well as in the East, and enjoyed the illustrious reputation of the faith, in teaching, as he did, the whole world to be righteous. And when he came to the remotest limits of the West, he underwent his martyrdom before the governors of mankind; and thus freed from this world, went to his holy place, the most brilliant example of steadfastness that we possess," (c. 5.)

The first question that here suggests itself is, why is Paul's journey into Europe and Paul's martyrdom at Rome, so pointedly stated in the very same paragraph in which nothing more is said of Peter's travels or of Peter's martyrdom than what manifestly pre-supposes the Scripture account about his going to the Jews of the Dispersion, as he was directed by his divine Master, and about his being put to death at Babylon, as his own epistles intimate? How is it that Clement makes no allusion to a residence in Europe, or even to a martyrdom there for the apostle of the circumcision as well as for the apostle of the Gentiles? Peter's martyrdom took place in Clement's lifetime. How is it that Clement never heard of anything connected with it at variance with the facts that are laid before us in the Scriptures? But we do not inquire for the evidences of Peter's having lived and died as is indicated in the sacred text. Our inquiry is for the alleged evidence of his not having done so.

Father M'Corry's view of Clement's words is wholly founded upon a textual misapprehension, very pardonable under the solicitude that he naturally felt about the question in which he was engaged, though avoided by all his more cautious predecessors. He supposes St. Clement to speak of the martyrs that had fallen in his own CITY; whereas Clement speaks of those who had fallen within the memory of that present generation. "Let us look at the illustrious examples OF OUR OWN AGE," says the bishop of Rome; "let us take, for instance, the apostles."

The Correspondent in the *Times*, Mr. Baratier, and others, adopt another view of the passage. They argue that if Peter was put to death at all by the Jews, it must have been in Europe;—that it was not likely that Nero either would or could persecute the Christians through the Jews within the territories of Parthia, of which Babylonia was a province, or in short, anywhere except in Europe; and that, therefore, as Peter fell in Nero's persecution, he must have perished to the west of Judæa. Whereas, it can be proved from Romancatholic records that Babylon was, at the time of Peter's martyrdom, in the most abject dependence upon the will of Nero; that Nero's persecution of the Christians was carried on not only by imperial edict, which took effect throughout all the Asiatic provinces of the empire, but that it was also carried on within the jurisdiction of the states dependent upon the empire; and that there was, during that persecution, a large and violent faction of the Jews at Babylon in an extreme state of exasperation against the leaders of the Christians in that city. I shall presently adduce evidence upon these three points; but let us first attend, once for all, to the facts which we have in Scripture, as to Peter's martyrdom, and the country in which it occurred. We shall then be in a better condition to judge of the amount of testimony requisite to meet the inferences drawn from Clement's words by the Correspondent in the *Times*, Father M'Corry, Baratier, and the other writers on their side.

In John xxi. 18 and 19, we have our Lord's prediction that Peter was to be crucified with his head downwards, in his old age. The manner of the crucifixion we gather from the GIRDLE (or zone) put on after the person was fastened to the cross by the hands and feet with nails, or by the wrists and ancles with cords. In the ordinary posture of crucifixion the body was not sustained (as is commonly supposed), and could not possibly be sustained, by the fastenings of the hands alone, but was also supported by a seat, or rest, at the middle of the cross, as we learn from Justin Martyr, and other early writers. This is well known to divines. "On the middle of the upright part of the cross," says Mr. Barnes, on the New Testament (Matt. xxvii. 35), "there was a projection or seat, on which the person crucified sat, or, as it were, rode. This was necessary, as the hands were not alone strong enough to bear the weight of the body, as the body was left exposed often many days." Horne, also, in his Introduction to the Holy Scriptures (in the chapter on Crucifixion), says: "There was a piece of wood that projected from the middle of the cross, on which the person sat as on a sort of saddle, and by which the whole body was supported. Justin Martyr, in his Dialogue with Trypho the Jew, gives this description. . . . . The person was permitted to hang (the whole weight of his body being borne up by his nailed hands and feet, and by the projecting piece in the middle of the cross) until he perished through agony and want of food." When the posture of the body was reversed it was necessary to adopt a different expedient for supporting its weight. This is the girdle alluded to in our Lord's words, with which the whole body at the hips was bound to the cross, and which was put on before the cross was set up in the hole dug for it. "The limbs of persons crucified," says Mr. Barnes, on our Lord's prediction of Peter's death, "were often bound or tied to the cross, instead of being nailed; and even the body was sometimes girded to the cross." Mr. Barnes does not seem to perceive the intention of the "girding;" but that this posture was considered (at least as late as the middle ages,) to be implied in our Lord's prediction, may be seen in the work on "the Destruction of Jerusalem," which was once erroneously attributed to Hegesippus— "Peter was crucified (says this book) with his head downwards, at his own request; either because it was so it was to happen, AS CHRIST HAD PREDICTED IT, or because his persecutors willingly granted him an increase of torture." (De excidio Urbis Hierosol. iii. 2.) And with regard to this mode of crucifying the Christians with the head downwards, Eusebius (A.D. 340) tells us in the eighth and twelfth chapters of his eighth Book, that it was not a very unusual practice in the countries in which the Jews had the ascendancy; and that on the Euphrates, even a little before his own time, in the districts around Babylon, smoking wood was often placed near the head of the victim thus suspended, in order to aggravate the sufferings or to accelerate the death.

Then as to the scriptural indication of Parthia, as the scene of Peter's martyrdom. In Matthew xxiii. 34, our Lord told the Jews that among their other misdeeds they would crucify some of his apostles, and all the fathers understood Peter to be one of these here referred to as martyrs to be crucified in cities where the Jewish population had sufficient authority for that purpose. St. Jerome, in his commentary on these words, illustrates them by saying,—"They crucified Peter." Nicolaus de Lyra, an eminent theologian of the 14th century, paraphrases the verse thus: "Some of them you will kill, as James, and Stephen, and many more; and others you will crucify, as Peter and Andrew." But it is unnecessary to enlarge on this. No Roman-catholic writer has ever denied that what our Lord here says, he says of Peter and to the Jews.

Again, from the following texts, Matthew, x. 5, 6, and 23; xxviii. 19. Mark, xvi. 15. John, xxi. 15, 16, and 17.

Acts, ii. 5; ix. 15; xi. 2 and 3. Galat. ii. 7, &c.; 1 Pet. ii. 25; v. 1, &c., we learn that our Lord told Peter to confine himself in his travels as much as possible to the Jews of the Dispersion, and to those cities in which these were in the greatest numbers; to seek out these cities of Israel in whatever nation of the earth they were to be found, but to confine himself to them (other apostles being appointed for the Gentiles); not, indeed, to reject the Gentiles when they came, yet not to go to Gentile nations, and not to stop even in Samaria, though he must of course pass through it, but to go rather to "the lost sheep of the house of Israel;" an expression which the prophets of old applied only to the Jews of Babylon and the adjoining provinces, and which no Jewish Christian would otherwise interpret. The Scripture records on this point are too explicit to require any comment.

Finally, from 1 Pet. i. 1; iv. 12; v. 13; and from 2 Pet. i. 14, we learn that this indefatigable apostle fulfilled to the letter our Lord's commands. After having taken one of the much-frequented routes from Antioch to Mesopotamia, we find him established, and Mark the Evangelist with him, upon the Euphrates, amidst all the ancestral associations and desolate magnificence of Babylon, the head quarters of the Dispersion, and where the hereditary patriarch of the Dispersion lived— seeking there to spiritualize the expectations of the Parthian Jews, who still looked with impatience for the conquest of the world —writing letters from there, exhorting "the lost sheep" in the surrounding provinces to return to their "Shepherd" (meaning Christ), announcing to them that the fulfilment of our Lord's prediction respecting him (Peter) was at hand; that Nero's persecution of the Christians, from which they were all suffering, had reached Parthia where he was; and that he was looking forward to an almost immediate martyrdom, but that he would endeavour to have them kept in remembrance of his advice after his death: in consequence of which, the First Epistle General of St. John, who survived Peter some twenty or thirty years, originally appeared as "The Epistle to the Parthians," is so described still in many of the early MSS., and is now looked upon as such by all the Roman clergy. With these scriptural indications before us, we cannot wonder if we find that so early a writer as Clement had heard nothing of the alleged residence "in the West," or of the alleged martyrdom "before the sovereigns of mankind."

Let us now attend to the argument put forward by such of the Roman clergy as rely, with the Correspondent in the *Times* and Baratier, on this passage of Clemens Romanus for Peter's not having been put to death at Babylon. It resolves itself, as has been seen, into these two propositions: that the king of Parthia would not have submitted to Nero's dictation; and that Nero himself did not seek to persecute the Christian churches beyond the confines of Europe. On the first point the chief authorities are Josephus, Tacitus, and Dio Cassius; on the second, Orosius, Sulpitius, the Younger Pliny, and Tertullian; all which authorities are approved of and quoted upon these two points, though upon occasions somewhat different, by Father Palma, Cardinal Baronius, Father Calmet, Father Tillemont, and all the rest of the Roman clergy who have written upon this persecution.

1. As to the relations between Parthia and Rome, the account given by Tacitus is transcribed in most of its details, by Tillemont in his "History of the Emperors," where, in his reigns of Claudius and Nero, this writer states that Vardanes was king of Parthia, and holding his court at Babylon, when Apollonius of Tyana was there in the early part of the reign of Claudius; that the Parthians sent an embassy to Claudius to beg of him to restore to the throne of Parthia the young Parthian prince, who was at that time a hostage at Rome; that Claudius sent the prince to Cassius, his governor in Syria, which adjoined Parthia, to convey him safe into the hands of the Parthian nobles at Zeugma, a frontier town on the Euphrates, the usual rendezvous between

the authorities of Rome and Parthia; that this manœuvre being unsuccessful, Vologeses was made king of Parthia, and conferred two of his provinces as kingdoms upon his two brothers, giving Armenia to Tiridates and Media to Pacorus, A.D. 51. Tillemont then proceeds to tell of the war carried on by the Parthians and Armenians against Corbulo, the distinguished general that Nero had on the Euphrates, respecting the crown of Armenia, which Nero had taken from the King of Parthia and his brother—of the complete success of the imperial army—and of the King of Parthia's being compelled to send his brother, Tiridates, with hostages to Rome, to Nero, to conclude a peace with him, and to receive from the Emperor the disputed crown, A.D. 66. Tillemont adds, that on that occasion Nero closed the Temple of Janus, as the peace of the empire was secured by this submission of the king of Parthia; and that it was in the middle of the following year that Peter's martyrdom took place.

This event Niebuhr thus records: " Another war which occurred in the reign of Nero is that of Corbulo against the Parthians. Corbulo conducted it with uniform success, and the Parthian king was compelled to consent to holding his kingdom as a fief of the Roman emperor. Tiridates himself came to Rome, and was received in the most magnificent manner, and obtained the diadem (of Armenia) from Nero."

Dio Cassius (lib. lxiii. c. 1) says: " When Tiridates came to Rome, he had with him not only his own sons, but those of his brother, the king of Parthia; those also of his other brother, the king of Media, and those of Monobazus, the king of Adiabene (another state dependent upon Parthia); and their whole journey from the Euphrates was like a triumphal progress." We are not told that these children returned with Tiridates.

Josephus gives us, in his Wars, ii. 2, a report of King Agrippa's speech to the Jews of Jerusalem (A.D. 66), from which the following passages are selected, urging them to remain in submission to Nero, and warning them to reflect that even the Parthians had their hostages at Rome. This was the Jewish king before whom St. Paul made his celebrated appeal to Nero. . . . "Numberless other nations (said Agrippa) armed with higher claims to freedom than you have, receive the yoke. You alone disdain servitude to those to whom the whole universe has submitted. . . . Will you not reflect on the empire of the Romans? Will you not measure your own weakness? . . . For the entire Euphrates has not sufficed them on the east, nor the Danube on the north. . . . What of the five hundred cities of Asia? Do they not, though ungarrisoned, do homage to the emperor and to the fasces of the consuls? . . . How strong a plea may Bithynia and Cappadocia put in for freedom? and yet they pay their tribute without force of arms. . . . But why need I enlarge, while even the Parthians, that most warlike race, lords of so many nations, and invested with so mighty a dominion, send hostages to Rome? And thus in Italy you may behold under the guise of peace, the noblest born of the East in submission to the yoke. . . . What help then will you obtain from the uninhabited quarters of the earth, for all the inhabited portion BELONGS TO ROME? unless, possibly, some of you extend your hopes beyond the Euphrates, and suppose that your kindred will bring you aid from Adiabene. But they will neither involve themselves on any frivolous pretext in a war so serious, nor were they so unadvisedly disposed, would the king of Parthia permit them, for he is careful to maintain the truce with the Romans, and would deem himself a violator of the treaty, should any under him rise in arms against them." (Where see much more to the same effect.)

We have here, in glaring colours, not only the utter subjection of the Parthians to Nero, and of the Jews of Babylon to the Parthians, about the time of Peter's death among them, but ample evidence of the two great factions which at this time subsisted among the Jews in all the cities of the East, and of which, no doubt, Nero's emissaries availed themselves in the persecution of the

Christians,—one faction intent upon submission to the emperor, the other upon war; and the Christian church at Babylon, inculcating, as Peter did, submission, was placed between these two parties, as it were between two fires. For on the one hand it was exposed to the co-operation of the peaceable Jews at Babylon, with the commissioners of the emperor, and on the other to the bitterest hostility of the discontented Jews there, who, with the distinguished Silas at their head, were straining every nerve (as Josephus elsewhere informs us) to arouse their fellow-citizens to a war with Rome. It may also be observed, that Josephus further attests the abject condition of the Parthians, with respect to the Romans at this time, when he subsequently states that even four years later, after Jerusalem had fallen, the same Vologeses, the king of Parthia, sent an embassy of congratulation to meet Titus at Zeugma, on the Euphrates, and to present him with a crown of gold.

2. As to the extent of the persecution, Cardinal Baronius says, in his "Ecclesiastical Annals," (A.D. 68, paragraph 45), "It was not only at Rome and in the places adjoining to that city, but IN OTHER STATES and in other provinces (sed in aliis civitatibus atque provinciis), that we find the Christians to have suffered martyrdom in this reign of Nero; for Orosius, the historian, tells us that orders were given by Nero that the Christians should be persecuted throughout all the dependencies of the empire with as much severity as at Rome (pari persecutione.) The names of these martyrs have been almost all lost, as the Ecclesiastical Records were burnt by the Emperor Diocletian; so that only very few of them are mentioned in the Roman Martyrology. But to say nothing of the rest, (for we cannot undertake to give an account of all the martyrs of all the churches,) let us now treat of the events which took place in our own church." And again (A.D. 69, paragraph 46), "That Nero's persecution was carried on with the greatest imaginable severity, not only in the capital, but throughout the whole world then under

the sway of Rome (toto orbe Romano), has been clearly shown," &c. &c.

Orosius, the ancient historian referred to by the cardinal, says: (7.6) "Nero was the first who visited the Christians at Rome with penalties and death; and he gave orders that they should be persecuted with equal severity throughout all the territories that were dependent upon Rome."

Sulpitius Severus, another ancient writer, says to the same effect (lib. ii):—"General laws were passed (datis legibus) to forbid the religion, and imperial proclamations were issued, (palam edietis propositis) prohibiting mankind from professing Christianity."

Father Calmet, in his "Dictionary of the Bible," also admits that it was not confined to Italy. "Nero," says he, "permitted his own gardens to be the scene of all these cruelties (immediately after the fire, A.D. 64). From this time edicts were published against the Christians, and many martyrs suffered, especially in Italy. We have mentioned the death of St. Peter and St. Paul consequent on this persecution, which probably continued to the demise of Nero, A.D. 68, the 14th year of his reign."

Father Palma, of the College of the Propaganda at Rome, says, in the first volume of his "Ecclesiastical History," (p. 32, &c.) "But it must not be supposed that this affliction of the Christian church was circumscribed within the limits of the capital, for it cannot be doubted that the Christians were then persecuted in all the countries conquered by the Romans (in universis Imperii Romani provinciis)." Again, of the notion that martyrdoms only took place in Europe, he adds: "That this notion is manifestly false and utterly at variance with the history of those times, has been shown with the clearest evidence." He also cites the chapter from Tacitus upon this persecution, from which he says, "it is evident that Nero's cruelties were not confined to the church of Rome, but extended, without exception, to all the Christian churches that were within the territories subject to his authority, not so much in consequence of the fire attributed to the Christians, as because they were looked upon as the common enemies of mankind." He also aptly illustrates the point with the case of Bithynia, one of the provinces of the Dispersion with which Peter was in communication, as being dependent upon the Jewish patriarch of Babylon; and where Pliny the Younger, half a century after Nero's time, found the same laws and edicts still in force against the Christians. But these authorities on this persecution are familiar to most readers. Pliny's Correspondence with the Emperor Trajan, on the laws in question, is thus referred to by Tertullian (A.D. 250): "Those statutes, which only the unjust and impious carry out against us, and which to some extent were annulled by Trajan, when he gave orders to the authorities that they should not ENDEAVOUR TO FIND OUT the Christians." (Vetando inquiri Christianos, chap. v.)

Thus we see that Nero's persecution was universal; that Parthia was in complete subjection to Nero at the time of Peter's crucifixion there; that it was usual for the imperial commissioners, at that time, not only to put to death the Christians that were brought to them, but to track them out and arrest them wherever they could be found; and that the Christian church at Babylon, as well as in all the other Jewish cities, had the whole of the war party in the fiercest hostility against it. It is evident, therefore, that when Clemens Romanus merely says that Peter was put to death, he does not contradict the intimations given us in Scripture, about his having been put to death in Parthia, but confirms them.

There will be found in the third chapter on Eusebius, some important particulars respecting the condition of Babylon at the period of Peter's martyrdom there, which have been collected from the writings of his contemporaries, and which have been unaccountably overlooked by the generality of modern writers. Suffice it to say here, that Babylon was then the same peculiarly constructed city as ever; consisting, as from its first foundation, of an enclosed area of about 200 square miles; of which the greater part was, as it always had been, laid out in pasture, tillage, and plantations, little more than a twentieth part of the whole being occupied with the dwellings of the inhabitants, and these for the most part detached from one another; that it was then, as has been seen, within the Parthian territory; that it was used as a country residence by the kings of Parthia, one of its palaces being not only kept in repair, but handsomely decorated; that its population was not much less than half a million, and that half of these were Jews; that though not adapted for military purposes, the kings of Parthia kept a garrison there; and that even half a century after Peter's time, when the Emperor Trajan went there, he was obliged to take it by force of arms, as Dio Cassius and Eutropius inform us, and placed a Roman garrison in it, in order to retain it. Theodoret (A.D. 459), one of the bishops on the Euphrates, remarks, in his Commentary on the thirteenth chapter of Isaiah, that Babylon in his day was wholly inhabited by Jews; and St. Chrysostom reminds us that there were Jews from Babylon among those Parthians who were at Jerusalem when St. Peter commenced his foundation of the churches at the Feast of Pentecost, immediately after the Ascension (Acts ii. 9).

V.

IGNATIUS (A.D. 107), archbishop of Antioch, in his letter to the Romans, dated from Smyrna, where he was at the time, says, that he does not think himself entitled to address a Christian church with as much authority as Peter and Paul did, because they were apostles, which he was not. "Not as Peter and Paul," said Ignatius, "do I give you directions. They are apostles; I am condemned. They are free; I am still a slave. But if I suffer, I also shall be free." (chap. iv.) Bishop Pearson and Mr. Baratier, to whom the Correspondent in the *Times* refers us, considered that these words afford reason to suppose that Ignatius thought Peter had been in Europe at some period of his history, as well as Paul, whether we suppose this to have been after or before he went to Babylon. "If it were not so," asks Baratier, "why did Ignatius name the two apostles together? or why did he name Peter at all, if Peter had no more to do with Roman Christians than St. James or St. John, who never were at Rome?"

The answer to the first question is, that in the fathers of this period Peter is, as all admit, and as we have already had occasion to observe, very frequently named alone as representative of all the twelve apostles of our Lord, who were mainly and primarily to occupy themselves with the conversion of the Jews, partly for the convenience of the expression, and partly because he was considered, as Eusebius tells us, one of the most able and energetic of the twelve, (it not being imagined until long subsequently, that our Lord had assigned him an ascendancy above the rest), just in the same way as although there were many apostles of the Gentiles, Paul is constantly named alone as their representative. So that these two names combined, as they so frequently are in the Fathers, were merely used to designate in a brief form *all* the original instructors of the Christian churches; and the reader will perceive that this expression has, from its frequency, greatly contributed (as Pearson and Baratier here so ingenuously avow), to the preposterous inference that, as the one apostle certainly was in Europe, the other apostle must have been there likewise. The answer to the second question is, that even if Peter had nothing to do with the Roman Christians, and had never taught any of them, Ignatius might nevertheless have very naturally said, "I do not give you directions as if I were Peter (or as Peter might have done), for I am not an apostle." This language would not in the least imply that Peter had ever addressed a word to the Roman Christians. But besides

this, it is quite a mistake to assume that Peter could
have had no connexion with the Roman Christians—
could never have addressed—never have converted any
of them, if he had strictly obeyed our Lord's commands,
in confining himself to the cities that were most frequented by the Jews. We learn, from the second chapter of the Acts of the Apostles, (as I shall show more
at large in the section on Irenæus,) that, before he ever
left Judæa, he, "standing up with the Eleven," made
the first converts, laid the first foundations, and taught
the first doctrines of the church of Rome; nor shall we
be mistaken if we assume that a very large (if not the
larger) portion of the Romans, who were Christians, when
St. Paul wrote to them, had been at one time or another
Peter's auditors at Jerusalem. Thus, even if the words
of Ignatius must be supposed to imply that Peter, as
well as Paul, addressed discourses to the Romans, we
find from Scripture that he did so without having
neglected for that purpose the special mission entrusted
to him by our Lord.

Neither Cardinal Baronius nor Cardinal Bellarmine,
nor even Father Feuardent, considered that much dependence was to be placed upon anything in Ignatius to
prove the point they were so anxious to establish, for they
do not mention him; nor do I know of any Roman-catholic
writer, except Father M'Corry, and the Correspondent
in the *Times*, who adopts this very unsatisfactory argument of Baratier's, as a "demonstration" that St. Peter
must have left the East and gone into Europe at some
period of his history.

VI.

PAPIAS (A.D. 110), bishop of Hieropolis, in Phrygia, is
regarded by Baronius, and all the writers on his side,
as very valuable testimony about Peter's having been
with Mark in Europe; but most fortunately for that
great scriptural fact, which this writer is supposed to

contradict, we have his own very words, and in them he says nothing whatever about Peter's having left Babylon. He only mentions Mark's having composed, from what he could recollect of Peter's lectures, that gospel which he wrote, as the Fathers tell us, in Egypt, at the universal request of those enthusiastic converts in Babylon, Jerusalem, Alexandria, and even Rome, and in all the other Christian cities who had, at different times, constituted Peter's crowded auditories in the East. What Baronius, and those who have followed him, suppose Papias to say, is, that Peter was in Europe while he was delivering those lectures from which Mark wrote. The words of this bishop are preserved by Eusebius, (iii. 39) and are as follows: "John, the Presbyter, also said that Mark, who was Peter's interpreter, gave from his recollection of what Peter used to tell, an accurate but not a systematic account of the sayings and doings of our Lord. For he neither heard nor followed our Lord; but subsequently, as I have said, accompanied Peter, who communicated the different facts to his hearers as occasion required; not, however, just as one who was giving a consecutive history of our Lord's discourses. So that Mark's account is not the less correct, from his having written some of the circumstances in the same order in which he remembered Peter to have told them. For he was careful not to omit or misstate anything that he had heard from the apostle." To which words Eusebius adds: "This is what Papius says of Mark." Every one can see that in this statement there is nothing whatever about Peter's having abandoned the Jews of the Dispersion. The modern Roman clergy who suppose, with some of the first adversaries of the Reformation, that Peter came into Europe, suppose also that Mark came with him, and (contrary to what the Fathers tell us) wrote his gospel while he was there with Peter. It is evident, however, that the words of Papius give no countenance to that story; nay, that they clearly prove Peter not to have been with Mark when this Evangelist wrote his gospel, which fact will in a future page be found further corroborated by all the Fathers.

Cardinal Bellarmine, and some other writers, have likewise, from their misconception of a passage in Eusebius (ii. 15), fallen into the mistaken notion that Papias said "Babylon" stood for "Rome" in Peter's First Epistle; and that this being the case, it was most probable that Peter went to Europe instead of to Parthia when he left the Holy Land. But our task is here easy, for the Roman-catholic commentators on Eusebius admit that the name of Papias is not connected in this passage with the *on-dit* of the fourth century, about Babylon meaning Rome in Peter's First Epistle; and several Roman Catholics, of the highest celebrity in their church, frankly confess that the *on-dit* itself is unworthy of their church, too improbable, too late, nay, even too absurd and too unnatural, to be allowed for an instant to take the place of the plain account given to us in the Holy Scriptures on this subject.

Henry de Valois (A.D. 1676), commonly called by his Latin name, Valesius,—the most celebrated Roman-catholic commentator on Eusebius, and whose authority as a Greek scholar all the clergy of his church accept, translates as follows the passage of Eusebius, referred to by Bellarmine: "This story (about Mark's gospel having been written at the request of all those who had been delighted with Peter's doctrines and eloquence in the East) is given by Clement of Alexandria, and corroborated by Papias. There is, moreover, a report that it is this Mark, the evangelist, that Peter mentions in his First Epistle; which it is also pretended (contendunt) was written at Rome, and that Peter intimates this himself by using the term 'Babylon' in a metaphorical sense for Rome." (Euseb. ii. 15.)

Valesius remarks on the whole of the clause beginning, "There is, moreover," "Ruffinus understood this as if it was related by Papias; and Musculus, in his translation adopted the same error. But these words are to be kept perfectly distinct (omnino sejunximus) from the preceding, and I find that this has been carefully done even by St. Jerome and Nicephorus."

Father Dupin also, in his Preliminary Dissertation, (Notes on Sec. 4,) says of this interpretation of Peter's language: "Some have thought that Papias, and St. Clement of Alexandria, cited in this chapter by Eusebius, were of this opinion; but it is not upon this point that Eusebius cites them."

It is unnecessary to add anything more to prove that the Greek passage in Eusebius affords not the slightest pretext for supposing that Papias had ever heard of the rumour mentioned in it. Eusebius, without vouching for the truth of this rumour, merely mentions it as the interpretation of some people in the fourth century, when he was writing, it being an opinion, then not uncommon among some of the Jews, that Babylon stood for Rome in the prophecies of Isaiah. But as this *on-dit*, and the grounds of it, will be fully examined when we are reviewing the testimonies of the fourth century, I shall here only observe that the Roman-catholic Archbishop Peter de Marca (A.D. 1662), whose learning and attachment to the Roman church were most conspicuous, is one of the many distinguished Roman-catholic writers, (of whom Father Calmet mentions several in his Preliminary Discourse, 1 Peter,) who refused to substitute a vague rumour of the fourth century for the plain language of the Holy Scriptures. "St. Peter went to Antioch," says Archbishop de Marca, "and from there to Babylon, where the hereditary patriarch of the first Dispersion of the Jews resided. When established in that city he wrote his First Epistle, as is clear from the words, 'the Church at Babylon salutes you.'" (De Marca, de Concordia, lib. vi. c. 1.)

Father Dupin is another of these more accurate writers of the Roman church. "Peter's First Epistle," says he, in the Preliminary Dissertation, "was written from Babylon. Some were of opinion that Rome was meant by this name; but that interpretation is not natural (mais ce sens n'est pas naturel). We cannot precisely name the time when it was written, but we may say that it was written at Babylon, A.D. 45."

Our present point, however, is not as to the abandonment of this *on-dit* by the more enlightened portion of the Roman clergy themselves, but as to whether we have any reason to think that Papias had ever heard of it, and after the foregoing analysis of this and the other point respecting what Papias says of Mark, let the conscientious Roman Catholic reflect upon the words of Father M'Corry, which, to do him justice, are but what he has read in Baronius and Bellarmine: "Papias tells us that Mark records in his Gospel what he had heard from St. Peter at Rome; and he moreover tells us that St. Peter wrote his Epistle from Rome, calling that city by the mystic appellation of Babylon."

VII.

HERACLEON (A.D. 126), of whose writings but very few words have come down to us, is adduced as evidence of the supposed event, merely because he had seen the work called "Peter's Proclamation;" and yet did not contradict the statement that it is supposed to have contained upon this point. This reason for thinking that Peter had left Babylon is peculiar to Mr. Baratier, and is, therefore, one of those which the Correspondent in the *Times* puts forward as "thorough proof" and "demonstration" of it. To say nothing of the absurdity of inferring from the few words of Heracleon's that have come down to us, what was or what was not contradicted in his works, we have seen that as far as we know anything about it, "Peter's Proclamation" did not contain the alleged statement, and that therefore Heracleon had no occasion to have contradicted that document upon that point. What will the reader think of a cause that is supposed to derive assistance from such evidence as this? The following is another instance of what the Roman-catholic Correspondent in the *Times* so erroneously supposes to be "thorough proof" and "demonstration."

VIII.

"THE RECOGNITIONS" is a work assigned by Mr. Barntier to the second century, though unquestionably belonging to the middle ages; and is represented by him as stating that Peter went in person into Europe in pursuit of Simon Magus; whereas it not only makes no such statement, but most distinctly records the contrary. In this work, which is a sort of historical romance, in no less than ten books, Peter, after a contest with the magician at Cæsarea, and the latter's departure for Rome, is introduced (Book iii.) saying that he must follow him *immediately* to that city of the Gentiles (è vestigio insequi), in order to refute him *at once*, ("ut continuo confutetur a nobis,") and that for this purpose, as Peter could not then personally leave Cæsarea, he would despatch twelve ordained persons to Rome after him, in order that the magician might perceive that by them the apostle was always present with him (ut *me* in ipsis semper *secum* esse sentiat), at Rome or wherever else he went to; and that he would himself proceed into Europe in three months afterwards. We are then told that the twelve missionaries were ordained and sent to Rome, and that Peter, having remained three months at Cæsarea, *did not* go to Rome, as he is made to say he would; that on the contrary, he then went from Cæsarea to Tripoli (Book iv.); and that, having remained at Tripoli for six months, he then went to Antioch (Book vi.), having Clemens Romanus with him the whole time, at which town the narrative concludes with events which occupy the four last books of the work, and without the slightest further allusion to any intention on Peter's part of going in any other sense to Rome. I do not insist upon the authority of the "Recognitions," for the facts here stated. The work has been approved of by Mr. Barntier and the Correspondent in the *Times*, as very clear proof upon the point at issue. I therefore refer to it to show how utterly mistaken they are, and that it not only does not say that Peter went to

Rome in person, but that it says the exact contrary, viz., that he did not go there; or, which is the same thing, that he only went there in the persons of his twelve evangelists or missionaries; and that that was considered by the writer of the romance as equivalent in the middle ages to his having been there in person.

IX.

"THE CLEMENTINA" is a work supposed by Baratier to have been originally written in the second century, but which he acknowledges to have undergone great changes in after times, and to be full of interpolations (admodum interpolatum et mutatum, p. 6). Yet he and the Roman-catholic Correspondent in the *Times* do not scruple to speak of it as some of the very best evidence that they could find of Peter's having been in Europe. It appears to me that their own account of this work, as given by the former and sanctioned by the latter, must annul its testimony in the eyes of all the more earnest of the Roman-catholic body. But I proceed to show, further, that all the more enlightened of the Roman clergy have always admitted that it is so full of these interpolations of the middle ages, so altered from what it originally was, and so replete with fictions and absurdities, that it cannot be regarded as affording any evidence upon this, or upon any other subject. The only passage in it I may, however, first observe, that could possibly be mistaken to mean that Peter ever left the East, occurs in the part called "The Epitome of the Recognitions," and is evidently no more than an allusion to what was said in the "Recognitions" itself, about Peter's having followed the Samaritan impostor to Rome, in the persons of his twelve missionaries, as any one can perceive by comparing the two passages. The words are, — "But after Peter had in this manner . . . . arrived at Rome, and had there taught the worship of the true God against the Samaritan, and made many converts, ... he at length went to his heavenly home." Instead of enlarging upon the obvious sense of these words, I confine myself to showing that Baronius and Ceillier, in short, all the Roman-catholic writers, are unanimous in describing the "Clementina," in unmeasured terms, as a mere tissue of lies and nonsense, and as a work that none of the Fathers of the church would have considered as testimony that they could rely on, of Peter's having been in person in Europe, even if it had existed in their day, and contained a statement to that effect.

Father Tillemont says of the "Clementina,"—"We need not say much about this work—full as it is of fallacies and fables."

Father Dupin says,—"The last work attributed to St. Clement of Rome is a collection of divers pieces, entitled, 'Clementina.' Perhaps this is the second part of the 'Recognitions,' for it is a continuation of what is called 'The Acts of St. Peter.' All these writings are only a series of fictions and idle stories."

The Dominican Fathers in the "Bibliothèque Sacrée" write thus: "The works falsely ascribed to St. Clement of Rome are, 1. 'The Apostolic Constitutions,' an ancient document into which various changes and additions have been introduced from age to age. 2. 'The Recognitions,' an old apocryphal writing, full of faults and fictions. Also, 3. 'The Clementina,' which is perhaps the second part of the 'Recognitions.'"

Father Ceillier says,—"There is a work extant, under the name of St. Clement of Rome, containing nineteen conversations, which is commonly called the 'Clementina.' Cotelier thinks that they may be another edition of the 'Recognitions.' What is certain is, that we find several things (plusieurs traits) in it that we also read of in the 'Recognitions.' It has the same inventions and the same mis-statements, and the plan of the two works is the same. In every part of it, we find proofs that St. Clement of Rome had nothing to do with the writing of it."

Cardinal Baronius frequently condemns this book, as

incompetent to prove anything, and as unknown to the Fathers. He says that it "abounds in falsehoods," (Mendaciis confertus, A.D. 41, paragraph 10); is "full of stupid fictions," (insulsis fabulis refertus, A.D. 102, paragraph 22), "full of corruptions," (depravatus, corruptus, paragraph 21), and that "any one accustomed to read the Fathers must see that they never mention it or allude to it," (Temperasse quidem l'atres ab eorundem librorum usu, nemo est qui antiquorum libris assuetus non intelligat. *Ibid.*)

It is clear that when such a character attaches to a work, all inquiry as to what it states is superseded; and we have here, as I have said, another opportunity of seeing the kind of testimony which Mr. Baratier considered himself obliged to have recourse to, and which the Correspondent in the *Times* calls "thorough proof" of Peter's having left the East.

X.

"THE APOSTOLIC CONSTITUTIONS" is another work whose testimony is adduced by Baratier in favour of the supposition that Peter must have left the East, although no Roman-catholic writer (except that singularly enthusiastic one, the Correspondent in the *Times*) pretends that it can be considered as affording any evidence whatever on the subject. The passage selected by Baratier as the strongest is that in which he states that Clement, who was a native of Rome, converted by Barnabas, and ordained by Peter, after a long residence with this latter apostle in the East, was the second bishop of the Roman church; as if Clement could not have been sent by Peter from Asia to be bishop of Rome, but that Peter must himself have gone over with him to instal him! a supposition so contrary to all usage, modern and ancient, that it would seem childish to discuss it. The Roman Catholics tell us, that Mark was ordained and sent to Alexandria by Peter to be bishop of the church there; but no Roman Catholic has ever pretended that Peter went there with him to instal him. The passage in "The Constitutions" is as follows:—" Now concerning those bishops who have been ordained in our lifetime, we make known to you that they are these; . . . . of Antioch, Evodius, ordained by me, Peter, and Ignatius by Paul. . . . . Of the church of Rome, Linus, the son of Claudia, was the first, ordained by Paul; and Clement, after Linus's death, the second, ordained by me, Peter. . . . . These are the bishops who are intrusted by us with the parishes in the Lord," &c.

XI.

DIONYSIUS CORINTHUS, (about A.D. 170,) a bishop of Corinth, is relied upon as the clearest possible proof that Peter's martyrdom took place in Europe, and not, as is intimated in the Scriptures, at Babylon. He does not, however, say anything of the kind. He only says that it occurred ABOUT THE SAME TIME as Paul's martyrdom, which we know from other sources took place at Rome. He also adverts to the principle laid down by Paul, (1 Cor. iii. 8,) that he who watered a planted church, was as much a planter of that church as he who originally planted it; and reminds the Romans that, although no Corinthians are mentioned in the Acts (chap. ii.) as being with them among the first Christian converts made by Peter at Jerusalem, and although, therefore, strictly speaking, Paul was, as he himself says, (1 Cor. iii. 6—10, also iv. 15), the original planter of the Corinthian church, yet as there were subsequently Corinthian converts with St. Peter at Jerusalem, through whom this apostle's instructions were conveyed to Corinth, the church of Corinth was therefore to be considered as having been planted by our Lord's twelve apostles while they were at Jerusalem, as well as the church of Rome was,—a community of origin which Dionysius assigns as a reason for good-fellowship between the Roman and Corinthian Christians. The following is the extract cited from this bishop's letter to the Romans; it has been preserved by Eusebius (ii. 25):—" By your recent exhortation, ye blend, as it were, the plant of the Romans and Corinthians, which was propagated by Peter and Paul; for it was not until after both these apostles had planted us in this Corinth of ours, as well as in Italy, by addressing their instructions, both of them, to the same cities (ὁμόσε διδάξαντες) that they were put to death for the faith, as they were about the same time." Some of the translators introduce here words equivalent to "went," or "came;" which gave rise to the impression that Dionysius supposed Peter to have gone to Corinth and to Rome with Paul to plant Christianity there, but no such word of any kind is to be found in the original, nor have we the slightest trace any where of Peter's having gone to Corinth. Father M‘Corry appears, as the reader will observe, to have been singularly deceived about this Greek passage.

XII.

HEGESIPPUS (A.D. 180) says not one word about Peter's having left the East, nor do any of the learned pretend to say he does. On this point Baronius, Bellarmine, Pearson, and Baratier, are all agreed. The only extracts that have been preserved from his writings may be seen in Eusebius, and in them he does not even mention Peter's name. When Father M‘Corry and the Correspondent in the *Times* adduce this author as evidence of Peter's being in Italy, it is because they suppose him to be the author of the little work of the middle ages, on the Destruction of Jerusalem, in which there are some extracts from Jacques de Voragine's story about the Learned Dogs and the Fiery Chariot at Rome, and which work was sometimes inscribed with the name of Hegesippus, by corruption for Josephus, from whose writings part of it was compiled. It is unnecessary to enter into much proof that this little romance was not written by Hegesippus. All well-informed writers without exception, Roman-catholic as well as Protestant, acknowledge that it was not. From its contents it is admitted to have been composed at least after the tenth century. But the portions about Peter and the Golden Legend are manifestly copied from the Pseudo-Abdias, a work commonly assigned to the fourteenth or fifteenth. The following Roman-catholic authorities will suffice:

The Benedictine Fathers, in the Bibliothèque Sacrée, say: "We have a History of the Destruction of Jerusalem in five books, under the name of this ancient Hegesippus, the author of which lived at least two hundred years after him. It appears to be only a work compiled from Josephus, the Jewish historian, whose name was corrupted into that of Hegesippus."

Father Dupin says: "We have besides, under the name of Hegesippus, a history of the taking of Jerusalem, divided into five books. But it is certain that this work does not belong to Hegesippus, it being evident that it was written by some one who lived after the reign of Constantine the Great. . . . Others, as Vossius and Miræus, affirm that this book was compiled after the tenth century. Be that as it may, whoever wrote this book is only a transcriber or translator of Josephus, who made a kind of imperfect epitome of his history, giving it the title of Joseppi or Josippi, and the copyists, not understanding this word, substituted Igisippi or Egesippi in its stead, as appears from some of the MSS."

Father Ceillier says: "As to the five books on the destruction of Jerusalem, which pass under the name of Hegesippus, it is agreed on all hands now-a-days, that they were written by some one of a much more recentage."

Father Tillemont (49th note on Peter) observes: "I have not ventured to quote what is said of St. Peter in the History of the Jews that passes under the name of Hegesippus. We do not know who that writer was, nor in what time he lived."

It is then evident that Hegesippus affords no evidence upon this subject; and as to the story about the Learned Dogs and the Fiery Chariot, extracts of which are contained in the work of the middle ages that used to bear his name, Father M'Corry and the Correspondent in the

Times are the only modern members of their church that depend upon it for proof of Peter's not having remained at Babylon. I do not mention here what this story is, as it will be found at full length in the last chapter of this work.

XIII.

VICTOR (about A.D. 200), a bishop of Rome, is supposed by Baratier to have written two letters on Easter, which no other writer attributes to him, in which letters the usual form of expressing the authenticity of the Roman doctrine occurs: " This was the doctrine taught at Rome by Peter." " It is manifest, therefore," says Baratier, "that Peter was at Rome." I appeal to any impartial reader, at all acquainted with the ecclesiastical phraseology of those times, whether this might not mean quite as well " the doctrine which Peter caused to be taught at Rome," as that " which he himself personally taught there," and whether the expression in question might not have been used if Peter had never left Jerusalem. Salvianus and St. Augustine, African writers, fathers of the church, use the same expression respecting Peter's having taught at Carthage, where no writer pretended that Peter or any one of the apostles ever was. How then can it be so manifest from such words that Peter was at Rome? But this is not the only remark to be here made. No other writer except Baratier— neither Baronius, nor Coillier, nor Bellarmine, nor any other, either among Roman-catholics or Protestants, speaks of these supposed letters of Victor's as anything but the clumsiest forgeries, and as the production of some much later writer. Baratier only says that he sees no very good reason why they should be so! " It is evident," says he, "that Victor wrote letters upon this subject (of Easter). Why may not some of them be extant? and if any are extant, why may not these be they, since there is nothing in them but what may have been Victor's?" This the Correspondent in the *Times* must concede is not what is commonly meant by "demonstration." For the sake of brevity in a case so very evident, I only cite Salvianus and Baronius on the expression, and Father Ceillier on the letters.

Salvianus (A.D. 400) says: "Carthage—which our Lord's apostles formerly instructed in their doctrines." (Quam quondam doctrinis suis Apostoli instituerant. De Gubernatione Dei, lib. vii.)

Baronius remarks: "Augustine and Salvianus frequently say that the African churches had received the Gospel from our Lord's apostles." (A.D. 44, paragraph 38.)

Ceillier says on Victor: "There are four letters still extant in these days that pass under his name, two of which are among the false decretals. The other two are also forgeries. The writer does not even seem to know what occurred in Victor's time about Easter, which is the subject of the letters." (Vol. ii.)

XIV.

IRENÆUS (A.D. 200), bishop of Lyons, in France, is supposed to afford more decisive proof than any other ancient writer, that Peter must have left the East and come into Europe. To those, therefore, who attend minutely to it, it will, for that very reason, afford the *stronger* proof of the contrary; for they will see that what is most depended upon as proof of the Papal story is, in reality, to be as little depended upon as what is put forward with diffidence and uncertainty.

Irenæus says that Peter had a share with Paul in making the first converts, in engaging the first teachers, and in promoting the extension of the Roman church; or, as this writer expresses himself, in "founding," and in "edifying" it. This, say some Roman-catholic writers, he could not have done, without having gone himself into Europe. Of Irenæus's three passages to the same effect, the strongest is that cited by the Correspondent in the *Times*, and is the one usually cited on this occasion: "The greatest and most ancient church founded and built by the two glorious apostles, Paul and Peter." (iii. 3.) Another of these passages is as follows: "Matthew published his Gospel among the Hebrews in their own language, while Peter and Paul were engaged in evangelizing and founding the Christian church at Rome. And after their death (some translate it their final departure from Judæa, when all the apostles separated), Mark, also the disciple and interpreter of Peter, gave us in writing what Peter made the peculiar subject of his proclamations to the Dispersion." (iii. 1.) The third passage from this writer is thus: "The blessed apostles having founded and edified (or built) that church (of Rome), gave the ministration of its episcopal duties to Linus. This is the Linus whom Paul mentions in his Epistles to Timothy." (iii. 3.)

That Peter was one of those who laid the foundations of Christ's church at Rome, as Irenæus here states, there neither is nor ever was any doubt. There is not, however, in this fact the slightest pretext for supposing that he or any of the rest of the apostles (and they all co-operated with him) came into Europe to lay these foundations. A short and complete proof of this is that Cardinal Baronius, whose authority upon that point no Roman Catholic will refuse, acknowledges that there is not, and that the apostle's presence in a city was not at all necessary to enable him to found, plant, erect, or evangelize a church there. The Cardinal's own unambiguous words will be found a few pages farther on; but (as in the former case about Peter's martyrdom), I shall here first place before the reader the scriptural account of this transaction as it was understood by the fathers, and by Baronius also; from which it will be seen that Peter was not in Europe, nor even supposed to be in Europe, when he was laying the foundations of the Roman church; that the thing was done at Jerusalem, and that all our Lord's apostles, as well as Peter, assisted and co-operated; that it took place, at least, that it commenced, immediately after the Ascension, immediately after those memorable words,

"Go, teach all nations"—that it took place, in short, when Peter, standing up with the eleven at Jerusalem, pronounced that energetic appeal whereby, we are told, that simultaneously all the most ancient churches of the earth were founded.

From the second chapter of the Acts of the Apostles, we learn that a body of Roman Jews (some of them Jews by birth, others by conversion) who were making a temporary stay at Jerusalem at that time (v. 10 and 14), were converted to Christianity by Peter's exhortations (v. 37), and baptized at Jerusalem into the church of Christ (v. 41), thus receiving, as Peter had promised them (v. 38), "the gift of the Holy Ghost;"—that these Romans, as long as they remained at Jerusalem, near the apostles, continued steadfastly in the apostles' doctrine and fellowship, and in the breaking of bread and in prayers" (v. 42); and that not long afterwards, in the same year, a persecution breaking out at Jerusalem about Stephen (viii. 1; and xi. 19), these Roman converts, with "the gift of the Holy Ghost" fresh upon them, went back, a Christian church, to their native city, "preaching the word" (viii. 4).

It is true that the Roman Jews must have been but a small portion of Peter's auditors upon this and the two or three subsequent occasions of his addressing them, prior to the general dispersion of the Christians from Jerusalem; but it is not improbable that they amounted to at least 100, for Baronius calculates, as will be seen presently, that all the Jewish converts who left Jerusalem upon that persecution to return to their different homes throughout the world, must have been upwards of 15,000. But even if the Roman converts did not amount to 100, as the proportion of Jews at Rome was very small, there being but 8000 at Rome (Josephus Ant. xvii. 11), while there were a million at Alexandria alone (Philo. de Virt.), and several millions in Babylon and its vicinity (Josephus and Philo. *ibid.*), yet it cannot be said that even fifty Roman Christians returning from Judæa and preaching the word, could hardly be what Irenæus meant to speak of as "a church."

The early Fathers considered that a Christian church did not at all depend on numbers. "One or two persons," says Tertullian, "constitute a church." (In uno et altero Ecclesia est. De Penitentia, c. x.) And in another place: "Three persons, even if they are not ordained, constitute a church." (Ubi tres ecclesia est, licet laici. De Castit.) The apostles themselves, also, often speak of a single Christian household, or of the Christian congregation assembling at one person's house, as an apostolic church, (Rom. xvi. 3 and 5; Col. iv. 15; Phil. i. 2), and our Lord had taught them to do so, when He said, "Where two or three are gathered together, there am I in the midst of them." But we have no reason to suppose that the Roman church at its first foundation had much less than at least 100 members, if it had not a great many more; two of whom Paul mentions in his Epistle to that church, at a much later period: "Salute Andronicus and Junia, my kinsmen and my fellow-prisoners, who are of note among the apostles, who also were in Christ BEFORE ME."

Such, then, is the Scripture history of the Christian church founded at Rome by Peter (as the fathers understood it to be founded by him), almost immediately after our Lord's ascension, while Pilate was still governor of Judæa, Tiberius still emperor, and upwards of a year before the conversion of St. Paul,—a period long antecedent to that at which the Roman clergy suppose that any of our Lord's apostles could have come into Europe. We see also from the Scripture History of this transaction, that the foundations of the Roman church were laid, not by Peter only of the twelve, as some have weakly imagined, but by Peter and his eleven colleagues,—a most important fact in connexion with this subject, which obtains too little attention from the general reader. In this passage of Irenæus, as so often elsewhere, we find Peter's name set down alone to represent all the twelve apostles of the circumcision. No Roman-catholic supposes, or is taught by his clergy to suppose, that it was not on behalf of his colleagues as well as on his own behalf, that Peter delivered his address on the occasion I advert to. "He pronounced that discourse," says Father Tillemont, "in the name of the other apostles, who all spoke by his mouth, and who authorized him by their presence. For they could not all speak at once"—a remark in which this learned priest was preceded by St. Chrysostom. "They allowed Peter to speak for them," says St. Chrysostom, in his Fourth Homily on the Acts of the Apostles, "for they could not all speak together." We must not lose sight of this.

Nor do the scriptures warrant the supposition that it was only as its founders that the apostles, with Peter for their representative and deputy, were at this time related to the church at Rome; and that after they had once laid its first foundations, they neither added to these, nor did anything else while they continued at Jerusalem, to edify and advance it—a strange notion, entertained, however, by some of the Roman-catholics. On the contrary, there can be no doubt, from what St. Luke tells us in the Acts, that, as long as the apostles remained together there, they occupied themselves in not only strengthening the foundations of the Roman Church, by their intercourse with the Roman converts already made, but that they also contributed to its extension and "edification," by sending over, from time to time, fresh supplies of converts from the Roman Jews—either from those of them who, Philo informs us (De Virtut. p. 1014), repaired to Jerusalem with the proceeds of the First Fruit Offerings every year, or from such other Roman Jews as for any other purpose visited that city, in which, for their accommodation, there was a Roman synagogue with a school attached to it. There can, I say, be no doubt that in this way the apostles added to that church daily; and that, not converts only, but persons whom they deputed to preach for them on their return, and to baptize for them at Rome. And this daily care of the apostles for the churches continued about twelve years. Their departure (or Exodus) out of Judæa is not mentioned by Baronius as having taken place much before that time; and

Jerusalem, the great centre of the Jewish world, afforded such advantages for the proclamation of the Gospel in every city, as could not have been expected to attend the personal presence of the apostles anywhere else. Whence it will be seen that Paul was converted soon enough to have a share in the earlier converts of the church of Rome, as is stated in this passage of Irenæus, for his conversion took place, as all the Roman clergy are agreed, less than two years after our Lord left his apostles. (Baronius and Calmet place it A.D. 34.) And as to Paul's part in the edification or extension of that church, we know from the Scriptures that he wrote letters to it, and that he even resided at Rome for two whole years, preaching there; besides which, it is clear that he co-operated with the twelve in their exertions at Jerusalem on its behalf, until Peter went to Babylon and the rest elsewhere, after which period Paul seems to have been unaided by the apostles of the circumcision, in his continued efforts to extend and edify the church of Rome.

I have confined these scriptural statements to this church of Rome; but as we learn from the same passages of the Acts, this was not the only church founded by the apostles at Jerusalem, immediately after the ascension. Far from it. The churches of Babylon and Pontus, of Carthage and Cyrene, of Colosse and Alexandria, of Antioch and Cyprus, with innumerable others, began all then their bright career. In fact, in every place where there was a synagogue, by those few words of Peter, a Christian church was founded; for from almost every synagogue in the world there seems to have been at that time a deputation at Jerusalem, which was sent back by Peter gifted with the Holy Ghost and preaching the word. It is to this simultaneousness in the foundation of the churches that Peter himself alludes when he speaks of the churches of the provincial Dispersion as having been founded at the same time as that of Babylon, the capital—(1 Pet. i. 1; v. 13)—a peculiarity in the foundation of all the earliest churches, which renders it, if possible, still more absurd to suppose that

F

Peter founded them by being himself personally present in the different cities.

And it is in this scriptural sense that all the Fathers, Latin as well as Greek, understood the Roman church to have been founded. Gregory, the bishop of Nyssa, in Cappadocia (about A.D. 390), thus mentions the first Roman Christians, in his Sermon upon Stephen: "From this time the disciples of the twelve began to traverse the whole world, and this was the beginning of the diffusion of the Gospel in all quarters. For if the Jews had not thus persecuted the first Christians after Stephen's murder, perhaps THE BLESSINGS OF THE GOSPEL MIGHT HAVE BEEN CONFINED TO JERUSALEM. But now that the Jews persecuted them, these first Christians were dispersed over the whole world, most of them going to different countries, expelling the father of evil by the doctrines of Christ. In this way it was that Samaria received the word. . . . Thus, also, the Egyptians, Syrians, Parthians, (in whose territory Babylon then was,) and the Mesopotamians, THE ITALIANS also, and the Illyrians and the Macedonians began to have their churches (Christum agnoscunt), and the Gospel traversing all nations, brought all the nations into the fold."

Irenæus, whose words we are now considering, says the same thing (b. iii. chap. xii.) After quoting portions of Peter's addresses, from the second and subsequent chapters of the Acts, he goes on thus: "These are the words of that church at Jerusalem, by which EVERY OTHER CHURCH WAS FOUNDED (or, from which every other church derived its foundation). These are the words of the Parent Church—of those who are the denizens of the New Testament—the words of the apostles —the words of the disciples of our Lord—of those who indeed were perfect disciples, made perfect by the Spirit after the ascension of the Lord."

St. Jerome, also, in his commentary upon the second chapter of Haggai, after mentioning the earthquake that occurred at our Lord's crucifixion, says: "And by this concussion every nation of the earth was shaken. Be-

cause then the voice of our Lord's apostles went forth
—went forth and found its way into the remotest regions
of the world. But why were the nations shaken? That
they might yield all the elect and whatever is to be found
foremost in the faith. The elect of Corinth, for instance,
for in Corinth God had many of his people. The elect
of Macedonia, for there was a large church assembled in
Thessalonica. The elect of Ephesus, that they should
know the mysteries of God. What more need I add?
All the nations were convulsed—all to whom the Saviour
sent his apostles when he said, 'Go, teach all nations'—
all were shaken, and the few that were chosen out of the
many that were called, constructed the churches of the
first Christians. Hence the apostle Peter says 'The
church at Babylon, that is elect, salutes you.' Hence
the apostle John writes to 'The lady that is elect,' and
afterwards mentions 'the children of her elect sister.' In
this way the nations were convulsed—unable to withstand
the brightness of the word, and the elect of all the nations
were put forward. It was then that was complete the
glory of the Lord's House, which is the church of the
living God."

Baronius quotes others of the fathers to the same
effect. "You have it stated," says St. Athanasius, the
patriarch of Alexandria, in his sermon De Sementi—
"you have it stated in the Acts of the Apostles, after
the stoning of Stephen, that the disciples of the twelve
were scattered, and as it were sown over the earth; not
that these primitive Christians were thus dispersed
through pusillanimity, but in the interests of the
faith. For they were scattered in this way in order that
in their travels over the whole world they might diffuse,
and as it were sow the Christian churches, the powers
and excellencies that are in the doctrine of life."

The Cardinal also quotes the following words from St.
Chrysostom's Homilies upon the Acts of the Apostles:
"Peter pleaded the cause of Christ upon behalf of our
Lord's other eleven apostles, as well as upon his own. . .
He was the first who collected a church, and that not of

the Jews only who belonged to Jerusalem and to the country round, but of the Jews of Parthia (in whose country Babylon was in the apostolic times), and of the Medes, and of the Phrygians, of the Africans (near Carthage), of the Egyptians (*i.e.* Alexandrians), and of the Arabs, OF THE ROMANS, and of others. He who was expressly appointed by our Lord as the shepherd of the lost sheep, began then to collect these scattered flocks out of all nations. He also taught them to renounce all things, and to meet together for the breaking of bread and for prayers."

St. Chrysostom again, also, makes the following allusion to this sudden creation of the Christian churches everywhere:—" For though it is a little thing to say " I shall build my church," do not hasten over the words as if they were nothing, but unfold them to your understanding, and reflect how immense an act it was in this rapid manner to fill with so many churches every portion of the earth that is inhabited by mankind, and to erect altars everywhere,—in the country of the Romans and of the Persians (within which, in Chrysostom's day, stood Babylon), in Scythia, in Mauritania (where Carthage was), and upon the Indus. But what am I saying? This fact went even beyond this world of ours. For the British Isles, which are situated beyond our sea— which lie, in fact, in the very ocean—these felt the power of those mighty words; for even there—even in those islands, churches and altars were then erected, and the words so spoken were realized in every heart. Thus it was that His apostles built our Lord's churches everywhere."—(Chrysos. vol. i. pp. 701 and 702.)

Instead of illustrating any further the undisputed unanimity of the fathers upon this point, I give Baronius's own account of this foundation, or first creation of the Christian churches: " In the 35th year," says he, " after the birth of Christ, all the Christians except the apostles were compelled to leave Jerusalem on Stephen's death, when they proceeded into different countries, the most widely separated from one another. In these countries they preached the gospel, and ENABLED THE APOSTLES IN THIS MANNER TO MULTIPLY UNDER FAVOURABLE CIRCUMSTANCES THE CHURCHES OF GOD. For it was not only into Judæa and Samaria, as Luke mentions chap. viii., that these first Christians travelled. He also tells us most distinctly that they passed the frontiers of Palestine and went into other countries (see Acts xi. 19). We find that an immense number of these first Jewish converts went into Asia, to whom Peter afterwards wrote his Epistles, inscribed to those scattered throughout Pontus, Galatia and Cappadocia, Asia and Bithynia. .... For the Jews lived far and wide, in Asia and Africa, and even Europe, as well as within the limits of the Holy Land; and that the number of these first Christians was very great, is evident; for if any one will only calculate them and reflect that none but the apostles remained at Jerusalem, he will find that several thousand Christians must have been scattered over the world upon that occasion." And again, after specifying the result of Peter's addresses as indicated in the 2nd, 4th, 5th, and 6th chapters of the Acts, he sums up thus: "If, therefore, we reckon all these, we shall not be very wrong if we suppose 15,000 men to have been then dispersed; so that we cannot wonder to find from Peter and others, that they had passed into the most distant and different lands." (Annals, A.D. 35, paragraphs, 1, 2, and 3.)

But enough has been said to show that in the Scriptural account of the foundation of the church of Rome, as understood by the Roman Catholics as well as by all the Fathers, there is not the slightest pretext for supposing that Peter left the East to effect it. It remains to show that even the Roman clergy admit that his personal presence was not necessary for such a purpose. And happily one brief testimony settles this. Baronius himself, even in the case of Antioch, in which there was no motive for a strained opinion (as the apostles were often there), admits that Peter's presence was not essential to the foundation of his churches. "For what does it mean," says Baronius (A.D. 39, paragraph 16), "when Peter is said to have founded the church of Antioch? They are quite wrong who think that Peter must have gone to Antioch for that purpose." (Errant men sententia qui existimarent, ad hoc, opus fuisse ut Petrus petierit Antiochiam.) Again: "As Peter's chair at Alexandria, in which it cannot be made to appear that Peter ever was, was founded by that apostle, it is quite evident that his presence was not necessary to found even a patriarchal see." (Non præsentiam Petri, sed potissimum requisitam esse auctoritatem ad constituendam sedem aliquam Patriarchalem.) Again: "When, therefore, we say that Peter founded the See (or Chair) of Antioch, this must not be supposed to imply that Peter was among any of the first who preached there, for that, it is quite evident, was done exclusively by those Christians who, on Stephen's death, were driven from Jerusalem." He further admits that these first Christians founded the churches wherever they went. "If others preached at Antioch before Peter, and were thus considered to have founded that church, (a quibus jactum videretur ecclesiæ fundamentum,) Peter and Paul cannot in that sense be said to be its founders," (hac exparte fundatores.) And again: "But if on the other hand, Peter is to be considered to have founded the church of Antioch, notwithstanding that it was not he who introduced the gospel there, Paul is certainly entitled to being considered in this light quite as much as Peter; for Paul did quite as much as Peter to promote that object. So that St. Ignatius, writing to the Magnesians, says that Paul had as much to do with the foundation of the church at Antioch as Peter had, and that the church of Antioch was founded by both of them," (ab utroque esse fundatam ecclesiam Antiochenam.)

The reader sees, also, in these passages that the See (or Chair) of Alexandria, was also considered to have been founded by St. Peter, although it is admitted by all parties that the apostle never was in that city. Nor is this view of the origin of that See peculiar to Baronius. We find that this was the general doctrine of the popes. They considered that it was for this purpose St. Peter sent Mark to Alexandria. Father Tillemont, speaking of the popes in his thirty-first note on Peter, says: "They hold that St. Peter founded the See of Alexandria; and that he did so through the instrumentality of Mark." This learned priest also adverts, in his twenty-fifth note on Peter, to what Baronius here says of Antioch: "Cardinal Baronius considered that Peter was able to found his Chair of Antioch, and to establish his See in that city without going there," (sans y aller.) In addition to which I may observe that a large majority of the Roman clergy are, by their peculiar view of Peter's history at this period, reduced to the necessity of admitting that Peter's foundation of the church of Rome took place while he was in the East. It will be seen in Part II. Section II. of the present Treatise, that Father Ceillier, Stephen Baluze, Father Pagi, Father Calmet, and a large majority of the writers in communion with the church of Rome, were of opinion that Peter could not have left the East for at least twenty years after our Lord's ascension; yet none of these writers considered that the capital of the empire was without its church during all that time, or that Paul's letter to the Roman church was not written for upwards of twenty years after the ascension. These writers, therefore, have no alternative. They frankly admit that Peter's foundation of their church took place while he was in the East. But the authority of Irenæus himself on this point obviates the necessity of adducing any other. Irenæus knew that the church of Rome was founded without the personal presence of St. Paul; for St. Paul, in his letter to it, speaks of it as a flourishing church, and alludes at the same time to his not having yet been able to go to Rome; still Irenæus, nevertheless, says in the very passage we are considering, that Paul was one of those who laid the foundations of the church at Rome. Here is the clearest and concisest evidence imaginable that this Father did not mean to imply Peter's absence from the East in Peter's foundation of the church at Rome. Again: Irenæus says, in this same passage, that the Roman church was one of the first founded—one of the earliest and most ancient churches. But the Roman clergy tell us, as may be seen in the quotations just given from Baronius, that the church of Antioch and all the most ancient churches were founded within a year after the Ascension. Does not Irenæus then plainly state, upon this showing of the Roman clergy themselves, that Rome also had its church from the apostles, during that first year, and therefore that it was founded by them without their presence at Rome? Is it not doing violence to his words to suppose them consistent with the supposition that Rome was at least a dozen years later than the earliest and most ancient of the churches in his time? And again: Irenæus says that Matthew's Gospel was written at the time this church was being founded, and the Roman clergy consider that it was written in, or even much before the year A.D. 41, four years, at least, before any of them think that Peter left the East. Baronius, with whom Calmet and Ceillier agree, says in his Annals, at the year A.D. 41 (paragraph 15), "In this same year Matthew wrote his Gospel." And immediately afterwards, speaking of Peter's supposed journey from the East, he says: "And this took place in the second year of Claudius, A.D. 45, four years after the publication of Matthew's Gospel." Father Tillemont and others of the Roman clergy, as well as the Protestant writers, assign a much earlier date to this gospel. "It seems necessary to mention here," says Father Tillemont, "that Matthew wrote only *three* years after our Lord's death." He then combats the opinion of Baronius, and says, in his fifth note on Matthew, that even A.D. 39 is too late a date to assign to the first appearance of this gospel. Horne, in his Introduction, says: "Tiberius died in the spring of A.D. 37, and it is highly probable that Matthew's gospel was written by that time." Thus Baronius has the latest date, but even with that date we see that Irenæus KNEW Peter was at Jerusalem when he says that this apostle was founding the church that was at Rome.

The Greek term "evangelizing," found in one of Irenæus's passages, denotes, as may be seen in the lexicons, to instruct a church by written documents, as well as orally, and was ultimately almost exclusively applied to written instructions. The Roman-catholic, as well as Protestant critics, indicate another sense of this expression. "In the beginning of Christianity," says Father Calmet, in his Dictionary, "there were evangelists and preachers who, without being fixed to any church, preached wherever they were led by the Holy Spirit." "We learn from Eusebius (v. 9,) and other writers cited by Suicer," says Dr. Bloomfield, to the same effect, in his New Testament, "that in the Apostolic Church, 'evangelists' was the appellation given to those preachers who aided the labours of the apostles, not by taking charge of any particular church, but by acting as itinerant preachers and teachers wherever their labours might be needed, and thus building on a foundation previously laid by the apostles."

At the risk of seeming tedious on a point so evident, I shall here observe that we hear much of this church in the history of Tiberius, as he happened to have a sort of controversy with the Senate respecting its encouragement. It appears that in consequence of despatches received from Pilate, Tiberius, apparently from pure good will to the Roman church, proposed to the Senate that our Lord should be worshipped among the gods of Rome. The Senate sought to flatter Tiberius by objecting to this proposal, upon the ground that he had previously considered himself undeserving of that honour. Some say, and with an appearance of truth, that the secret cause of their objecting was the emperor's having proposed a measure which it was their own exclusive prerogative to propose. Be that as it may, Tiberius did not persist in his proposal; but contented himself with neutralizing a law that the Senate had passed for the expulsion of the Christian church from Rome. This he effected by issuing an imperial edict, with very heavy penalties annexed, that there should be no more informations lodged against the members of that church. This account will be found given at length in Tertullian (Apol. v.), Eusebius (ii. 2), and many other writers. It is also admitted by the Roman clergy to be true.

Orosius, the historian, in relating this, says: "The Senate not only refused this apotheosis of the Saviour, but passed a law for the expulsion of the Christian church from Rome (edicto constituit exterminandos esse Urbe Christianos.) Tiberius, however, by a countermandate, threatened death to those who should lay the necessary accusations against the members of this community." (Lib. vii. c. 4.)

Father Calmet says, in his Dictionary: "Tiberius continued to show his good inclinations towards the Christians, and even threatened those with death who gave them any disturbance. In short, we do not find any persecution of the church under this emperor."

The foregoing illustrations show not only that Peter was in the East, and was considered by the fathers to be in the East whenever they speak of his founding the church at Rome, but they also show us the unreasonableness of inferring that Peter was present in any country or city merely from his ecclesiastical relations to its church being mentioned. When we hear of his having his chair anywhere—of the chair there being founded upon him—of his having sat in it—of his having died in it—of a city being Peter's see—of his instructing the church there—of his having many hearers in that city—of his proclaiming the gospel in it—of his ordaining one of its bishops—of his succession being there—of his baptizing or being bishop there—of his prayers being felt there, &c. &c., we must clearly, even upon the showing of the Roman clergy, understand all such expressions to apply to the agency of those disciples of all the twelve apostles, who left Jerusalem, from time to time, for their various homes during the ten or twelve years that the apostles themselves remained in Jerusalem. Thus, as will be seen in the course of these pages, Salvianus says that the apostles taught at Carthage; St. Gildas, the monk, that Canterbury was the see of St. Peter, or Peter's chair; Gregory the Great, that Alexandria was Peter's see; he and the other popes, that the church of Alexandria was founded by this apostle; Optatus, that Carthage was Peter's chair; Dionysius, bishop of Corinth, that his church of Corinth was planted by St. Peter; Irenæus, bishop of Lyons, that the church of Lyons had Peter's succession; Clement of Alexandria, that the church of Alexandria had it; Tertullian, that our Lord's apostles baptized in the Tyber with as much efficacy as John the Baptist had done in the Jordan. The old Roman Calendar and St. Jerome, who is supposed to have published it, that Peter entered upon the bishopric of Rome under the emperor Tiberius, and immediately after the ascension of our Lord; St. Chrysostom, that the church of England was founded by St. Peter, and that many of his hearers were in Alexandria; Baronius, that he founded his see of Antioch without being present there at the time; Aubespine, bishop of Orleans, that all the orthodox churches were sees of St. Peter; and all the Roman-catholic writers that the first bishop of Alexandria was ordained by Peter. It would be evidently absurd to infer from such expressions, that Peter had been in these cities and countries; yet this kind of inference is constantly being drawn by the Roman clergy with reference to Rome; and it may not be an uninteresting or inappropriate illustration for the general reader, to find a celebrated English priest and Jesuit engaged in this sort of work with regard to England.

Father Personius, (Anglicé, Robert Parsons), an English Jesuit, in the time of Elizabeth, eminent alike for his great learning and his great zeal, wrote a work called "The Three Conversions," in which he adduces, from testimonies of the foregoing character, what he and several others of his church considered to be demonstration and clear proof of Peter's having been at Canterbury. Father Parsons enjoyed the favour of Pope Gregory XIII. to such an extent, that he was made rector of the college founded at Rome expressly for proselytizing England,—was soon after sent over himself from Rome to contribute to the same end,—and was subsequently sent on a special mission from Rome to Madrid to Philip II. of Spain, to obtain a mitigation of the severities practised by that prince against the Spanish Jesuits,—a mission in which the favourite of the Vatican had great success. Among his most zealous friends he reckoned Cardinal Allen, and died at Rome, A.D. 1610. After going over the proofs that there are of the existence of the Christian church in England very soon after our Lord's ascension, this learned priest thus proceeds:—" And thus much of the time and occasion whereby the Christian religion began first in Britain within the first fifty years after Christ's ascension, whereto also we may add the testimony of Nicephorus, and, before him, of Theodoretus and Sophronius, ancient writers, who do testify that '*the British Islands fell in division among the apostles in their first partition which they made of the world.*' And it is most like that St. Peter, being come to Rome to teach and convert the western parts of the world, as Italy, Spain, and France, these Islands also received the same benefit from him. And so say our authors, whom afterwards I shall allege, for his being in Britain. And this is another point of obligation betwixt England and Rome, to wit, that the first bishop of Rome went in person to convert our country, as afterwards we shall hear grave authors affirm, to whom I remit me." Here occurs a long parenthesis as to the names of those of the laity who preached the gospel in England before Peter, after which the learned Jesuit thus goes on:—" Wherefore, to let this pass, and to speak of the first ecclesiastical teachers of the Christian religion in England, who, through the great perturbation of wars (as hath been said), were not so well known, nor distinctly observed, nor delivered to writing in those days, as otherwise they might have been; yet find I some mention, though dispersed, of three several apostles of Christ to have preached there, to wit, St. Peter, St. Paul, and St. Symon of Chananey, surnamed the Zealous;—two apostolical men also in these first troubled times to have been sent thither,—Aristobulus, a Roman whom St. Paul named in his Epistle to the Romans, and Joseph of Arimathea, a nobleman of Jury that buried Christ. Of all which five we shall speak somewhat in order. And, first, of St. Peter himself to have been in England (or Britain) and preached, founded churches, and ordained priests and deacons therein, is recorded, out of Greek antiquities by Metaphrastes, a Grecian, (Metaph. apud Surium, p. 862,) and it seemeth to be somewhat confirmed by that which Innocentius I., bishop of Rome, hath left written, above a thousand and two hundred years ago, saying, '*That the first churches of Italy, France, Spain, Africa, Sicilia, and the islands that lie betwixt them, were founded by St. Peter, or his scholars or successors.*' (Innoc. Epist. ad Decent.) For which cause Gulichnus Eysengrenius, in his 'First Centuria, or Hundred Years,' doth write also, '*That the first Christian churches of England were founded by St. Peter under Nero.*' (Eyseng. cent. i. part 7, dist. 6.) Whereunto it may be thought that the foresaid Gildas had relation, when expostulating with the British priests of his time for their wickedness, (for which the wrath of God had brought in the English Saxons upon them,) he objecteth, among other things, '*quod sedem Petri apostoli inverecundis pedibus usurpassent,*' (Gild. p. 2, de Excid. Brit.,) that they had usurped the seat of St. Peter with unshamefaced feet; meaning thereby, either the whole church of Britain first founded by him, or some particular place of devotion or church which he had erected; and finally Abredus Rienvallus, an English abbot of the order of Cisterce, left written, about five hundred years ago, a certain revelation, or apparition, of St. Peter to a holy man in the time of Edward the Confessor, showing him how he had preached himself in England, and consequently the particular care he had of that church and nation, &c. (Alred. apud Sur. p. 131.) If any man ask what time it might be that St. Peter left Rome and went into Britain, and other countries round about, Cardinal Baronius, (vol. i. p. 512,) a famous learned historiographer of our time, thinketh that it was then when Claudius, the emperor, banished all the Jews out of Rome, (as in the Acts of the Apostles it is recorded,) among whom it is like that St. Peter also, being by nation a Jew, retired himself, and took that occasion to go into divers pagan countries to preach the faith of Christ, that thing belonging especially to his charge, as head of the apostles, according to his own words himself, 'God hath chosen and appointed that Gentiles should hear and believe the word of the gospel by my mouth,' (Acts xv.) This, then, was the cause why he was so diligent and careful to go and preach everywhere the Christian religion, to the end he might fulfil and accomplish this will and ordination of his Master; and this was one cause, also, (to wit, his absence from Rome,) why, according to Baronius and other learned men, St. Paul, writing to the Romans, did not name or salute him in his Epistle, whereof our heretics do brabble much; and thus much of St. Peter. Of St. Paul's being in Britain there are not so many particular testimonies, yet the foresaid Theodoretus doth affirm," &c. &c.

Father Parsons, in imitation of Baronius about Peter's being at Rome, frequently afterwards alludes to the foregoing proof as complete and incontrovertible:—" Of Joseph of Arimathea's coming into France, and his sending thence into Great Britain, either by St. Philip, (as some say,) who preached then in Gaul, or (as OTHERS hold) by Peter himself, as he passed that way to and from Britain, and how he obtained," &c. &c. Again,— "Albeit St. Joseph came not immediately from Rome, nor was a Roman by birth, (as none of the apostles were,) yet he taught in England the Roman faith; that is to say, the same faith that St. Peter, and St. Paul, and Aristobulus, that came immediately from Rome, had taught before him, or did teach jointly with him in Britain." Again,—" For if this first preaching and first faith, taught in England by our first preachers, was the Roman faith, and derived principally from the city and church of Rome by the preaching of St. Peter and St. Paul, Aristobulus and others, as hath been declared, and if," &c.; and again,—" Besides the proofs set down in the former chapter, how the chief of our first preachers came from Rome immediately, as St. Peter, St. Paul, and St. Aristobulus, and that the other," &c. (Treatise on the Three Conversions of England. Part i. chaps. i. and ii.)

We have in all this a curious instance of the lengths to which the Roman clergy carry the practice of inferring Peter's personal presence in any city from the mere expression in the Fathers of his ecclesiastical relations to its church. But to return. I appeal to any Catholic, Roman or Protestant, who is in earnest in this inquiry, whether it has not been clearly shown, both from the Scriptures and from the fathers, from the acknowledged opinion of the Roman church herself, and from the common history of the Roman empire, that Peter's having founded the church at Rome is not to be supposed to imply his having come into Europe, or intermitted for a single day, that mission to the Jews of the Dispersion with which Paul so often reminds us that this apostle had been specially entrusted by our Lord.

XV.

LUCIANUS CHARINUS, (placed by Baratier in the second century, by others in the sixth,) wrote a work called "The Travels of the Apostles," which is wholly lost, and from which no one pretends to adduce any extract with the slightest reference to the present inquiry. "The whole book," says Photius, bishop of Constantinople, (A.D. 891,) in whose days it was to be seen, "contains nothing but childish and prodigious things, malicious fables, fallacies, follies, contradictions, and impieties." Mr. Barntier, (to whose collection of evidence the Correspondent in the *Times* attaches so much value,) after adverting at some length to Lucianus Charinus as an important authority on the subject, says that he is convinced this writer described Peter as having come into Europe, that many reasons convince him of it, but that he thinks it unnecessary to mention any of these reasons, as no one would think that writer worth attending to! Must not that be a very doubtful historical fact, which can be supposed to receive the slightest support from such a witness?

XVI.

CLEMENS ALEXANDRINUS, (about A.D. 217,) archbishop of Alexandria, is still relied on by a few of the Roman clergy, but certainly not with quite so much expectation as Irenæus is, for making it appear that Peter must have left the East in the earlier years of his mission. In the same manner as Irenæus, in a work purporting to treat only of the local church of Rome, had said that Mark's Gospel was written after St. Peter had founded that church; so Clement of Alexandria, in a statement purporting to have been derived from Irenæus, says that it was written "after Peter had effected the proclamation of the gospel at Rome." Peter could not have effected this, argue some of the Roman clergy, unless he had come into Europe for the purpose.

The passage in question is one in which it is stated, —1st. That the Gospel which Mark wrote, as St. Chrysostom assures us, in Egypt, was written at the instance of several of those Jewish converts who, "out of every nation under heaven," had been from time to time with Peter at Jerusalem, hanging with affection and delight upon the inspired eloquence of that apostle, among whom there were even Alexandrians applying for it, as Chrysostom informs us; and Romans, as we learn from Jerome and Epiphanius. 2nd. That the reason for Mark's being selected by them for this purpose, was his having been Peter's companion from an early period, which naturally afforded him more opportunity than others had of ascertaining the facts of our Lord's history from this apostle. 3rdly. That the want of this gospel does not appear to have been felt until Peter had discontinued his general proclamation of the gospel in the different cities of the East and West, through those Jews that were constantly passing and re-passing between these cities and Jerusalem, in which last city he was stationed,—in other words, that it was written after Peter, by his departure to Babylon, had broken off that general relation with the churches in which he was placed by his central residence at Jerusalem; and 4thly, that Mark wrote it either before or after he was living at Babylon with St. Peter, as he wrote it from memory, and as Peter did not hear of it until it was finished. Eusebius thus puts this passage (vi. 14): "Again, in the same work, Clement also gives us a tradition respecting the order in which the gospels were written, derived from the elders of the preceding age, to this effect:— The gospels containing the genealogies were, it was said, first composed, and Mark's had the following origin:— After Peter had made proclamation of the word at Rome, and had announced it to all nations, with the assistance of the Spirit, those who had been with the apostle himself, and who amounted to a considerable number, urged Mark, as he had been Peter's companion from an early period and could remember his words, to commit to writing what he had taught them. Whereupon Mark composed his gospel, and gave copies of it to the applicants; which gospel, when Peter came to hear of its existence, he in the first instance neither prohibited nor recommended."

The whole of the argument which the Roman clergy have founded upon this passage, proceeds upon the supposition that, when we speak of "making proclamation of a thing anywhere," these words imply the personal presence of the party by whom this is said to have been effected. One single testimony will prove that this is a mistaken notion. Of the word which represents this expression in the Greek text, Henry Stephens says, in his Thesaurus, that it very frequently signifies to cause proclamation to be made of anything, as well as to be actually the proclaiming party. "Not only those," says he, "who literally use their voice in publicly announcing anything, but also those who authorize them to do so, are said " to proclaim;" and this use of the Greek term is frequent." (κηρυσσειν dicuntur sæpe non ipsi κηρυκις, sed ii qui eos κηρυσσειν jubent.) This authority alone shows the mistake into which the few of the Roman clergy we now speak of have fallen respecting the use of this Greek term, and will abundantly satisfy every conscientious inquirer upon the present subject. It may however be remarked that the same interpretation of the word is given in other Greek Lexicons, and that in the popular Lexicon of Dr. Donnegan, it is explained as meaning "to make publicly known," "to promulgate," "to announce openly;" none of which expressions imply the personal presence of the principal party mentioned, but merely the same kind of action as is implied when we say that the Prime-minister of England did so-and-so at Madrid. Of this common use of the term, as explained by Henry Stephens, we have an appropriate illustration in Thucydides, (i. 27.) "The Corinthian government proclaimed a colonizing expedition to Epidamnus." This it is evident does not mean that the different members of the Corinthian government went themselves over the country uttering words to that effect, but merely that they adopted whatever was the usual or most effectual method of solemn and general proclamation for the purpose. So, also, when the Roman clergy admit that the eight synagogues and 8000 Jews at this time (as Josephus tells us) at Rome, were sending up their deputations every year with their first fruit offerings to Jerusalem, and that Peter and the apostles were teaching the gospel to each succeeding deputation, in order that it should be again taught by them at Rome; and that this continued for nearly a dozen years, would it not be very unreasonable to argue that Peter was not in this way proclaiming (κηρυσσειν) the gospel in that city, and that he must have gone there to have enabled him to do so? Accordingly we find that even the vigilant Baronius did not see anything available in that expression.

Cardinal Bellarmine and some others have put forward another supposition connected with this passage. They suppose that Clemens here asserts that Mark wrote his gospel at Rome! and that Peter was with him at the time he wrote it! It will be at once seen that the words we are considering have nothing resembling either of these assertions, which are merely those fictions of the 14th and 15th centuries already adverted to in the chapter upon Papias, and in which the ideas of these writers appear to have been entangled. But it may be of use to show, *en passant*, that on both these points the exact contrary was the opinion of ALL the Fathers, although undoubtedly some of them say that Peter's Roman, as well as Alexandrian hearers, were among the most zealous of Mark's applicants. St. Chrysostom, in his allusion to the story, says in his first Homily upon Matthew: "It is said that Matthew, at the request of the Jewish converts, committed to writing for them what he taught orally, and that he composed that gospel in the Hebrew tongue; and that Mark also did the same thing in Egypt, at the request of the disciples there." Jerome, apparently from misunderstanding Eusebius, says that the Romans also made an application to Mark when he was among them, for the Gospel which he afterwards wrote in Egypt. (Rogatus Romæ a fratribus .... breve scripsit evangelium. *De vir. illus.*) Epiphanius repeats this: "After the Hebrews made Matthew write, Mark, Peter's fellow traveller, was solicited at Rome to do the same; and as soon as it was completed, he was invested with apostolic functions in Egypt by St. Peter."—(*Epiphan. against the heresy of the Alogi*, 51.) This is very far from saying that Mark's Gospel was not written in Egypt, and still farther from saying that it was written at Rome. Nor do any of the Fathers contradict Chrysostom upon the point in question. All agree that, wherever else Mark may have been petitioned on the subject, the Gospel that he wrote was written at Alexandria, and as much to gratify

Peter's auditors in that as in any other city. Then, as to Peter's being with Mark at the time the latter wrote, all the Fathers agree in acknowledging that he was not. Papias says plainly that Mark had to write from memory; Irenæus that Mark did not write until after Peter's death; Clemens Alexandrinus is reported as repeating what Papias said, adding that the existence of Mark's Gospel did not come to Peter's knowledge for some time after it was written; Eusebius repeats this addition of Clemens, and says that it was by divine revelation the thing came to Peter's knowledge; all which expressions are allowed to be inconsistent with the supposition that Peter was then with Mark, and neither Jerome nor Epiphanius, nor any subsequent Father, has ever pretended to say he was. Thus, in no way can it be shown that Clemens Alexandrinus lends the slightest countenance to the story about Peter's having left the East.

XVII.

CAIUS (A.D. 218), an ecclesiastical writer and a Roman, makes nearly the same statement as Irenæus. He says that our Lord's apostles founded the church of Rome; and from this it is inferred, as in the case of Irenæus, that Peter (although here his name is not even mentioned) must have come from Jerusalem into Europe before he went to Babylon.

Caius seems to have been boasting of the genuineness of his church, and of the veneration in which the apostles were held at Rome—veneration so great that there seem to have been already two sets of monuments erected to their memory in that city; one (the original one, no doubt) in the catacombs, the entrance of which was between the Via Appia, and the road to Ostia; the other on Mount Vaticanus, where the churches were first built as soon as they were allowed to be built above the ground. The work of Caius is lost, but his words on this point are preserved by Eusebius (ii. 25), who remarks that the two parts of Rome, here mentioned by Caius as having trophies of our Lord's apostles in the beginning of the 3rd century, were the same as those in which two handsome temples had just been placed by the Emperor Constantine, in the beginning of the 4th, in each of which buildings Sylvester, the bishop of Rome at that time, had just deposited equal portions of some supposed relics that he possessed of St. Peter and St. Paul. "Caius speaks thus," says Eusebius, " of the places in which Paul's and Peter's relics have been deposited: ' I can show you the trophies —the martyrs' monuments—erected to the memory of our Lord's apostles; for if you go to the hill called Vaticanus, or even to the road that leads to the harbour of Ostia, you will be able to find the trophies—the victorious records of those by whom this church was founded.'"

In the Greek text (as I have said) there is no special mention whatever of St. Peter, of the importance of which omission the Roman clergy are very sensible; for some of the more zealous of them boldly introduce his name when they quote these words. He is, nevertheless, unquestionably included among the rest of the apostles, all of whom are represented in the Roman Martyrologies as having had trophies—as having borne witness to the faith, either in their lives or in their deaths, and are so described by Eusebius himself in his Commentary on the Psalms. For even St. John's tomb, whenever it was constructed anywhere, had the " trophy," or emblems of martyrdom upon it, in consequence of all he suffered in his lifetime (Rev. i. 9), although it is universally admitted that he died a natural death at Ephesus. Eusebius says, on Psalm lxxi.: " Every one of the apostles had a different termination allotted to his testimony." ποικίλον ὑπέμεινε το τοῦ μαρτυρίου τέλος. (He does not, however, say as Father Butler supposes, in his Life of St. Thomas, that every one of them died in consequence of the testimony he afforded); and Montfaucon, the eminent Benedictine editor of that work, says: " It is now generally admitted that all the apostles underwent some kind of martyrdom," (apostolos omnes pro Christo passos esse.) All the apostles are also often spoken of in the Fathers as having "trophies" at Rome. "There is there," says St. Jerome, in one of his letters to Marcella, "there is there a holy church. There are there trophies of the apostles and of the martyrs." And again, in his Commentary on the Fortieth Chapter of Ezekiel, he says: "When I was a boy, and pursuing my studies at Rome, I used to go on Sundays with other boys of the same disposition to visit the sepulchres of the apostles and the martyrs, and frequently went into the catacombs." The Roman clergy would not, I think, pretend to assume that the only apostles meant in such passages are Peter and Paul, the two patron saints of the Roman church; but even if they do, even if we must understand that Caius meant to exclude the other eleven apostles from all share in the foundation of that church, and to speak of Peter and Paul as the only apostles who had trophies at Rome, we have already seen, in the section on Irenæus, that this supposition, strained as it is, affords not the slightest reason for thinking that Peter ever was in Europe. We have seen that his part in the foundation of that church might as well have been performed in the East as Paul's, and that (as Baronius long ago acknowledged) the scriptural account of the foundation of the churches is utterly at variance with the theory of those few who hold that Peter must have been present in every city in the foundation of whose church he was considered to have a share.

There is a second argument founded upon these words of Caius, one which is scarcely, indeed, defended by any Roman Catholic writer that I have met with; but as the point which the Roman clergy think so important about Peter's not having been put to death at Babylon, where he himself speaks of his martyrdom as at hand, is supposed to gain an air of probability in the eyes of the general reader from this argument, they put forward that portion of the passage with more emphasis than, in reference to this question, it is entitled to. The argument is this: As Peter's trophy, or martyr's tomb, (μαρτυριον,) was at Rome, some of his relics must have been there; and, as his relics were there, he must have been put to death there. Why should his body, or any portion of it, have been there, (ask the uninitiated,) if he was not put to death there? Why should his trophy be there, if his body, or some portion of it was not? It will be seen from the following quotations, that trophies, or martyr's monuments, were constantly erected in cities where those to whose memory they were erected had neither lived nor died; that the bodies of martyrs were constantly removed to cities and places at a very great distance from the scene of their martyrdoms, and trophies there erected to their memory; and that it was no unusual thing for a martyrium, or martyr's tomb, to have no body, or even part of a body, in it. All which points are fully acknowledged by all the Roman clergy. It will be seen, for instance, that there was a trophy of St. Stephen's at Ancona, not very far from Rome, constructed immediately after his martyrdom, which took place in the East, and that neither his body, nor any part of it, was deposited beneath this trophy. It will be seen that St. Peter had another trophy at Constantinople, at the very time Eusebius was writing, and that no portion of Peter's body was there. We shall find, also, that the trophy of St. Laurentius was at Ravenna, although his body was not there, and although it was not there that he had been put to death; that St. Andrew, Peter's brother, had a trophy at Constantinople, and that his remains were lying there in Eusebius's time, although it was at a distance of some hundred miles from that city that he was murdered; and that, among numberless other cases of this description, Ignatius had his trophy at Antioch, with all that could be saved of his body placed beneath it, immediately after his martyrdom, which, it is well known, took place at Rome. It is no wonder, therefore, that the Roman clergy do not consider a trophy as any proof of the locality of a martyrdom, and that, as we shall see, even St. Augustine acknowledged it to be a matter of considerable uncertainty whether St. Peter's body was at Rome at all.

The following is the account given by Eusebius of the

magnificent martyrium, or martyr's tomb, built by Constantine, at Constantinople, to the memory of all our Lord's apostles, about the same time as he rebuilt Peter's martyrium at Rome. The account occurs in the fourth book of the life of that emperor by Eusebius.

"Chap. lviii.—On the Building of the Martyrium (Μαρτυριον) of the Apostles at Constantinople.

"After this he (the Emperor Constantine) proceeded to erect the martyrium to the memory of the apostles, in the city called by his own name. It was he who carried the whole of the sacred temple to its immense height, and brilliantly decorated it, by covering it from the foundation to the very roof with all kinds of coloured stones, in a sort of Mosaic work. He also made the ceiling of the lightest kind of filigree, richly gilt. The roof which protected the structure from the weather, was of copper instead of tiles; and this also was profusely gilt, so as to dazzle one when the sun shone on it; and a sort of tracery, of copper and gold, beautifully carved, was placed all round the dome.

"Chap. lix.—A further description of the same Martyrium.

"The temple was thus magnificently adorned by the emperor; and there was around it an uncovered space of great extent, without any buildings in it. In a quadrangular form round this, there ran a piazza, which enclosed this area for the temple; and national buildings, laid out in baths and caravansaries for pilgrims, extended all along this piazza, besides several other apartments for the use of those who were in charge of the place."

"Chap. lx.—That he also erected his own monument in it.

"All these structures the emperor consecrated, for the purpose of perpetuating among all men the memory of the apostles of our Lord. He had, however, another object; one at first unknown, but afterwards evident to every one. He prepared a place there for himself when he should die, intending, with an extraordinary amount of Christian fervour, that his relics should participate, after death, in the designation of the church as that of the apostles; so that after this life he might, as it were, profit by the prayers which, out of honour to the apostles, would be offered up to the Almighty in that place. He therefore constructed there twelve tombs — sacred monuments — to the honour and memory of all our Lord's apostles, and placed a coffin for himself in the middle of them, so that six of the apostles were deposited (or *lay*) on each side of it. He thus wisely provided a place, as I have said, where his body, after this life, was to rest; but he arranged these things, and consecrated this temple to the apostles long beforehand, in the hope that while he lived it would promote his eternal welfare to honour their memory in this way."

St. Chrysostom, the archbishop of Constantinople, (for Constantinople, Babylon, Jerusalem, Alexandria, and Antioch, were all archbishoprics,) often afterwards alludes to this as St. Peter's tomb, or trophy to which great multitudes of pilgrims came; and considers, that by its construction Constantinople was, with regard to this apostle, placed upon exactly the same footing as Rome. In his 26th Homily, on 2 Corinth., (*vol.* x. *p.* 741, *Benedictine Edition*, 1834,) after speaking of the tombs of our Lord's apostles in some cities as surpassing in splendour the residences of the emperors, he goes on thus:—" For he who wears the purple goes to those monuments to kiss them, and, putting aside his ornaments, begs of the saints to intercede for him with God, (this was in the fifth century.) Yes, crowned though he be, he entreats the dead fisherman and the tent-maker to be his friends: .... and this is to be seen, not only at Rome, but at Constantinople. For at Constantinople the son of the great Constantine thought that he conferred a high honour on his father when he deposited his body in the vestibule of the fisherman; so that the emperors performed in their sepulchre that office for the fishermen which the door-keepers performed in the palaces for the emperors." And again, to the same effect, in his Homily " Quod Christus sit Deus," (*vol.* i. *p.* 697,) speaking of the veneration in which our Lord's apostles were everywhere held, and especially in the two great capitals of the empire, the archbishop says:—" See how it is at Rome; the emperors, the consuls, the generals, leave all their state and repair to the tombs of the fisherman and the tent-maker; and, at Constantinople, those who wore the crown thought it a happy thing to have their bodies buried, not even close to the apostles, but in the space outside their doors, and thus the emperors became thenceforth the doorkeepers of the fishermen. And again, in his Homily "Against the Games and Theatres," on the occasion of a great storm which occurred at Constantinople, three days before he was speaking, he says:—" Prayers were offered up to the Almighty, and our whole city rushed to where the apostles were, and took refuge with the holy Peter and and his blessed brother Andrew, that apostolic union, with Paul also and Timothy. And when the storm was over, we (the inhabitants of Constantinople) boldly traversed the floods, and ran to the leaders of the apostles—to Peter, the foundation of the faith—to Paul, the vessel of election,—celebrating a spiritual festival, and proclaiming their contests and their trophies." The Benedictine editors suppose Chrysostom here to allude, in the second clause, to a second martyrium of St. Peter's, on the *other* side of the Bosphorus, within the archbishopric. It is unnecessary to add, that no one ever considered Peter to have been put to death in any part of the Bosphorus, and but very few that his body was deposited in any of the martyr's tombs that were erected in that neighbourhood to his memory.

Nor did St. Augustine consider that a martyrium implied the presence of the martyr's body. With all his enthusiasm for the church at Rome, he does not scruple to mention it as a mere saying and an uncertainty that Peter's reliquiæ were lying at Rome, although there never was a doubt that this apostle had one of his martyria with its trophy there from the very earliest period, whether as a little oratory in the catacombs, or as a stately church upon the Vatican Hill. "Men speak," says St. Augustine, "as if Peter's relics were at Rome;" or, "It is said that Peter's relics are at Rome." (Jacet

Petri corpus Romæ, DICUNT HOMINES. *Serm.* 296.) Would he have used such an expression if it were an ascertained fact that Peter's body had been deposited at Rome, or even if it were supposed that the martyrium implied the relics? He also states in the most unreserved and open manner that in his day Laurentius the martyr had a martyr's tomb at Ravenna, though he was not put to death there (Laurentii memoria apud Ravennam. Serm. 322), but that the remains of this martyr were at that very time deposited at Rome (Laurentii corpus Romæ jacet. Serm. 296.)

The foregoing quotations are sufficient to show us how little the erection of an apostle's martyrium or trophy in a city had, in the judgment of the fathers, to do with his having been put to death there, or even with the presence there of the smallest portion of the body. Let us now attend to the opinions and statements of the Roman clergy on this subject.

Baronius says in his Index: "The least fragment of the relics of any saint is equivalent to the entire of that saint's body." (Minima pars reliquiarum alicujus sancti eandem vim habet quam totum corpus.) And again (A.D. 55, *paragraph* 15): "As there is in the smallest portion of any martyr's relics the same efficacy as there would be in his whole body, the body of one martyr was usually divided into several small portions, and was thus placed under different altars; for in the martyria, or temples of the martyrs, the altars are their tombs. And doubtless it was from the various minute portions of the body being dispersed in different places, and having in each the same efficacy as if they were all there together, that the body of one and the same martyr was supposed to be deposited in several different cities; a mistake which we may well excuse, as it arose not from human imposture but from the divine bounty; for EACH CITY IMAGINED ITSELF POSSESSED OF THE MARTYR'S BODY, ON ACCOUNT OF THE TROPHY OR TOMB ERECTED in consequence of this efficacy; and, as we have said, the tomb was always the altar of the martyr's oratory, or martyrium, as it was called in the Greek language." (Cum igitur eandem virtutem in exiguâ parte reliquiarum martyris, quæ in toto sit corpore, inesse, experimento ipse (Gregorius Nazianzenes) testetur; inde evenit ut corpus unius martyris in plures interdum partes dividi soleret, recondique in diversis altaribus, quæ sepulchra sunt martyrum; indeque fortasse accidit ut cum unius ejusdemque martyris diversis in locis reliquiæ conditæ haberentur, et æque ac si integrum corpus ubique horum locorum conditum esset, eadem miracula sint operatæ, unius ejusdemque martyris corpus diversis in locis haberi dicatur. Tolerabilis error cui non hominum impostura, sed exuberans divina largitas præbuit occasionem; dum quod, ob virtutis præstantiam, diversis in locis sit unius ejusdemque martyris erecta memoria, vel excitatum sepulchrum (quod esse consuevit sacrum altare) quisque apud se corpus illius habere est opinatus. A.D. 55, *paragraph* 15;) where see much more to the same effect.

We here see, upon the authority of the Roman church herself that martyrs' tombs were built, and the bodies of martyrs constantly supposed to be in cities where the martyrs did not suffer, and where there was nothing more than some very small portion of their bodies, or of something belonging to them; and this, the cardinal tells us, was quite usual. The following quotations will afford the general reader some illustrations of it. He will also see from them that nothing was of more ordinary occurrence than to remove the whole of the remains from the country of the martyrdom to very distant places, either after the lapse of years, or immediately upon the martyrdom having taken place, and to erect trophies over them,—for the trophy was the palm-leaf, the cross, &c., placed upon the monument of the martyr.

We learn from the venerable Bede, (who is a canonized saint of the Roman church,) that the remains (he uses the word denoting the *whole* of the remains,) of St. Peter, together with those of other martyrs who had trophies at Rome, were deposited at Canterbury, A.D. 656, a fact which does not appear to be generally known. Yet we have Pope Vitalian's letter to king Oswy of England, which accompanied these remains to our shores; and Baronius does not attempt to deny the truth of the account nor the authenticity of the letter. He says, as might be expected, very little on the subject; neither whether they were ever returned, nor whether it was all or only a part of each saint that was sent. The pope writes thus: "We have ordered the blessings of the Saints—for so we call the remains (reliquius)—of the blessed apostles Peter and Paul, and of the holy martyrs (not apostles) St. Lawrence, St. John, and St. Paul, St. Gregory, and St. Pancras, to be delivered to your messengers, (who are also the bearers of this, our letter,) to be by them again delivered faithfully to your Highness. For even to your royal consort, our spiritual daughter, we have by the aforesaid messengers sent," &c. &c. (*Hist. Eccles.* iii. 29.) Father Butler adds, (upon what authority he does not say,) "that it was only a *portion* of St. Pancras's body that was sent to England upon this occasion."

St. Andrew, the brother of St. Peter, is believed by the Roman clergy to have suffered his martyrdom at Patræ, in Peloponnesus. After stating this, Butler (in his Lives of the Saints) thus proceeds: "The body of St. Andrew was translated from Patræ to Constantinople, A.D. 357, together with those of St. Luke and St. Timothy, and deposited in the church of the apostles, which Constantine the Great had built a little before. . . . . The churches of Milan, Nola, Brescia, and some other places, were at the same time enriched with SMALL PORTIONS of these relics, as we are informed by St. Ambrose, St. Gaudentius, St. Paulinus, and others. When the city of Constantinople was taken by the French, Cardinal Peter, of Capua, brought the relics of St. Andrew thence into Italy, and deposited them in the cathedral of Amalphi, where they still remain."

Butler also writes thus (in his article on Luke): "St. Hippolytus says, St. Luke was crucified at Elæa, in Peloponnesus, near Achaia . . . . . The bones of St. Luke were translated from Patræ, in Achaia, A.D. 357, by order of the Emperor Constantius, and deposited in the church of the Apostles at Constantinople, together with those of St. Andrew and St. Timothy. On the occasion of this translation, SOME DISTRIBUTION was made of the relics of St. Luke. St. Gaudentius procured a part for his church at Brescia; St. Paulinus possessed a portion in St. Felix's church at Nola, and with a part enriched a church which he built at Fondi. The magnificent church of the Apostles at Constantinople was built by Constantine the Great, whose body was deposited in the porch, in a chest of gold, the twelve apostles standing round his tomb. When this church was repaired, by an order of Justinian, the masons found three wooden chests or coffins, in which, as the inscriptions proved, the bodies of St. Luke, St. Andrew, and St. Timothy were interred. Baronius mentions that the head of St. Luke was brought by St. Gregory from Constantinople to Rome, and laid in the church of his monastery of St. Andrew. Some of his relics are kept in the great Grecian monastery on Mount Athos, in Greece."

Baronius (in his Annals, A.D. 637, paragraph 1,) says: "It is certain that at this time SEVERAL bodies of saints, both martyrs and confessors, were brought into Europe and placed in different cities, either at Rome or Venice, or elsewhere. There is a general report that Ignatius's remains were then brought to Rome from Antioch..... Moreover, St. Mark's body was brought over at a still later period to Venice from Alexandria."

We have an account in Butler's "Lives of the Saints," of five of the martyria (memoriæ, or oratories) that were erected to the memory of St. Stephen in places at various distances from Jerusalem, in which city he was put to death; in the earliest and most famous of which it will be seen that there was no portion whatever of St. Stephen's body. This writer states that Stephen was not buried at Jerusalem, where he was stoned, but at a place about twenty miles from Jerusalem, called Caphargamala, or borough of Gamaliel; that after Stephen was stoned by the Jews, outside the north gate of Jerusalem, his body was left exposed one day and one night upon the spot where he died; that Gamaliel, who instructed

Paul, the apostle, in the law, had it carried off in the night-time to Caphargamala, where he lived, and that he had it interred there, twenty miles from the scene of the martyrdom; that it was discovered there A.D. 415, for the first time, and part of it at once taken possession of by the archbishop of Jerusalem, as it was found in his diocese, the rest being left in the martyrium at Caphargamala.

Butler then proceeds thus: "The relics of this saint (Stephen) were SOON DISPERSED IN MANY PLACES. Portions of them were brought with great devotion into Europe and Africa. Avitus, a Spanish priest, who then lived in Palestine, obtained of Lucian (the priest of Caphargamala), out of the part which he had reserved for himself, some of the dust of the flesh, and a little portion of the small bones of the martyr, which he sent to Palconius, bishop of Braga (in Spain), his native place."

Again: "Some of the martyr's blood contained in a vial, and some small fragments of his bones, which certain monks had procured from Palestine, arrived at Uzalis, in Africa; and before the oratory of the relics of St. Stephen, at Uzalis, was placed a veil on which the saint was painted carrying a cross upon his shoulders." These relics, we hear, performed great cures, and attracted immense pilgrimages of the faithful.

Butler also mentions that at Calama, another city of Africa, in Numidia, there was another martyrium or chapel of St. Stephen, enriched with some of his relics, the cures effected by which are almost incredible.

Butler also writes thus: "The church of Hippo (in Africa), was enriched with a portion of these relics, A.D. 425. St. Augustine (the bishop of Hippo), in his 317th sermon, says those relics consisted of a little dust into which his sacred flesh was reduced, shut up in a case. An altar was there raised, not to St. Stephen, but to God, over the relics of St. Stephen."

And thus: "St. Augustine relates (sermon 323), that a certain person, who was present at the martyrdom of St. Stephen, picked up one of the stones that had struck the martyr's arm, and brought it afterwards to Ancona, in Italy, where from that time there began to be there a *trophy* or *memoriæ*, as it was called—that is, an oratory, of St. Stephen's, says that Father. When the Christians had the liberty to erect churches, a famous one, in honour of St. Stephen, was built on this account, near Ancona, which is mentioned by St. Gregory." Pilgrims innumerable from all parts of Christendom flocked to this shrine.

The only other case I shall mention is that of Ignatius. "He arrived at Rome the 20th of December," says Butler in his Life, "the last day of the public entertainments. He was hurried into the amphitheatre. Two fierce lions being let out upon him, they instantly devoured him, leaving nothing of his body but the larger bones .... His bones were taken up and carried to Antioch, and there laid in a chest as an inestimable treasure. They were first laid in the cemetery outside the Daphnitic gate (of Antioch), but in the reign of Theodosius the Younger, A.D. 438, were translated thence with great pomp to a church in the city, which had been a temple of Fortune, but from this time bore his name. They are now at Rome. The regular canons at Arouaise, near Bapaume, in Artois, the Benedictine monks at Licasse, in Haynault, and some other churches, have obtained each some bone of this glorious martyr. His martyrdom happened A.D. 107."

Baronius says: "When Ignatius had undergone his martyrdom in the theatre at Rome, his body was immediately conveyed to Antioch, from city to city, upon the shoulders of the faithful," (A.D. 55, *paragraph* 17,) and this fact is stated or alluded to in many of the Fathers.

Thus we see that the Roman clergy do not consider that the mere circumstance of Peter's having had a martyrium or oratory at Rome, was the slightest reason for supposing that he was put to death there (whatever other reason they may have for thinking so), and that (as St. Augustine tells us) it was not even a reason for supposing that his body, or any portion of his body, was lying there.

The Correspondent in the *Times* goes farther than any other commentator on this passage of the writer Caius. He is not satisfied with suggesting that there may have been relics beneath the trophies. He boldly says, that Caius here states that it was the Vatican hill that was the depository of Peter's, and that the Ostian road was the place allotted to St. Paul's!—a distinction of which there is not the slightest trace in the original, in which it is not even said that there were any portions at all of the bodies of the apostles beneath their trophies at Rome.

XVIII.

St. Hippolytus about (A.D. 250), an eastern bishop, it is not known exactly of what place, is supposed to be described in a little poem by Prudentius, a Spanish poet, in the fifth century, as speaking of "Peter's chair," but without saying anything that would lead us to suppose that he thereby meant either the Roman or any one other local church, or, in fact, in any way connecting the name of Rome with it; and this Baronius brings forward as satisfactory, nay, as "brilliant" evidence of Peter's having made a journey into Europe, either before or after he went to Babylon.

In the *first* place, however, it is to be observed, that the testimony is that only of Prudentius, in the fifth century, and not at all that of St. Hippolytus in the third, who said nothing whatever on the subject in his works. In the *second* place, the words occur in a Latin poem, written in metre, without the slightest pretension to historical accuracy. *Thirdly*, the words "Let no faith flourish but that which Peter's chair and Paul preserve," (Prud. in Peristeph. 11,) do not even suggest Rome, or the church there, except to the mind already irresistibly imbued with the misconception,—as the same words are, we have seen, constantly applied to numberless other churches. *Fourthly*, even if it was the local church at Rome only, and not the whole church of Christ that was meant here by the expression, that would evidently not prove that Peter had been in Europe, as we know that the church of Carthage was called "Peter's chair," though Peter never was at Carthage, and that Alexandria was called the "chair," as well as the "see of St. Peter," although Peter never was in Egypt; nay, that in the very time of Prudentius, Canterbury was called "Peter's chair," although Peter never was in England. But, *fifthly*, even if all this were otherwise, almost every writer admits that the Hippolytus mentioned by Prudentius was some priest of that name, and not the bishop. Nor is that all. Baronius himself, upon another occasion, acknowledged that it was very evident to him that the poet had confounded three very different persons under the same name,—a priest, a bishop, and a soldier! "It must not be forgotten," says the cardinal, on the Roman Martyrology, "that this writer has confounded together three persons named Hippolytus,—a soldier, a priest, and a bishop,—and that he has related, as of one party, the acts of the three." How, then, could anything said by the Hippolytus of this poem be laid before an enlightened public as having been said by St. Hippolytus the bishop?

XIX.

AN ANONYMOUS AUTHOR (in Eusebius, v. 28, and placed by Baratier in the early part of the third century) speaks of a person as being "the thirteenth bishop of Rome from the times of the apostle Peter." It is thence inferred, but I must say, only by those who are inexperienced in the language of the Fathers, that the apostle Peter must have been bishop of Rome, and therefore that he must have lived there.

In reply to this argument for Peter's having left the East, it is sufficient to state that all the ecclesiastical historians date the transactions of the churches from the apostles, without thereby meaning to imply that the apostles were bishops of those churches. St. Theodoret begins his "Ecclesiastical History" with this remark: "As Eusebius began his history from the blessed apostles, to record all that occurred in the churches until the reign of Constantine, I shall begin my work from the end of his." And this account of the expression is admitted by all the Roman-catholic commentators. Carminus Finianus, royal professor of theology at Naples, and to whom we are indebted for a very fine edition of the works of archbishop De Marca, writes as follows, in the preface to the fourth volume of that work: "When Eusebius says that any one was third or sixth bishop of Rome 'after Peter and Paul,' or 'from the apostles,' he does not mean that these apostles, or that all the apostles, were bishops of Rome. That all the apostles who lived at Jerusalem were bishops of Jerusalem, is what nobody thought. Eusebius himself did not think so; for he considered only James to be its bishop. Nevertheless, this very Eusebius says that Narcissus was the thirteenth bishop of Jerusalem from the apostles. St. Jerome in his catalogue of ecclesiastical writers, says that James was the bishop of Jerusalem after the apostles. Now, as it is agreed on all hands that the apostles were not bishops of Jerusalem, and that only James was so, it necessarily follows that neither the expression 'from the apostles,' nor the expression 'after the apostles,' is any reason for supposing that the apostles were bishops of Jerusalem. And by a like process of reasoning (pari modo), when Eusebius says that any one was bishop of Rome 'after Peter and Paul,' or third, fifth, seventh, 'from the apostles,' it is not from such expressions that we can infer the episcopal character of these apostles." Valesius also acknowledges that however frequently Eusebius used this language with reference to Rome, he never meant to imply in it, that any of the apostles was a bishop of that church. Valesius writes thus: "Irenæus and Eusebius say that Peter and Paul laid the first foundations of the church of Rome, but they nowhere reckon them among the bishops of that church." (Eos in Episcoporum ordine NEQUAQUAM recensent. *Valesius on Euseb.* iii. 21.) And again,— "It must not be forgotten that Eusebius never speaks of any of the apostles as a bishop." (Sciendum est Eusebium apostolos in ordine Episcoporum minime numerare ut supra notavi. *Ibid.*) As it is admitted, therefore, by the Roman Catholics, that the phrase in question does not involve the supposed sense, it cannot be inferred from it, in any case, that Peter lived at Rome. And that Peter's name, as so often elsewhere, is above employed by this anonymous writer to represent *all* the apostles, and not Peter alone, is proved by Eusebius (iv. 5), where, in a clause exactly parallel, Telesphorus is said to be "the eighth bishop of Rome from the apostles." He even says (iv. 1) that "Primus was the fourth bishop from the apostles at Alexandria;" where not one of the apostles ever was.

But over and above all this, with which every classical scholar is well acquainted, and which will be further illustrated in the fifth section on Eusebius, Cardinal Bellarmine very honestly and ingenuously acknowledges that Peter's being considered bishop of Rome would not be a legitimate indication of his having ever resided in that city. Several persons whom Bellarmine enumerates, and whose names will be found in another page, were, this cardinal reminds us, spoken of and considered as the bishops at Rome, although, as he truly adds, they never in their lives had even seen Rome; and we know that with respect to Asiatic bishoprics, a similar practice still prevails in the Roman church. I cite Bellarmine here, not because I have any doubt as to whether the Roman-catholic reader will consider what has been above said abundantly sufficient to show the utter emptiness of the alleged testimony, but because it is important that he should be made to see the miserable shifts (if they will pardon me the expression) to which his clergy are reduced in their efforts—conscientious efforts it may often be—to show that Peter was supposed by the ancients to have been in person at Rome. To do this in the present case they are compelled to ignore the most ordinary usages of their church, and the most ordinary principles of patristic phraseology.

XX.

SEXTUS JULIUS AFRICANUS, the writer of a chronology, (about A.D. 250,) is supposed to have said in his work, now lost, that Peter was put to death at Rome. The grounds of this supposition, as stated by Barutier, are that a barbarous writer of a much later period, or a writer named Barbarus, (for it is not known which,) has left us a chronology, consisting of extracts from the similar works of Sextus Julius Africanus, Eusebius, and others; and that as this writer, "Barbarus," mentions something about Peter's having been put to death at Rome, which is not mentioned in Eusebius, he must therefore have taken this from Sextus Julius Africanus! This is one of the testimonies of young Barntier, described by the Correspondent in the *Times* as constituting "thorough proof." I need only reply, what is obvious to every one, that "Barbarus" may have taken his statement from some of the other and much later writers to whom he had access, and from whom Scaliger, his only editor, says that he gave extracts.

XXI.

TERTULLIAN (about A.D. 250), a priest of Carthage, who is admitted on all hands to write in a highly figurative and turgid style, with Rome intervening between him and the church of Jerusalem, and who naturally sought to array in every kind of attractive imagery that one of the first churches to which, purely on account (as he himself says,) of its proximity, Carthage was in the habit of appealing in her controversies, makes two metaphorical allusions to St. Peter's scriptural connexion with the church of Rome. In one of these the apostle is said to have baptized in the Gentile rivers, and therefore in the Tyber; in the other to have been a martyr in the Gentile as well as Jewish churches, and therefore (as the Roman clergy understand the passage) to have died in the church of Rome. It is supposed that this language of Tertullian is much more to be depended on for Peter's history than those passages in Scripture in which we read of the apostle's special mission to the countries in which there were most Jews, and of his residence at Babylon, when his martyrdom was at hand, —and this, although up to this time (the middle of the third century) no writer of any kind had called in question the scriptural account of his mission or his death.

The character given by the Roman clergy of Tertullian's manner of expressing himself is as follows: "He was (says Father Dupin) of a very quick, sprightly, and sharp temper; but he had not all that exactness and clearness that might have been wished. He often stretches things too far. He is warm and transported almost upon everything. He is full of figures and hyperboles. If he does not persuade by his reasonings, he at least forces consent by that pompous way of expression whereby he sets them out." "As to Tertullian's style," says Father Coillier, "it cannot be denied that it is harsh, unpolished, obscure, and sometimes too inflated," (trop enflé.) We surely are entitled to take some account of so very marked a style of composition.

On one occasion when this writer is insisting, with his usual vehemence, that it is unimportant as to what water we are baptized in, and that there is no difference in this respect between the Jewish and the Gentile river—between John the Baptist, who was restricted to the Jordan, and the twelve apostles of our Lord, who had all the rivers of the earth before them (Matt. xxviii. 19)—he puts the matter briefly thus: "Can there be any difference between those whom John baptized in the Jordan and Peter in the Tyber?" (*De Baptism.* c. 4.) No reader of history, no sincere inquirer after religious truth, will look upon such a passage as in itself a plain indication that Peter was supposed to have come into Europe. It may lead such a person to inquire whether it was supposed that Peter had done so; but it will not lead him to conclude that Tertullian certainly understood he had. Every one will admit that the same words might have been used in a metaphorical sense, and that if Peter's disciples baptized in the Tyber, it was in effect the same thing as if Peter himself had done so. But besides all this, which is so obvious to the most careless reader, Tertullian himself, though fond of metaphor, and perhaps exactly because he was so, often takes more pains not to have this style of writing misunderstood than more prosaic writers would have done, and he does so here. With regard to this particular case of Peter's being said to do things (tingere, Κηρυσσειν, &c.) in the different cities in which there were local churches, Tertullian offers the following very appropriate remark a few chapters further on, in the same treatise in which the passage occurs that we are now considering: " Our Lord came, they say, and did not baptize, (for John the evangelist says, although Jesus himself baptized not, but his disciples) as if it was meant that our Lord would baptize literally with his own hands (revera suis manibus tincturum). The expression, however, is not to be understood in this literal way, but in the natural and ordinary sense of such expressions; (non utique sic intelligendum est sed simpliciter, dictum, MORE COMNUNI,) as when we say, for instance, the emperor proclaimed a decree, or the governor scourged some prisoner, are we to suppose that it was the emperor himself, or the governor himself, who did this? Certainly not. A thing is ALWAYS said to be done by the person through whose deputy it is done;" (c. 11.) and that Tertullian understood this to apply to those Roman converts whom Peter sent from Jerusalem to Rome, " preaching the word," is further proved by his adding almost immediately afterwards: " I take it for granted that he who was permitted to proclaim was permitted also to baptize." (c. 14) So that not only is the expression itself opposed to the literal interpretation which some of the Roman clergy have deceived themselves into supposing it to bear, but Tertullian himself, who used it, warns us against that very interpretation. Those, therefore, if there be any, who still think that the words under consideration must mean that Peter baptized literally with his own hands in the Tyber, and could not possibly mean anything else, are bound at least to tell us upon what grounds they depend for this peculiar opinion. Neither Baronius nor Bellarmine, nor even Father McCorry, considered that this passage afforded any evidence.

The other passage, in any sense that we take it, has a less marked reference to Rome itself. The most that can be made of it is to the effect that Peter died in the church of Rome—THAT HE WAS CRUCIFIED A FOUNDER OF THAT CHURCH—that his martyrdom belonged to it as well as to any other—and from this they infer that he must have died within the very walls of the imperial city. But upon what principle can it be pretended that the mere fact of his having, in ecclesiastical language, died in the Roman church, necessarily implies that he must have died at Rome? Had the Roman church then none of its members, none of its founders, scattered and martyred in other countries? The passage is "Happy church!" supposed to be said exclusively of the Roman Christians. "Happy church! into which, with their lives, our Lord's apostles poured forth all their doctrine! In which St. Peter and his Master both suffered the same death! In which St. Paul was decapitated as well as John the Baptist! and in which St. John the evangelist was banished from Ephesus to Patmos, after rising unscathed from flaming oil." (See Father McCorry's translation in the Appendix.) The unbiassed reader will see at once that all this refers not to the local church of Rome, but to the universal church of Christ. Let us, however, first consider the passage in the limited sense in which the Roman clergy profess to understand it, as applied to the local church of Rome only. In the first place, Peter was in reality, and was always spoken of as one of the founders of the Roman church. He was always therefore, especially by the Africans and Romans, associated with it; and was always regarded by them in that light when his crucifixion is spoken of, although that, as he tells us, was at hand while he was at Babylon. When, therefore, we are told that he died *in* the Roman church, or *for* the Roman church (as the word "*ubi*," in reference to "ecclesiæ" here indicates either of these loose relations), what is there in such forms of expression to justify us in allowing ourselves to be thereby diverted from our steadfast faith in the plain narrative of our Holy Scriptures? In the second place, St. John the evangelist, one of the eleven who stood up with Peter to co-operate with him in the foundation of the churches, is here mentioned as having been banished from Ephesus to Patmos, *in* or *for* the Roman church, in the same sense and in the same way as Peter was crucified at Babylon, in it or for it (Felix ecclesia ubi Johannes relegatur), a banishment most unambiguously outside the *walls*, however much it may be regarded as within the *church*, of Rome. St. Chrysostom, in his first Homily on the Epistle to the Ephesians, says of their city: "St. John the evangelist resided there a long time. IT WAS THERE HE WAS WHEN HE WAS BANISHED. It was there he died. There also St. Paul left Timothy;" and in this statement of St. Chrysostom all the rest of the Fathers, without one single exception, acquiesce; nor do I know of any Roman-catholic writer who contradicts it Irenæus, Clement of Alexandria, Polycrates, one of the earliest bishops of the church of Ephesus, Origen, Eusebius, Jerome, and many more, mention St. John's banishment from Ephesus and his return to that city; none of them contradicting what St. Chrysostom says, that he was at Ephesus when this took place—none of them saying that he ever was at Rome then or at any other time. Is it not evident, then, that if St. John gave his life and doctrine to the church of Rome, and was one of its founders (as he undoubtedly was), when he was banished from Ephesus to Patmos, and when he died at Ephesus (as all the Roman clergy admit he did), is it not evident, I say, that Peter's being said to have given his life and his doctrine to the same church, and to have undergone his crucifixion in it, does not imply that it was within the walls of Rome that he did so? If St. John's banishment could be said to have taken place in the Roman church when John was, as all the Fathers tell us, at Ephesus, so Peter's crucifixion could have taken place in it when he was, as the Scriptures tell us, at Babylon. If one assertion is not contrary to what the Fathers say, there is no necessity for supposing that the other contradicts the Scriptures.

All this is so evident, that scarcely any of the Roman-catholic writers venture to dispute it. They have, therefore, set up another argument upon the passage. They pretend, that though St. John was at Ephesus when he was banished to Patmos and when he returned from his banishment, and also that it was at Ephesus he died; yet, with regard to the other occasion alluded to by Tertullian as having occurred prior to his banishment, the occasion of his having been thrown into flaming oil (for they understand this in a literal sense), there is, they pretend, mediæval evidence sufficient of this having occurred at Rome, and this they think is what Tertullian in this passage says took place there. But the slightest reflection—the very structure of the sentence, disproves that argument. For it is not "the church where John's alleged immersion took place prior to his banishment," but "the church where his banishment took place subsequent to his alleged immersion," that is in question. Any locality that is supposed to be conveyed in the term "church," is strictly confined to the banishment only. Yet even if this were not so,— even if the supposed immersion in the flaming oil were included with the banishment in the reference to the Roman church,—this leaves the above remarks untouched; for, whatever else may have taken place, if John's banishment can be said to have taken place in the Roman church, Peter's crucifixion at Babylon may equally be said to have taken place in it. All this is so very plain, that few, I think, of the more enlightened of the Roman clergy will now-a-days rely on such an argument for refuting the indications that the Scriptures give us respecting the place of Peter's martyrdom. They will still, no doubt, believe that there is sufficient mediæval evidence for thinking that John was thrown into the flaming oil in a literal sense, and that this happened (as the Pseudo-Prochorus, in the twelfth or thirteenth century, first relates) at Rome instead of Ephesus; but they will not pretend to deny, that whatever else Tertullian says, he distinctly says " THE CHURCH IN WHICH John was BANISHED FROM EPHESUS TO PATMOS;" and this is all that it is incumbent upon me to explain, for (as I have so often repeated) in the same sense in which John could be said to have been banished from Ephesus to Patmos in consequence of his fidelity to the Roman Christians, Peter may also be said to have been, in the same cause, crucified at Babylon.

I am, nevertheless, unwilling to pass over without notice this mediæval legend about John's alleged immersion in a tub of flaming oil, as I find an incredible amount of misconception existing as to what is said upon this subject in the fathers. Of its having, in a literal sense, occurred at all anywhere, we have no evidence of any kind, as Baronius reluctantly acknowledges, unless we regard the present passage as such, until the writings of the Pseudo-Prochorus in the middle ages; for Jerome, in his memoirs of St. John, says nothing whatever about it, and only mentions it elsewhere as a metaphor of Tertullian's, in illustration of Matt. xx. 32. None of the other Fathers ever mention it; nor does Tertullian himself do so anywhere else, except in the passage now under consideration—a universal silence which, in the case of so eminent an apostle as St. John, and so extraordinary an occurrence, can only be accounted for by the metaphorical nature of the statement. And as to its being at Rome instead of Ephesus that John was thrown into the flaming oil, there is not the slightest intimation of this in any of the Fathers, for Tertullian does not connect even the Roman church with the event, nor does Jerome when he repeats it; nor is there any other kind of evidence at all upon the subject, until the fictitious narrative of Prochorus made its appearance, towards the end of the middle ages. This fact is also candidly acknowledged by Baronius, (A.D. 92, paragraphs 1 and 2,) and the following passages, taken from this narrative of Prochorus will show what the Roman clergy hold upon the subject,—it is given in the Bibliotheca Patrum, (vol. ii.) After saying that the proconsul of the Ephesians brought over John to Rome in chains, by the orders of Domitian, in consequence of complaints transmitted to the Emperor against him, all which matters are given in detail, Prochorus, who pretends to have been his companion the whole time, adds, (chap. xi.)—" After these things the Roman senate, with the proconsul and the people of Rome, sat together before the Latin Gate, and ordered a tub full of *boiling* (not flaming) oil to be brought, into which they threw the apostle, on the day before the nones of May." Then, after describing how he experienced not the slightest pain or martyrdom of any kind under this operation, and that, when he was taken out, though nearly ninety years of age, he appeared to be quite refreshed and invigorated by it, Prochorus proceeds: " Then Domitian gave orders that the proconsul should not make any further attempts to torture John, but that he should take him back to his prison, in order to see what was best to be done with him." We are then informed that John had a vision, in which he was told, " You must go back again to Ephesus, for that city has still great need of you," &c. The narrative then proceeds thus:—" So we went again to live at Ephesus; and the rest of the idols were destroyed, and there was not a temple in Ephesus from which the abominations were not removed. These were some of the miracles performed at Ephesus by John, before he was sent into banishment,—ill-treated by the Jews, the Romans, and the Greeks, whom the devil thus excited against us. Then the pontiffs and authorities of the Ephesians sent another letter to Domitian as follows:— 'The inhabitants of Ephesus to Domitian, the sovereign of the world,—We beg of you to assist us. Certain persons, who have come here from Judæa, named John and Prochorus, have taken possession of our city, disseminating a new doctrine, and destroying by their witchcrafts the temples of the gods. We acquaint you with these things, in order to comply with your wish respecting them, for you are our Emperor.' When the Emperor read this despatch, he gave orders that both the offenders should be banished from Ephesus, and wrote back as follows:—' Domitian the Emperor to the authorities, and to the city of the Ephesians,—We wish those wicked impious wizards, John and Prochorus, to be banished, whom in our mercy we have endured too long. Therefore we order that they be banished to the Isle of Patmos,' &c. When this decree was brought to Ephesus, persons were sent to arrest us, I mean me, Prochorus, and St. John. Those who were sent were about one hundred, &c. At length they led us to the ship; and, when we got on board, orders were given that we should be placed in the middle of the ship, and be allowed, as our provisions, six ounces of bread and a small vessel of water, and a little vinegar. St. John consumed two ounces of bread in the day, and one-eighth part of the water. He left the rest for me," &c. " There was afterwards a dance on board," &c.

Thus it is evident, that John's being at Rome when he was banished to Patmos, is no part of the Roman legend on this subject, even in the absurdest writers; for although the Roman clergy accept the account given of St. John in these fictitious writings of Prochorus, they nevertheless frankly enough acknowledge that these writings are fictitious, and cannot be regarded as good authority, either of his having been at Rome, or of any particular respecting that supposed event. The Abbé Rohrbacher evidently considered them not entitled to the least attention. In his "Universal History of the

Church," (vol. iv. p. 490,) he says:—" We are not told in what year, nor in what way, nor for what purpose, the apostle John should have come to Rome, when he was so very old."

Father Tillemont (A.D. 1650) says,—" The narrative of Prochorus is full of ridiculous fictions, and is supposed to have been written only about 300 years ago."

Cardinal Baronius says,—" The writer of this narrative is proved to have, in many cases, written the grossest falsehoods," (in multis mendaciissimus fuisse convincitur, A.D. 92, paragraph 1.)

Father Ceillier says,—" The two books that we have under the name of St. Linus, about the martyrdoms of St. Peter and St. Paul, and the life of St. John, supposed to have been written by Prochorus, one of the seven first deacons, (Acts vi. 5,) are compositions full of absurd inventions, which are not even worth being read."

The Benedictine fathers, in their Bibliothèque Sacrée, say: " We have a history of St. John the Evangelist, supposed to have been written by the Deacon Prochorus. But it is evidently a modern composition, and full of fabulous anecdotes, unworthy of the deacon whose name it bears."

I may mention here, that all the fathers speak of John's banishment, whether it was a voluntary one or otherwise, as his martyrdom, and that they constantly speak of him as a martyr in allusion to it; yet that by some singular mistake, the Roman clergy speak of his martyrdom as having taken place in this ecclesiastical miracle, although they tell us that he was so far from suffering either in mind or body during its performance, that he seemed to have been in every way greatly refreshed by it.

But to return. As I have said, our present question respecting John exclusively concerns his banishment from Ephesus, as Tertullian is supposed to have said that this took place with reference to the Roman church in the same sort of way as Peter's crucifixion at Babylon might be said to have taken place with reference to the same church; and the attentive reader will see, from the facts to which his attention has been drawn, that there is not the slightest room for inferring from Tertullian's passage, even as the Roman clergy understand it, that Peter's death did not take place, as the Scriptures intimate, at Babylon. There is even another sense in which this highly figurative writer might have used the words in question, still supposing, as the Roman clergy pretend, that he does not here mean by " ecclesia " a COMMUNITY OF PERSONS, but some LOCALITY from which these derive their name. Whatever was done by the Roman government was constantly said to have been done at Rome, whether it was the union of separate provinces, the restoration of dethroned princes, or any other act of government. I merely advert thus little to this sense, because although a very common one, it would involve too much unnecessary illustration here. According to it, however, Tertullian might have said that John was banished at Rome and Peter martyred there, as well as Paul beheaded within the very walls of that city. But are the Roman clergy prepared to show that Tertullian is in this passage speaking of the Roman church at all? Whoever will be at the pains of reading the treatise in the original, will, I think, see that he is not; or, that this is at the least a very doubtful matter, and that there is quite as much, if not more, reason to suppose that he is speaking of the whole Christian church in contradistinction to the heretics, saying that she had martyrs to prove the truth of what she taught — a happiness of which the heretics could not boast — that the local church of Alexandria, his own church of Carthage, and all the other African local churches, were in harmony with her, and that the heresies which sprang from this universal church of the apostles and the martyrs, were no more to be in any way identified with her than the wild fig-tree with the cultivated fig-tree. which, amidst the mysteries of nature, sprang often both from the same seed. The whole treatise is against the heretics of those times, and one of the main arguments which recurs in every page is the disunion of these heretics on the one hand, and the universal oneness of the church of the apostles on the other. In chapter xx. he describes the foundation of this church in all its different localities, citing it as the first act of the apostles (stated in their "Acts," by St. Luke), and often insists that but one church was then founded by the apostles everywhere. "All these local bodies," says he, "great and many as they were, constituted that one first church founded by the apostles, to which one they all belonged. So that they were all the first church, and all apostolical, because they were all one church (omnes prima—una omnes); and this oneness of all these societies is proved by the peace, the brotherhood, the harmony of intercourse that reigns among them, which conditions arise from nothing else but the singleness of their faith." In chapters xxi. xxii. and xxiii. he reiterates this oneness of Christ's church, and for the first time in the treatise mentions John, and Paul, and Peter as joint agents in the building of it, dwelling also upon the too often forgotten fact that Peter's special mission was to the most Jewish districts of the earth (Petrus in circumcisionem; Paulus in nationes). This oneness of "the church" is argued in every variety of forms to the last page of the treatise; nor is the term "church" ever once used without some qualifying words, except when speaking of this one universal church. In chapter xxxiii. Tertullian points out how the church under the apostles foretold and denounced the heresies, and here again he names its three great martyrs and apostles. Paul, he says, denounced those who, like Marcion and Apelles, denied the resurrection (1 Cor. xv. 12), and discouraged marriage (1 Tim. iv. 3). John, he says, denounced those who, like Marcion, "eat things sacrificed to idols" (Rev. ii. 14), or, like Hebion, denied that Christ had "come in the flesh." And Peter, he adds, condemned the worship of the angels, which was among the tenets of the Gnostics. In chapter xxxiv. he again adverts to the church as it existed under the apostles, saying that it not only condemned what it named, but still more what it left unnamed, as these were still later heresies, and "so much the more corrupt," he says, "as not being even named by the apostles." In chapters xxxv. and xxxvi. he again speaks of this universal church as the anti-heretical church, saying that it was the true one because it was the first; and that it was the church of the apostles because it had their sanction while they lived, and now the sanction of those local bodies in which the chairs of the apostles were, *i.e.* (as he says, chapter xxxii.), the chairs in which the first bishops were men ordained and sent by the apostles. He then enumerates some of these localities, which naturally remind him of the three apostles he so often mentioned before—Rome, Philippi, &c., of Paul; Ephesus, of John; and all, of Peter, for it was by his orations that the apostles founded the church in most of these localities. He finally exclaims, "Happy church, to which the great apostles gave both their doctrine and their lives," &c., adding, that from this universal church of Christ the heresies came forth, as in nature it sometimes happened that what was impure sprang from what was pure. This is the context; the following is a literal translation of that portion of the context immediately adjoining the present passage. "Our system—the doctrine of our church (nostra disciplina—nostra res) is not of a later date than theirs (the heretics')—nay, it is earlier, it is before them all. And that is the proof that it is the true church, for in such cases truth is always first, and the apostles not only did not denounce it, they defended it, and this is our proof that what we now have was theirs. For the church that the apostles did not condemn, as they condemned all that was not theirs, is thereby proved to be their own, and to have the sanction of THEIR TEACHING and THEIR BLOOD. Refer to some of the apostolic localities, you who may wish to employ your curiosity to your advantage in the cause of your redemption, and you will see that it is as I tell you. Go to the cities in which the very chairs which the apostles founded are still occupied as they were, in which the very letters that they wrote are still publicly read from authentic copies, conveying to us as it were the very sound of their voice, the very expression of their features. There are plenty of these places. If you live next Achaia, you have the city of Corinth to go to; if near Macedonia, you have the town of Philippi and you have Thessalonica; if you can go so far eastward as Asia Minor, you have the advantage of Ephesus; and if you live near Italy, you have the city of Rome, whither we also send up our appeals. Yes, happy—truly happy is that church, into which with their lives the apostles poured forth all their doctrine; in which Peter and his divine Master both suffered the same death—in which Paul, like the Baptist, is beheaded—in which St. John the Evangelist is banished from Ephesus to Patmos (after coming forth unhurt from the flaming oil). Let us consider what she has learned from the apostles, what she has taught to us. She recognises but one God, the Creator of the universe, and Jesus Christ his Son, born of the Virgin Mary; she recognises also the resurrection of the dead; she unites the law and the prophets with the writings of the evangelists and of the apostles. From them she learns what she believes; and this she seals with baptism—this she clothes with the Holy Spirit—this she sustains with the Eucharist. She exhorts all to steadfastness in the trials of their faith, and receives no one who conforms not to this teaching. Such is the church which not only foretold the heresies, but out of which the heresies proceeded. They did not, however, belong to her, inasmuch as they set themselves in army against her. From the nut of the cultivated olive the wild olive springs; from the seed of the most delicious fig the empty and useless wild fig rises: and thus the heresies have grown out of our church. They grew from our fruit, yet not of the same kind as we are; from the seed of truth, indeed, but untrue and wild. In order, then, that the truth of our principles should be seen, which are those that the church has handed down from the apostles, the apostles from Christ, and Christ from God, heretics must not be allowed to appeal to scripture, as without scripture we can prove that they have no right to appeal to it."

It cannot appear to any one so very evident that all this applies to the local church of Rome. To many it must be evident, for various reasons, that it does not. No one, for instance, has pretended that it was at Rome that the heresies here condemned by Tertullian took their rise; and the Roman clergy show that they also have their misgivings; for they introduce the word "Rome" or "Roman" in the passage where it is not in the original, in order to fasten this sense upon the words. I do not here argue that Tertullian shows clearly what church he speaks of, though I think he does; I only say that he leaves that point so *uncertain* as to render the apostrophe, "Happy church," &c., unavailable as evidence of Peter's not having died in the city whence he wrote his letters to the provinces of the Dispersion, even if that apostrophe would in any case have proved it, which, however, I have shown that it would not.

The other two passages, adduced from Tertullian's writings, afford no statement whatever—not even a metaphorical one—upon the subject of our inquiry, and have been supposed to do so only from the preconceived notions of those who cite them. In one of them it is said that our Lord's prediction respecting Peter's crucifixion was fulfilled, as every one admits, *at the period when* the first Roman persecution was being carried on (a persecution which we have already seen extended over the whole empire), and some writers look upon this as a sort of argument for supposing that it was fulfilled at the same *place* as the persecution originated. Tertullian's words run thus:—" We read the lives of the emperors. Nero was the first at Rome who dyed with blood the infant faith of Christendom. It was at that period that Peter 'was bound by another,' for he was then fastened to the cross. It was at that period also that Paul really became a citizen of Rome, for it was at Rome that his martyrdom—that second noble birth—took place." (Scorpiacum, c. 15.) Here we are not told that Peter became a citizen of Rome. Rome is not named as the scene of his martyrdom, although it is as that of Paul's; and although this was a case in which, for the sake of clearness, it would, if possible, have been so named, as Tertullian alludes here to the prediction mentioned by Peter in his letter from Babylon, upon that very subject. This passage will remind the reader of that in Clemens Romanus, where also Rome is mentioned as the scene of only one of the two martyrdoms.

In the other passage Tertullian merely says, "The Romans—to whom Peter and Paul left the gospel sealed with their blood." (Adv. Marcion. c. 6.) Is it, I ask, pretended that they did not leave the gospel so sealed to all other churches also? If all the Roman clergy were thoroughly convinced that Peter was crucified at Babylon, as his own words and our Lord's words so plainly intimate, would they not still consider it to be true, that he who had founded the church of Rome bequeathed the gospel to it sealed with his blood? Is there not something frivolous in inferring from such a statement that the scriptural intimations are not to be depended upon, and that after what Tertullian says, it cannot be supposed that Peter could possibly have undergone his martyrdom at Babylon?

XXII.

ST. CYPRIAN (about A.D. 250), bishop of Carthage, speaks of the church at Rome as "Peter's chair;" and this, which all admit to be all that he says of Peter in connexion with Rome, is looked upon as one of the most conclusive proofs that we have of the apostle's having left the East. That it is, however, not the slightest proof, or even intimation of this, is evident from the fact, that churches in places where Peter can be proved never to have been, and where it is allowed on all hands that he never was, are also called "Peter's chairs." St. Optatus, the bishop of Milevis, in Numidia, calls his small church of Milevis, "Peter's chair." (ii. 5. 9.) The church of Carthage, St. Cyprian's own church, some hundred miles distant from Milevis, is likewise called so by this same writer. (i. 10.)

Alexandria is called "Peter's chair" by St. Gregory the First, in his letter to Eulogius, one of its archbishops, (book vi. epist. 40,) and Hippo, St. Augustine's little church, on the African coast, is spoken of by St. Augustine as the chair of Peter. (lib. ii. contra literas Petiliani, c. 51.) Yet none of these writers, nor any other writer, Roman-catholic or Protestant, pretends that Peter was either at Milevis or at Carthage, at Alexandria or at Hippo. Even the remote church of England was called "Peter's chair" by St. Gildas, two or three centuries after Cyprian's time, yet no modern Roman Catholic affects thence to infer that Peter must have been to Canterbury. "Britain has her priests," says St. Gildas, (born A.D. 511,) in his epistle "On the Destruction of Britain," "but they are foolish; they sit in Peter's chair with unwashed feet, but fall into the place that more becomes them, the chair of the traitor Judas." (Script. Brit. p. 23.) Nor does the Roman church object to other churches being called "Peter's chairs." "It is justly," says the celebrated Aubespine, bishop of Orleans, in 1600—"It is justly that Optatus calls Carthage 'Peter's chair,' because, as Tertullian expresses it, it was begotten by St. Peter." (Quia Petrus eam genuit, ut loquitur Tertullianus. *Albaspinæus in Optat.*) And again, "In the church there is but one chair, which Christ gave to Peter, and which Peter has given TO EVERY BISHOP. This is what all the ancient writers teach us. It is not without good reason, therefore, that the chair of Carthage was called Peter's chair." (*Ibid.*) The Benedictine editors, also, of St. Gregory's works, say that "St. Peter's chair at Alexandria and St. Peter's chair at Rome was one and the same chair, belonging to one and the same apostle." (Unius esse atque unam. *in loc. supra citat.*) We find, in like manner, that "the chair of Moses," (cathedra Moysi) cited as a similar and explanatory expression by St. Augustine, was at Jerusalem, where Moses himself never was; and that the chair at Rome was also called "the chair of Christ," (Cathedra Christi;) and "the chair placed by our Lord at Rome," (cathedra quam Romæ Christus constituerat. *Aubespine on Optatus*,) although we know that our Lord when on earth was not at Rome. Peter's chair, therefore, being in Europe, is no more a sign of Peter's having left the East, than our Lord's chair being at Carthage or Rome is a reason for thinking that our Lord went to either of those cities, or that the chair of Moses being at Jerusalem is a sign that Moses himself must have been in the capital of Judæa.

Although this is all that we are here called upon to prove, yet as some of the less informed of the Roman clergy think, and lead others to think, that what Cyprian means by this expression is a chair which had been made at Rome by a joiner there, (not sent over, as some might imagine, by the apostle after he had been sitting in it at Babylon or Jerusalem, but which had never been outside the walls of Rome); and that Peter's having sat in a chair of this description is the clearest proof that he must have left the East;—as some, I say, of the less informed of the Roman clergy sometimes mention this wooden chair in their tracts, as the chair alluded to by St. Cyprian, the two or three following quotations from the fathers and the more enlightened of the Roman clergy will exhibit the preposterous character of this delusion and the true interpretation of the term "chair" in these expressions.

St. Jerome tells us distinctly, that in all such expressions, the word "chair" means doctrine or authority to teach. Per Cathedram—DOCTRINAM debemus accipere. (Commentary on Matthew, book 4.) And this figurative sense of the term is the only one that was pretended to by any of the writers of the Roman church until they became involved in the present controversy.

"Peter's chair, or the episcopal seat," says Father Dupin, "is the supreme authority of ruling the laity by the power of the priesthood." (Cathedra est auctoritas regendæ plebis vi Episcopatus. Commentary upon Optatus.)

"The chair of the scorner," and "the chair of the

traitor Judas," are often introduced by the fathers, as may be seen in the quotations from St. Gildas, St. Augustine, and others, to exemplify this use of the term "chair," to denote doctrine or authority; and in the same way "the chair of Moses" is and has always been understood. "By the chair of Moses," says Father Calmet (on Matthew xxiii.), "is here signified either his doctrine or his authority." And again, in his "Dictionary of the Bible:" "The chair of Moses expresses the authority of the doctors of the law, and their office of teaching." The Dominican fathers also, in their Bibliothèque Sacrée, say, "The chair of Moses means the authority to teach."

Accordingly, Tertullian, as it has been seen, considered that Peter's chair admitted of being generated (Petrus eam genuit. *in loc. supra cit.*) The bishop of Orleans also looked upon it in this remarkable light, and considered that it admitted of being multiplied *ad infinitum*. (Propagatæ et genitæ Cathedræ. *not. in Opt.*) What in the name of common sense can such expressions have to do with a wooden chair at Rome?

But that Cyprian himself did not mean by "Peter's chair" any particular wooden chair, either sent into Europe by Peter from Babylon, or in which the apostle literally *sat down*, but only any local church in which his doctrine was taught and his authority exercised, is clearly proved by St. Cyprian's own unequivocal explanation of his own expression as "the chair that rested upon—that was founded upon St. Peter." (Cathedra super Petrum fundata. Epist. 40.)

It may seem frivolous to have taken up so much space with a matter so obvious, and once so universally admitted; yet now-a-days, as the fate of the Papal power is found to depend upon Peter's having left the East, this calling the Roman church, or something in it, "Peter's chair," is one of the straws laid hold on by the clergy—one of the most incontrovertible proofs they tell us that they can find, or that we ought to require, of that great ecclesiastical supposition.

XXIII.

St. Firmilian, (about A.D. 250) bishop of Cæsarea, one of the churches which were founded by Peter in Cappadocia, at the same time as he founded the church at Babylon and the church at Rome, says in a very indignant letter to Cyprian, that Stephen, the bishop of Rome, endeavoured to persuade people that he had Peter's succession in his church of Rome quite as much as Firmilian himself had in Cappadocia, or as Cyprian had at Carthage: yet that this Stephen was not acting up to these pretensions; nay, that, on the contrary, he was a fool and a heretic.

From this it is inferred by Baratier, the Correspondent in the *Times*, and others, that Peter must have been at Rome, as "Peter's succession" could only be in some town where Peter was. St. Firmilian wrote as follows: "I have good reason to be indignant at the arrant folly of this bishop Stephen,—that he who boasts so much of the city in which he is bishop, and pretends (contendit) that he is one of those who have the succession of Peter, upon whom the foundations of the whole church are placed,—that he should bring in several other rocks beside Peter, and build several other churches beside that of Christ." Of the inference which it is attempted to draw from these words, there is abundant refutation in the single well known fact that Irenæus, bishop of Lyons, in France, a writer of great piety and eminence, spoke of himself as possessing at Lyons "the succession of the apostles," although it is known that the apostles never were at Lyons, nor even one of them for a single hour. "The work about the number Eight," says Eusebius, (v. 20,) "was also written by Irenæus; and in it he informs us that he had received the first succession of the apostles." Clemens, the bishop of Alexandria, who lived about the same time as Irenæus, makes a similar statement about himself, in almost the same language. "In his first book," says Eusebius, (vi. 13,) "Clemens tells us that he was one of the first in the succession of the apostles." And yet no Roman-catholic writer pretends that any of the apostles were at Alexandria. How, then, can any one suppose that Stephen's being said to have Peter's succession proves Peter to have been in Europe?

But I cannot forbear mentioning four other considerations which set this matter in quite as clear a light as the cases of Irenæus and Clemens, and which may serve to show how totally common sense has been outraged by these struggles to prove that Peter left the East. 1st. What could be more natural than that the line of bishops in every church founded by Peter and the apostles should call themselves "the bishops of Peter and the apostles," or simply "the apostles' succession of bishops," or "Peter's succession of bishops;" and this, even if neither Peter nor the apostles had ever been within their town? 2ndly. Would not such an expression be, if possible, still more appropriate and still more natural, in the case of a church to which Peter had himself sent one of its first bishops,—which is what it seems highly probable that Peter did for the church at Rome, and what all the Roman-catholic writers affirm that Peter really did do for that church? Would not those who succeeded this bishop be most truly "Peter's succession," without Peter's having ever left the East? 3rdly. The very passage quoted from St. Firmilian is so far from saying that Stephen really had Peter's succession, (as some have been led to think,) that Firmilian therein pretty distinctly intimates that he had it not; that his pretensions to it were not allowed; that he had at least some difficulty in enforcing them; that his conduct was incompatible with it, inasmuch as he was introducing strange rocks under the foundations of the church, and that he was no longer entitled to be spoken of with the respect that was due from one of Peter's bishops to another. But, 4thly, over and above each of these considerations, what can be more plain or conclusive upon this point (even if we had nothing else to guide us) than St. Firmilian's own explanation of the phrase, "Peter's succession," when, on again requiring to advert to this a few lines afterwards, and to the unreasonableness of Stephen's pretensions respecting it, he says, "Stephen, who gives out that he has by succession the chair of Peter"? It is evident from this expression alone, that "Peter's succession," as Firmilian understood it, was not confined to the cities in which Peter had resided, any more than Peter's chair was confined to them; and that therefore the church at Rome, being one of those that had his succession in Firmilian's sense, would be no proof, nor even the smallest sign, of his having been in Europe. As on former occasions, I indicate sundry reasons why the words do not prove what they are brought to prove. What I have mentioned, however, of Clemens and Irenæus, supersedes all else upon the present passage.

XXIV.

St. Stephen, bishop of Rome, (about A.D. 250,) does not say one word upon the supposed visit of Peter to Europe; and is merely introduced to augment the apparent "cloud of witnesses" respecting this supposed visit, on the ground, that it is to be presumed, from what Firmilian says, that Stephen really did pretend that he had Peter's succession as well as any one else, however much the bishops of other churches might dispute his having it; and that therefore he also considered the supposed visit to have taken place. But it is clear that this Roman bishop having set up a disputed claim to what was called Peter's succession, does not by any means prove that his claim was a well-founded one; and equally clear, from what has been said in the last chapter, that even if this Roman bishop had that "Peter's succession" to which he pretended, this would not prove Peter to have ever been in Europe.

XXV.

ORIGEN, (A.D. 254,) an ecclesiastical writer of Alexandria, is one of the authorities most depended upon by the Roman Clergy, for showing that the scriptural account of Peter's martyrdom, as having occurred when he was at Babylon, is not to be relied on. But Origen does not say one word to this effect. Eusebius, as it will be seen later, mentions, (ii. 25, and iii. 31,) what we learn also from other more recent sources, that some relics found in the catacombs in his day at Rome were supposed to be those of Peter; and is thence led to conjecture that perhaps this apostle was transferred from Babylon to Europe to be put to death, after he had written at Babylon his letters to the Jews of the Dispersion. The Roman clergy have imagined that Origen is described by Eusebius, on this occasion, as having been the author of this conjecture about the relics. But Origen, as will be seen, says nothing about it, nor does Eusebius say he does. This is now admitted by Valesius, the Roman-catholic commentator on Eusebius, and by Father De la Rue, the Benedictine editor of Origen's works, although the latter has inadvertently inserted the whole chapter from Eusebius as a portion of what Origen had written. The mistake, which seems to have begun with Baronius, even the English reader can judge of. Eusebius, who wrote in the fourth century, tells us (iii. 1), that there was in his day a tradition, or unauthenticated rumour, respecting such particulars of Thomas, Andrew, and John, as are not recorded in the Scripture; that for what is not there recorded of Peter we were limited to mere conjecture; but that there was the plain statement of Origen to go upon respecting Paul. What is here said of Paul, Baronius and most of the Roman clergy have confounded with what is said of Peter. The passage in Eusebius is as follows:—" The holy apostles and disciples of our Lord having been scattered over the whole world, Thomas, according to tradition, (παραδοσις) received Parthia (in which Babylon was not included in the time of Eusebius) as his allotted region; Andrew, Scythia; and John, Asia Minor; where, after continuing for some time, he died at Ephesus. There is some reason to think (ἰοικε) that Peter had proclaimed the gospel to the Jews of the Dispersion in Pontus, and Galatia, and Bithynia, in Cappadocia and Asia Minor, when, being ultimately at Rome, he was crucified with his head downwards, which was the way in which he himself understood he was to suffer. What need is there that we should tell where Paul went when spreading the gospel of Christ from Jerusalem to Illyria, and that he finally suffered martyrdom at Rome in the reign of Nero? These things are distinctly asserted (σαφως ειρηται) by Origen." The mistake into which Baronius fell was, that he confounded what Origen "distinctly asserted" with what Eusebius states as a conjecture. Some of the earlier critics supposed that the words "These things are distinctly asserted by Origen," referred to all the previous clauses, beginning at "the holy apostles," although they so obviously apply to the last only. Many of the moderns extend them to the clause respecting Peter. But Valesius frankly acknowledges that Eusebius does not tell us that Origen attested what is said about St. Peter, though Valesius himself seems to assume that Origen may have done so. "Eusebius," says he, "has not clearly pointed out what is the commencement of Origen's words; which remark Father De la Rue repeats in his edition of Origen. Both these writers, therefore, admit that we cannot infer from what Eusebius says, that Origen had ever heard of the conjecture that contradicts the scriptural account of Peter's martyrdom at Babylon.

The whole of Valesius's note is as follows:—"Cum Eusebius hic dicat superiora ex libro Origenis esse desumpta, dubitari merito potest unde incipiant Origenis verba; an a vocibus illis Θωμας μεν an potius ab istis Πετρος δε. Neque enim Eusebius satis distincte nobis notavit quodnam esset initium Origenis verborum."

Valesius here speaks of Origen's words; but no one pretends to produce any thing in Origen's own words upon this subject.

XXVI.

PETRUS ALEXANDRINUS, (A.D. 311,) archbishop of Alexandria, is supposed to have heard that Peter's martyrdom did not take place at Babylon, but at Rome, because there is a work now extant, "On Penance," in which a statement is made to this effect, and which work was once attributed to this archbishop. That this production, however, is of a much later date, and not his, is evident from two facts connected with it, and universally admitted by the Roman clergy, although they still continue to publish the work under his name. One of these facts is, that a portion of this work is discovered to have been taken, word for word, from another work, called a "Discourse on Easter," also attributed, until very lately, to this archbishop. Of this portion of the work on Penance, the Dominican Fathers, in their Bibliothèque Sacrée, observe: "It is nothing more than a passage taken from a discourse, written by Peter of Alexandria, about the feast of Easter." The discovery here stated was first made by Zonaras, a monk of Constantinople, in the eleventh century; and as long as the "Discourse on Easter" was considered to have been written by Petrus Alexandrinus, the authenticity of the work on Penance not only remained also undisputed, but was even looked upon as confirmed by this discovery. At length, however, a new fact turned up. The "Discourse on Easter" was discovered, by the Roman Catholics themselves, and by the librarians of the Vatican, to be of a date long subsequent to the times of this archbishop, extending at least to A.D. 451. The discovery I now speak of was made in this way:—A MS. with another portion of the "Discourse on Easter," that had not yet made its appearance, was found, not very long ago, in the Vatican library, some particulars respecting which are given by Father du Fresne, in his edition of the Paschalion, or

Chronicon Paschale, (Paris, 1688,) a very slight inspection of which MS. at once convinced all who saw it, and none more than the Roman clergy themselves, that the "Discourse on Easter" attributed to the archbishop of Alexandria, was written after the Council of Chalcedon, (A.D. 451,) and therefore not by him. Of the "Discourse on Easter" thus completed, Father Ceillier says: "A Discourse on Easter, in the form of a dialogue, and printed in the beginning of the Alexandrian Chronicle, is attributed to Petrus Alexandrinus; but there is no room for doubt (mais on ne peut douter) that this is the work of a much more recent writer..... He did not live until after the Councils of Ephesus and Chalcedon." (Ceill. vol. iv., Petr. Alex.) In a matter universally admitted as this is by the Roman clergy, it is unnecessary to load the statement with their opinions. It naturally follows from these two facts, that the work on Penance, which was to some extent compiled from the "Discourse on Easter," was at least of as late a date as that Discourse, and was therefore erroneously attributed, as it was during some centuries, to Petrus Alexandrinus.

In addition, however, to this irrefragable proof of the late period at which the work on Penance was written, I may observe, that there is no trace of the existence of this work at all until the Council of Constantinople, commonly called the Trullan Council, at the close of the seventh century, by which council the orthodoxy of the work was examined into and acknowledged, but without the least reference whatever to its authenticity; and that the original MS. title of this work on Penance, as presented to the Trullan Council, does not by any means describe it as the production of Petrus Alexandrinus, but only as having been compiled from a treatise imputed to him, "On those who Fall Away in Times of Persecution, and then Repent." The rules of penance introduced in this treatise are thus professedly set down afresh by some unknown person, who wrote between the Council of Chalcedon, A.D. 451, and the Trullan Council, A.D. 692. The title under which the work was examined by the latter council is as follows:—"Regulations introduced by Peter the Martyr, and archbishop of Alexandria, in his work on Penance, called 'Those who Fall Away in Times of Persecution, and then Repent.'" Thus, in no way that we approach this document is there a shadow of pretext for saying that Petrus Alexandrinus had ever heard that the apostle Peter was not put to death at Babylon.

XXVII.

ARNOBIUS, (about A.D. 330,) a pagan convert, and African writer of great eloquence, is supposed to have heard that Peter had been in Europe some twenty or thirty years before he was put to death at Babylon. The only ground that the Roman clergy assign for this supposition is, that in one of his enthusiastic addresses to the pagan world on behalf of his new faith, after alluding to its diffusion in the most distant countries, in our own Islands, in Egypt, in Cappadocia, and at Babylon, immediately on the first teaching of the apostles, he adds the Romans as a remarkable instance of conversion. "They hesitated not," says he, "to join the faith on that occasion; for they had *seen* the fiery steeds of the Magician scattered by the breath of Peter, (ore Petri,) and vanish at the name of Christ." On this passage the Roman clergy rely, as affording the clearest indication possible that Arnobius must have been under the impression that Peter came into Europe before he employed himself in the mission appointed for him by our Lord. But there is nothing of this kind implied in these words. "To *see* a thing happen," is an expression which we constantly apply to things which occur at the greatest distance from us. For instance, if it is said of Englishmen, "They have seen the Pope banished from his dominions: they have seen him restored by the bayonets of the President," this does not imply, either that there were Englishmen present at Rome or Naples at the time, nor that it was in England that the Pope took refuge, nor that Louis Napoleon went to Rome. The Romans, we are told, *saw* that the thing happened. It is mere sophistry to argue from such an expression that the thing must have happened at Rome. But, besides this, even if we must give the "had seen" of this passage a strictly literal sense, there were Romans of all classes scattered in great numbers throughout the East, and Arnobius gives us to understand that the thing happened *before* the apostles left Jerusalem, mentioning, moreover, the name of a town, apparently in connexion with the story, which is not known as having ever been the name of any European town. The whole passage is as follows:—

"Those miracles which were performed openly—that superhuman power which the Saviour exerted upon the natural world, made the Gentiles believe in Him, and made the most heterogeneous of the nations unite in that belief. For we can recount what happened, and it may be of use to you to hear; we can recount what happened—the churches that were founded—in the far East, among the Persians and among the Medes; we can recount what was done in Asia Minor and in Syria, among the Galatians, among the Parthians, (who had Babylon in Peter's day,) and among the Phrygians; we can tell you what happened in Achaia, in Macedonia, in Epirus, aye, and in every island, every province, upon which the rising or the setting sun sheds light; and, finally, at Rome, the mistress of the world—even there men were found, who, although intent upon the ancient superstitions of their Numa, did not scruple to abandon the religion of their country, and to become members of a Christian church; for they had seen the path of the Magician; they had seen his fiery chariot and four fire-winged coursers scattered by the breath of Peter, (ore Petri,) and vanish at the name of Christ. Yes, they had seen one who was betrayed by the false gods to whom he trusted, and who, by falling headlong when they forsook him, broke both his legs, and lay thus upon the ground. And, at a subsequent period, they saw this same man, after he had been transferred to Brunda, worn out with his sufferings and his shame, fling himself down from the highest point of a roof, and die. But all these things ye neither know nor wish to know, nor think that it could ever be of any use to you to know them. The false gods ye trust to are your own hearts," &c. (Lib. ii.)

Now, when it is considered that Brunda was not the name of any European town that has ever been heard of—that the Roman church, whose foundation is here mentioned as subsequent to the apparition of the fiery equipage, was existing under Tiberius, and before the general exodus of the apostles from Judæa, (as has already been shown from Tertullian, Eusebius, Orosius, and others, in the section on Irenæus) and that Judæa, as well as the whole country from Judæa to Babylon, was, at this time, constantly occupied by the Roman legions, and full of other Romans of all descriptions, it will, I think, be admitted by all parties, that even if "had seen" is to be taken in its strictly literal sense, Arnobius not only says nothing to indicate Europe as the place where the fiery chariot was presented in mid-air to the eyes of the astonished Romans, but even seems to designate the East, in a very pointed manner, as the scene of that astonishment, which we are here told, led, as a proximate cause, to the establishment of the Roman church. To which, it may be added, that none of the other Fathers, although they all considered this story as the most undisguised allegory, make any allusion to Rome as the scene of it. (See the sections on Cyril of Jerusalem, Theodoret, &c.)

I do not, it will be observed, raise any question in what I now say, as to whether the story of the fiery chariot, drawn, at a considerable elevation, by four wild horses winged with fire, at the mere word of an absurd impostor, was a pagan fable or an ecclesiastical miracle. What I now ask is, whether Arnobius states that it was in Europe that this took place? and on this point there is not the slightest room for any doubt. Arnobius does not say that it was there (wherever else it might have been), that the first Roman converts saw the chariot;

K

on the contrary, he very plainly gives us to understand that it was in Asia.

But besides all this, even if Arnobius gave the story as a fact, not as an allegory, and added, in a distinct manner, that it was in Europe that the phenomenon had been seen, how could we infer from the expression, "by the breath of Peter," or "by the prayers of Peter," (ore Petri) that the apostle was in personal attendance on the occasion? Would it not be a very weak and degrading argument to say that this fiery equipage could not possibly have been brought down by the prayers of the apostle Peter, unless he himself came from Babylon or Jerusalem, and was present on the spot? I appeal to the conscientious Roman Catholic. Would there not be something bordering upon an impious and reckless levity in such a supposition? If any satisfactory authority can be shown for believing this ecclesiastical miracle about the four horses with wings of fire, and the ascent of the enchanter into mid-air over Rome, towards heaven, in a chariot of flame from the top of the Capitoline hill, as the circumstances are usually described—if there be, I say, credible evidence for the literal reality of this transaction, what need would there be that we should suppose Peter present in person to bring back the triumphant Samaritan to the earth by prayer? Might the apostle's prayers not have been successful from the greatest distance, even from the banks of the Euphrates, as well as if he had stood beneath the very chariot as it passed? Or might not the prayers of the Roman church be here called the prayers of Peter? Will any one that is sincere pretend to say that the Christian church at Rome, of which Peter and the apostles at Jerusalem were the founders, might not be with perfect propriety designated the "breath of Peter," or "the prayers of Peter". on this occasion? Nay, was not that church, in fact and in truth, the voice of the apostles within the city of the Cæsars? Might not the bishop that Peter sent to Rome —might not the twelve missionaries or evangelists, which some of the apocryphal records of the Roman church represent Simon Peter, the apostle, as having sent there from Cæsarea after the impostor of Samaria—might not the document, called "Peter's proclamation," (το Κηρυγμα Πετρου) which is known to have been published at Rome in the reign of Claudius, expressly against the Gnostics, have been a sufficient representative of the apostle at Rome, to justify Arnobius in saying that what these effected was effected by the "breath of Peter?" Tertullian tells us that verified copies of Peter's letters, and of those of the other apostles, were carefully preserved at all the apostolic churches, for the purpose of arresting heresy. Will any one undertake to say that, even if this story of the chariot is not an allegory, these letters alone were not that "breath of Peter" at Rome—that teaching of the apostles, by which the fiery steeds of the heretic were arrested and scattered as they passed in their mad career above the capitol?

Thus, even if a literal sense be given to this passage, it affords not the slightest pretext for supposing that Peter was in Europe, or even that Arnobius thought he was. That the allegorical sense, however, is the only one that the statement will bear, is placed beyond all dispute by the unanimity of the Fathers on the subject. Justin Martyr (A.D. 167), St. Irenæus (A.D. 200), and Tertullian, men of research, and the only writers who for the first three centuries speak of the impostor of Samaria as living at Rome, after having been first the greater part of his life in the East, say nothing whatever of his passing above the imperial city, at any time, in a fiery chariot, nor of Simon Peter's presence in Europe on that or any other occasion. It strikes me that this will always be looked upon as insuperable evidence against the literal interpretation of the passage in Arnobius, for if they did not consider the story an allegory they would have related it; and when we add to this, that Eusebius (A.D. 340), the next writer, in the order of time, says not one word about this fiery chariot having ever been seen either in Europe or in Asia; and that he says that he relates in his history, every, the smallest, particular that had come down to his own times about St. Peter, we have the clearest possible assurance from the Fathers that the Samaritan impostor did not drive, in any literal sense, these four fire-winged horses, either in the West or in the East; and that, even if it could be shown from any other source that he did drive them, St. Peter was not personally present when he did so. Cyril of Jerusalem, and the one or two other post-Nicene Fathers, who do speak of a Gnostic chariot, confirm this. For they not only do not make Europe the scene of it, nor represent the great apostle of the Jews on the occasion as present, otherwise than in his prayers, but, as may be seen in the sections on these writers, they speak of it as a mere allegory, with which each was at liberty to combine any fresh circumstances he might think proper.

I have now to show that most of the Roman clergy have for a long time viewed this story in the same allegorical light as all the Fathers did, and as all Protestants have always done; and that they have for centuries abandoned as utterly untenable the literal interpretation given to it by Father M'Corry, and the Correspondent in the *Times*.

John Baptist Cotelier, one of the most learned doctors of the Sorbonne (A.D. 1686), says in his Notes upon the writings attributed to the early Fathers (*Apost. Const.* vi. 9): "No doubt you will ask me what we are to think of this amazing and much-talked-of downfal of the the Samaritan's chariot. I stick to the old proverb,— there is danger both in believing and in not believing. I neither maintain this story as a fact, nor do I positively reject it. I do what is called ιπιχω, I suspend my judgment on the matter. Whoever has a fancy for miracles of this kind (cui cordi erunt ejusmodi miracula), and there are many who have, he has in this case the support of many great names, both in the Greek and Latin churches. But those who are more inclined to look upon the story as an allegory, which is now-a-days the case with a LARGE PORTION (magna pars) of the learned of our church, will see reason for doing so, partly in the original source of the details, for these are taken from spurious and unauthentic writings; partly in the discrepancies which enter into the different accounts; partly from the silence of many writers, and especially of many of the popes, who do not generally omit what thus concerns the interests of the church. One thing certain is, that the 'Liber Pontificalis' shows that the thing was but very little and very vaguely talked of at Rome; and even the words mentioning that it was ever talked of are only found in some of the copies of that document."

Father Antony Austen Touttée, a Benedictine (A.D. 1720), says in his Notes upon Cyril of Jerusalem: "What is here related of the downfal of the Samaritan at the prayers of the apostles, IS NOT REGARDED BY MANY OF OUR MODERN WRITERS in the light of a fact; as well because Justin Martyr, Irenæus, Tertullian, and Eusebius, say nothing whatever about it, only spurious writings first vouching for its reality (propter primam historiæ fidem ex pseudepigraphis petitam); as on account of the great differences subsisting in the details of the different writers. For some say Paul's prayers, as well as Peter's, were employed on the occasion; others, Peter's alone; some, that prayer alone effected the downfal of the flying chariot; others, that fasting was employed as well as prayer; some, that the Samaritan had only his legs broken by the fall; others, that his whole body was dashed to pieces. All these discrepancies, however, would not prevent us from looking at the story as a fact, if it were confirmed as such by any satisfactory authorities. (si aliunde certis monumentis firmaretur.) But the reader will do well to see what Dr. Cotelier says about it."

The learned Charles Weis, (A.D. 1809), a Roman-catholic contributor to the "Bibliothèque Universelle," a work sanctioned and largely contributed to by the Roman church, says, after giving the usual story: "It is, however, GENERALLY AGREED UPON, (mais on s'accorde généralement,) now-a-days that this story is not to be looked upon as a fact."

The Abbé Pluquet, (A.D. 1780,) in his Dictionary of the Heresies, dedicated to a Roman-catholic archbishop, a friend of his, makes the same remark: " Nevertheless that story, as a fact, is regarded as unauthentic. For, to say nothing of the difficulty of supposing it consistent with history, it is quite certain that the downfal of this fiery chariot, through Peter's prayers, would have been too important an event to have escaped the knowledge of the Christian world, and to have been left unrecorded by the earlier Fathers; yet neither St. Justin, nor St. Irenæus, nor Tertullian, say one word about this chariot, —they who told us so much about the statue."

Thus, Father M'Corry and the Correspondent in the *Times* are bound to show upon what grounds they dissent from the majority of their own church respecting the allegorical character of this fiery chariot and of the various other little incidents connected with it by the writers of the 13th century—most of which are stated in the last section of this work; and not only upon what grounds they dissent, but also upon what grounds they expect that the enlightened classes of Great Britain and Ireland will in the 19th century accept as authentic history, what the church at Rome, even in its darkest ages—600 years ago—did not profess to regard in any other light than as a mere nursery tale, like St. George and the Dragon, and the other similar stories with which it was published.

But the main point to be at present attended to is, what Arnobius himself thought upon the subject; and he, it has been shown, neither says that it was in Europe that the first Roman converts saw the fiery horses in the air above their heads, nor that the apostle was present when they saw them,—nor does he say that it was not an allegory, nor that he derived the story from any other writer. We have not, therefore, the shadow of a reason to infer from the three or four words quoted from this African writer, that St. Peter abandoned for a single hour the great Jewish appointment assigned to him by our Lord.

XXVIII.

LACTANTIUS (about A.D. 330), another African, and said to have studied eloquence under Arnobius, but who enjoyed a much higher reputation as a writer than his master, is also supposed to have inferred from the Κηρυγμα Πετρου, already so often alluded to, that St. Peter came into Europe; because the following passage occurs in a chapter in which this writer is speaking of that written document, ascribed, as will be seen, by him and others to both Paul and Peter, and in which Lactantius says that the apostles repeated some of our Lord's predictions respecting the events that occurred in the siege of Jerusalem. Lactantius thus expresses himself (iv. 21):

"Our Lord also disclosed certain prophecies to his disciples which Peter and Paul published at Rome; and that publication having taken place in a written form, so as not to be forgotten—(Ea Prædicatio in memoriam scripta)—was still to be met with after all these things had happened. In it, among many other remarkable predictions, the apostles mentioned (in quâ dixerunt) that Providence would soon send a king to exterminate the Jews, &c., and so it was. After the apostles were dead,—after Nero had slain them,—Vespasian annihilated the name and nation of the Jews, and all those things happened which the apostles had foretold."

The commentators in communion with the church of Rome acknowledge, without any exception, that when Lactantius here speaks of Peter as promulgating Christianity in the capital of the empire, he alludes to the Κηρυγμα Πετρου—"Peter's Preaching," or "Proclamation," which, as Eusebius informs us, (ii. 14,) was sent to Rome by Peter for that purpose. Father Dufresnoy, in his edition of Lactantius, (Paris, 1748, iv. 21,) says of the document here mentioned: "This was the title of a work erroneously attributed to St. Peter, and now lost; for the particulars respecting which the reader is referred to Fabricius, in his 'Codex Apocryphus' of the New Testament, (p. 800.)

John Albert Fabricius, a distinguished scholar of the eighteenth century, says, in his *Codex Apocryphus*, "We may conclude from Clemens Alexandrinus, and from Lactantius, (iv. 21,) that 'Peter's Proclamation,' and 'Paul's Proclamation,' were one and the same document, which is sometimes quoted under the name of only one of them, and sometimes under the name of both. The reader is recommended to look at what has been collected on that subject by the illustrious Grabbe, in his 'Spicilegium' (vol. i.)"

John Ernest Grabius says, on this passage of Lactantius, in his "Spicilegium," (vol. i.)—"And Lactantius quotes these words from the written Proclamation of Peter and Paul, although I suspect, as I shall show presently, that they were taken from the Apocalypse of St. Peter." Where see much more on the same point.

Father (Edward) Xavier (A.D. 1617) also says upon this passage, (same edition): "A work which St. Jerome looks upon as apocryphal has appeared under this title of 'Peter's Preaching,' or 'Petri Prædicatio,' which is no longer extant."

Valesius, in allusion to the same work, says, (upon Eusebius iii. 3): "I wonder to find Eusebius say that the work which was called the Κηρυγμα Πετρου was not quoted by any of the ancients." And again: "As to the work which was called the Κηρυγμα, or 'Peter's Proclamation,' it is cited by Clemens Alexandrinus, and also by Lactantius, who mentions this document in the 20th chapter of his 4th book."

Thus the Roman church herself admits, that it was in and by this document that Peter published those predictions which Lactantius here says he published at Rome. This passage, therefore, affords no evidence whatever that Peter, at any period, forsook the lost sheep of the house of Israel to come into Europe, or that Lactantius inferred he did so, from the existence of this document. Cardinal Bellarmine, indeed, says that we have stronger evidence in the last clause of the foregoing passage, in which Lactantius says: "After Peter was dead, after Nero had slain him, Vespasian annihilated the nation of the Jews." But this requires no answer. I only draw attention to it to show the straits and contradictions to which the Roman clergy are reduced in their honest struggle to uphold the absurd pretensions and delusions in which they have been educated. Did the Roman emperors put no one to death except at Rome? Father Palma, as may be seen in the section on Clemens Romanus, exposes the absurdity of such a notion; and Father Dufresnoy admits, in his own note upon these words of Lactantius, that it was not certain that Peter was put to death at Rome, and that an expression of this kind does not show where either Paul or Peter died. "All that we know for certain upon this point," says he, "is, that Paul was put to death at Rome." (Certum est Paulum Romæ Martyrium passum case.)

The writer in the *Times* is singularly misinformed as to the testimony of Lactantius. He supposes this author to have thought that Peter had been in Europe, because there is a statement to that effect in a little tract of the 17th century, which was once, for a few years, attributed to Lactantius. But is not the writer in the *Times* aware, that nearly a century and a half ago this tract was discovered to be a forgery, and a very clumsy one,—so clumsily constructed, in short, for the part it had to play, that the Roman clergy endeavour now to make out that it could never have been even intended by the person who wrote it to have been passed off as having been written by Lactantius? Is he not aware that, as far back as A.D. 1710, Father Le Nourry, a Benedictine monk of great learning and celebrity, proved, in the clearest manner, that there was not the slightest reason for supposing it to be the production of Lactantius? Is he

not aware, that in these days not one of the Roman clergy
pretend to say it was? and that it is now regarded by them
as the work of some unknown writer, at some unknown
period? Father Palma of Rome, for instance, one of the
most recent writers in communion with that church, and
lately Professor of Ecclesiastical History at the College
of the Propaganda, says, in his "Prælections," (part i.
p. 38): "The book on the Deaths of the Persecutors,
which used to be attributed to Lactantius, was written
by some person named Cæcilius." But even Father
M'Corry, by not citing it, shows that he was aware of
its being spurious; or at least that he could find no
modern writer authorizing him to put it forward as
authentic. On a subject so universally acknowledged by
all the Roman clergy, as well as by the College of the
Propaganda at Rome, it might seem unnecessary to
add any other testimony to that of Father Palma; but
lest what the writer in the *Times* has said should mislead
any one as to the justice of the decision to which all the
learned have come respecting this document, and as to
the clearness of the grounds upon which they have rejected it, I subjoin the following particulars:—

The full name of Lactantius was, "Lucius Cæcilius
Firmianus Lactantius;" and though there are a few of
his MSS. upon which the whole name is thus inscribed,
there are also many upon which we only find "Firmianus
Lactantius." His work, "De Persecutione," mentioned
by St. Jerome as extant in his day, has never since been
found. In A.D. 1678, a MS. was produced at Moissac,
in France, in the department of the Tarn-et-Garonne, at
a monastery there, with the following title: "The Book
on the Deaths of the Persecutors," addressed to the Confessor Donatus, and written by Lycius Cecilius. Now,
one of the undisputed works of Lactantius, that "De
Ira," is also addressed to Donatus the Confessor, and no
one can dispute the plausibility that attaches in these
cases to the want of uniformity in the author's name. It
is a point that all forgers attend to, more or less, although

in this case, as will be seen, the *utter* dissimilarity of name seems very much to overhit its own mark. Stephen Baluze, a zealous Roman Catholic, of immense learning and immense fame, who had for many years the management of Colbert's library, immediately published this MS. as the lost work of Lactantius, although there was nothing whatever connected with the MS. to lead one to suppose that it was not the production of one of the monks of Moissac, except some very awkward allusion to what might have been the state of a person's feelings and circumstances when writing in those times, which, in the eyes of many, will only make the forgery more apparent. However that may be, the work contained the most unobjectionable statement, as Baluze then said, that had yet been found about Peter's being in Europe, and it was triumphantly received by the Roman clergy.

As there was but one MS., and this accessible to very few persons, every new edition was copied from its predecessor, so that the act of Stephen Baluze (in substituting the name " Lucius Cœcilius Firmianus Lactantius" for " Lycius Cecilius," and " De Persecutione" for " De Mortibus Persecutorum ") remained undetected about thirty years; until at length Father Le Nourry, seeing many improbabilities in the body of the work, and suspecting something wrong, looked into the MS. He saw at once what the over-zealous Baluze had done, and, with an amount of indignant spirit unusual in such cases, had a correct copy immediately published, with a fac-simile (to be now seen at the British Museum) of the title and first page of the MS., whereby the extraordinary conduct of Stephen Baluze, the librarian of the great Colbert, and the accepted antiquarian of the Roman church, was most unequivocally and for ever exposed. Father Le Nourry, a Benedictine, fervently devoted to the prerogatives of the see of Rome, is one of those who have attempted to show what the probabilities were of Peter's having been in Europe; but even he felt, that to defend his cause by such a stratagem as this, was to abandon it altogether. He therefore acknowledged that Lactantius affords no testimony upon this favourite theory of the Roman clergy.

Father Le Nourry's account of the discovery of this MS. will not be uninteresting:—" This MS. struggled for its existence among the moths and worms of the libraries until the great John Baptist Colbert gave directions to M. Foucault, then royal intendant of that part of France, which is now called the Tarn-et-Garonne, to search all the libraries of that district. In consequence of which, M. Foucault went in April, A.D. 1678, to Moissac, to an old Benedictine monastery that was there, called anciently the "Abbey of a Thousand Monks," but occupied in his days by what they call Secular Friars. After he had been hospitably received by these, they took him to a place, the atmosphere of which was most unfavourable to the preservation of MSS., (locum cuilibet cœli intemperiei aerisque inclementiæ expositum). He there found several masses of MSS., (plures acervos,) heaped together in a disgusting state, and with the parchment almost entirely destroyed. From these, however, he at once picked up two hundred and fifty MSS., older, and in a better state of preservation, than the rest, (vetustiores et saniores,) and among these the one in question, taking the greatest care to keep it apart from all the rest. He then procured the permission of the abbé and friars to send all these MSS. to Colbert's library in Paris, where they have been ever since. The learned Baluze, who had had for several years the management of Colbert's library, after having carefully looked through this one of the MSS., came to the conclusion that Lactantius must have been the person meant as the author of it. Therefore he had it printed the following year as the work of that writer." (Cecilius, by Le Nourry. Preface.)

The following disclosure as to the importance of this document to the church of Rome, if it could have been shown not to be a forgery, is from the pen of the learned, upright, and zealous papist who was first deceived about it, and is entitled to the attention of every earnest and conscientious Roman Catholic. Baluze writes as follows:—" Although I consider that it is useless to deny, as some do, Peter's journey to the city of Rome, which is proved by the clearest evidence, I nevertheless see very great uncertainty about the time he went there; for there are several very great difficulties connected with the notion of his having gone there in the reign of Claudius (as Baronius supposes), inasmuch as it obliges us to suppose that he went there twice, and had two contests there with the Samaritan heretic,—once under Claudius, and again under Nero. How PREPOSTEROUS SUCH A NOTION AS THIS IS, (Quæ res quam absurda sit,) when no ancient writer states it, those well know who are acquainted with this subject. For as Cardinal Baronius himself justly observes, every one disregards as untrue what a later writer states, without the authority of some one preceding him. If, therefore, I may be permitted to dissent from that notion, I should be disposed to prefer the statement of Lactantius (' On the Deaths of the Persecutors,' chap. ii.); I mean, I should fully grant that the apostle proclaimed the Gospel at Rome in person; not however in Claudius's, but in Nero's reign; for this view of the matter, the only true one as I think, being thus once established upon the indisputable authority of Lactantius, all controversy is immediately at an end, and that, too, without any disadvantage to the authority of the Pope; for it is not length of time, but Peter's being there at all that is required for the supremacy of our church." (Baluz. in Lact.)

Thus, over and above the proofs of spuriousness brought forward by Father Le Nourry and the various other Roman-catholic commentators, the four following suspicious circumstances have, we see, attended the discovery of the MS. in question. 1. The occasion upon which it made its appearance was one well known to afford great temptation to the forgery of MSS.; for Colbert, the celebrated minister of Louis XIV., had a little before commissioned his friends and agents, in the different provinces of

France, to search out and send him all the ancient MSS. they could find. 2. All the MSS. that were lying in the same place in which this one was—and we are told there were *several heaps* of them—were of a medieval or post-medieval date; insomuch, that not one of them appears to have been old enough to have been thought worth publishing. 3. It contains a statement about Peter's being in Europe, which Baluze (into whose hands it came, as Colbert's librarian), acknowledged to have been very much wanted, in support of the Papal supremacy, as the evidence they previously employed upon that point was no longer credible or satisfactory. 4. Although the cellar or place in which it was found was so damp as to have almost quite destroyed all the other MSS. that were there, this one is in the most perfect condition possible, the few words in it that are illegible being rendered so by some substance of a sticky nature having touched it on that spot, as Le Nourry mentions in his notes.

Accordingly, we find that from the very first there were doubts entertained as to the authenticity of this work. Bishop Pearson admitted, that although he thought it might be authentic, others might not be able to bring themselves to this conclusion, and Le Nourry, in his preface, says that various persons had already expressed their misgivings on the subject before any proofs had been laid before them. Even Father Ceillier, one of Le Nourry's contemporaries, does not appear to have entered into the delusions of Baluze about the authenticity of this work, although the writer in the *Times* gives us to understand he did. On the contrary, Ceillier hesitates to pronounce an opinion, acknowledging that there are arguments in favour of Le Nourry's view, stating what they are, and recommending them to attention. He writes thus: " M. Baluze was the first who published that document, and he did not scruple to attribute it to Lactantius. One of his reasons for believing him the author of it was, because he supposed that the title, " On the Deaths of the Persecutors," given to that work in the MS. he found, which is the only one we have, was of the same import as the title "On Persecution," which is cited by St. Jerome, in his list of Lactantius's writings. He also went upon the circumstance that the names Lucius Cæcilius, which were inscribed (Lycius Cecilius) upon the MS. in question, are found prefixed to those of Firmianus Lactantius, in another MS. of other works, known as certainly the productions of Lactantius. Finally, he thought he could discern the style of Lactantius in this document . . . . Father Le Nourry, the Benedictine, is almost the only one who has yet written on the other side. His arguments have been combated by several of the learned; but as there is some force in them, we have thought it might be of use to set them before our readers in an abridged form. He says then," &c. &c. (Ceillier in Lactant.) Accordingly, although Ceillier sometimes seems rather to incline to the opinion of Baluze, and not to consider this a production of the 17th century, he nowhere speaks of Lactantius as the author of it. He even adds: "We do not know who this Cecilius was; we only know that there was a whole family of distinction at Rome that bore that name." (On ignore qui était ce Cecilius. On sait seulement qu'il y avait une famille entière très illustre qui portait ce nom.—Ceill. *ibid.*) Thus, not even the great effort made upon this occasion, by Baluze and Colbert, has rendered the name of Lactantius available to the Roman clergy in this controversy. This is fully admitted by Father Palma, of Rome. Upon what grounds then does the Correspondent in the *Times* profess to contradict Father Palma and all the rest of the modern clergy of the church of Rome? Is the Roman-catholic church of these islands more credulous or less instructed than that of Italy? This would be a severe and unwarranted conclusion respecting it.

PART II.

EUSEBIUS.

I.

EUSEBIUS, bishop of Cæsarea, in Palestine, and one of the Greek Fathers (A.D. 340), wrote a history of the church, in which he tells us (iii. 31) that he gives all the facts that had come down to his times respecting the apostle Peter. In this history he is supposed to assert that St. Peter was in Europe, and that he was not put to death (as the Scriptures indicate) at Babylon. But it will be seen that he asserts neither of these alleged facts. Some of his translators, indeed, represent him as doing so; but every Greek scholar who is acquainted with the original, is aware that Eusebius has made no such assertions.

It is, however, perhaps here of equal, if not greater importance, to observe that if Eusebius had asserted what is here alleged, this could not be regarded as even a slight indication of the supposed facts. Eusebius, it must not be forgotten, wrote nearly three centuries after the events in question could have occurred, and had as we have seen no intervening record of them to advert to, although there were no less than *one hundred and fifty* ecclesiastical writers who preceded him, and some of them extremely voluminous. His sole authority, therefore, (for such it would have been,) could, under such circumstances, have had no weight whatever. No historical event—no event even merely traditional has ever been accepted, or ever could be accepted, as authentic upon the sole testimony of a writer who lived so many generations after the supposed period. This is an important consideration with regard to Eusebius, too much overlooked by some writers on this subject; but overlooked clearly from its having been hitherto erroneously supposed that writers long before the time of Eusebius had attested the event in question.

It need scarcely be observed that if a historian of the present day states now for the first time some remarkable fact respecting Henry VIII., without having any authority to assign for his statement, his testimony would be refused. No one would think it unreasonable to disbelieve such a statement; on the contrary, no one would think it at all reasonable to believe it. No one would be expected to take important steps in reference to it,—to establish institutions, to construct theories, confessedly of the gravest import, that were wholly founded upon such a statement. In one word, no one would or could believe it. I say, therefore, that even if Eusebius had made the statement imputed to him, it could have no weight as evidence with honest and earnest minds, inasmuch as it would have been the first statement of the event in any kind of writer for three centuries after it is supposed to have occurred. On this I presume that no one, Roman Catholic or Protestant, will entertain the least doubt. Eusebius, however, as I shall now show, does not make the statement imputed to him.

Before I proceed to correct the misconceptions abroad respecting this writer, it is proper to remove at once two fresh errors set up (no doubt inadvertently) by the Correspondent in the *Times*. In the first place, it is quite a mistake to suppose that Eusebius mentions anywhere "*several important transactions of this apostle in that city.*" The Correspondent is totally misinformed upon this point. Eusebius asserts no one thing, important or unimportant, that Peter is even ever said to have done in person at Rome. Not one day is indicated

L

that he passed there; not one spot on which he trod there; not one word stated that he uttered there; not one person mentioned to whom he spoke there. To suppose that Eusebius mentions anything of this kind is mere delusion, of which any one can easily satisfy himself, from the most careless English translation of the history. The utmost that we find upon this point in Eusebius is a mere conjecture, incidentally suggested by himself, that as Peter's relics had been found at Rome in the fourth century, when Constantine was there, the apostle might not, perhaps, have been put to death at Babylon; for it is to be observed, that Peter's Second Epistle, in which the apostle indicates (i. 14) his martyrdom as about to take place at Babylon, was not, in the days of Eusebius, universally acknowledged to be authentic by the churches. The conjecture of Eusebius, therefore, at that time, did not, as it now would, contradict the Bible. It did not take into account that Epistle. "What is called Peter's First Epistle," says Eusebius, (iii. 4,) "has been always acknowledged as authentic; and the earliest fathers have quoted it as indisputable authority. But that which is called his Second Epistle, is not considered by all of us to be authentic; although, as being a useful exhortation, it is esteemed and read with the other Scriptures." And, beyond this very loose conjecture, Eusebius will be found to give no countenance whatever to the story about Peter's having been in Europe. "He suggests no other reason," says Cardinal Bellarmine, (*De sum. Pont.*,) "except these relics, for supposing Peter to have died in Italy." It is also a great mistake to say that it is "*in several places*" that Eusebius adverts even to this conjecture. In this respect, also, the Roman Catholic in the *Times* is utterly and strangely misinformed. He mentions it but once in the whole ten books of his history, distinctly representing it, on that occasion, as a mere loose conjecture of his own, not supporting it by any authority, and never again adverting to it.

The passage in which he states it occurs in the first chapter of the third book. After having mentioned, towards the end of book ii., that Peter had undergone his predicted crucifixion during Nero's persecution when that emperor had conquered the masters of Babylon, (την ανατολην πασαν υποταξας, ii. 25,) and that his relics were supposed to have existed at Rome from Nero's time, the historian then says (iii. 1):—" It is not improbable (ιοικι, there is some reason to suspect) that Peter had written his proclamation of the gospel to the Jews of the Dispersion, in Pontus, and Galatia, and Bithynia, in Cappadocia and Asia, when being finally in Rome he was crucified, with his head downwards, he having himself also considered that it was in this posture he was to die."

That Eusebius here neither makes, nor intends to make, a positive statement as to the point in question, is as evident as language can make it. It is true that he adverts at the same time to two facts, of which there never was a question; but that circumstance, the attentive reader will see, makes no difference as to the purely conjectural character of the passage, and of the other allusion in it. There never was a doubt, in the early church, as to the fulfilment of our Lord's prediction respecting Peter's crucifixion with his head downwards, nor ever a doubt as to the authenticity of at least the first letter addressed (or proclamation issued) by St. Peter from Babylon to the adjoining provinces (παρπιδημοις). It is not to be supposed that these are the points to which Eusebius here alludes, as "seeming likely," and as "not impossible." These facts it would have been unscriptural to question; and that the mention of the Epistle here is merely to mark its being prior to that journey which Sylvester's discovery at Rome of Peter's supposed relics led Eusebius to conjecture as not impossible, is further clear from the use of the pluperfect infinitive, κεκηρυχιναι, before the participle, γινομινος, which introduces the only conjecture that there is in the passage. Then as certain relics supposed to be those of the apostle Peter, were discovered in the catacombs at Rome in the days of Eusebius and his patron, Constantine the Great, and were as such

deposited by the Emperor and the Roman bishop of that
day in three of the new churches that the Emperor then
built in that city, the historian, purely on account of
that circumstance, (as is admitted by Bellarmine,)
suggests, also as a conjecture of his own, although he
had never been at Rome, and was very ignorant about
the Western churches ("peu instruit de ce qui regardait
l'Occident."—Ceillier), that there was no reason for not
thinking that the apostle may even have suffered his
martyrdom in Europe. For, as has been already observed, the authenticity of Peter's Second Epistle, in
which this martyrdom is indicated as about to occur at
Babylon, was not yet then universally admitted.

I wish, on two points in connexion with this passage,
(on account of the importance attached to it,) to add
illustration. *First*, I wish to show that Eusebius himself
did not consider that it was known, even by tradition,
that it was at Rome that Peter was put to death. *Secondly*,
I wish to show, that even the Roman clergy themselves,
up to a very late period, did not consider that anything
more was known upon this point, (except as A CONJECTURE,) than what is mentioned in St. John's Gospel and
in St. Peter's two Epistles.

1. On the *first* of these points we derive the clearest
possible indication of the historian's meaning from
the context of the very passage we are considering;
for in this chapter he first tells us that there existed
a tradition in his day as to the places in which St.
Thomas, St. Andrew, and St. John lived and died,
using, to denote that idea, the ordinary Greek word for
tradition, (παραδοσις). He then abandons that term
to speak of Peter, and introduces what he says of him
with the usual Greek expression for denoting a conjecture, (ιοικι,), saying, that in addition to what the Scriptures inform us, he saw reason for thinking that Peter may
have died in Europe, after having written from Babylon to
the adjoining provinces of the Dispersion; adding that as
to Paul, it was historically recorded by Origen, both that
he had travelled in Illyria, and that he had died at Rome.
The conclusiveness of this illustration induces me to

transcribe here the whole passage from the original, a translation of which has been already given for the English reader in the section upon Origen.

Των δε ιερων του Σωτηρος ημων αποστολων τε και μαθητων εφ' απασαν κατασπαρεντων την οικουμενην Θωμας μεν, ως η παραδοσις περιεχει, την Παρθιαν ειληχεν, Ανδρεας δε την Σκυθιαν, Ιωαννης την Ασιαν, προς ους και διατριψας εν Εφεσω τελευτα. Πετρος δε εν Ποντω και Γαλατια, και Βιθυνια, Καππαδοκια τε και Ασια κεκηρυχεναι τοις εν διασπορα Ιουδαιοις εοικεν· ος και επι τελει εν 'Ρωμη γενομενος ανεσκολοπισθη κατα κεφαλης ουτως αυτος αξιωσας παθειν. Τι δει περι Παυλου λεγειν, απο 'Ιερουσαλημ μεχρι του Ιλλυρικου πεπληρωκοτος το ευαγγελιον του Χριστου, και υστερον εν τη 'Ρωμη επι Νερωνος μεμαρτυρηκοτος; Ταυτα Ωριγενει κατα λεξιν εν τριτω τομω των εις την γενεσιν εξηγητικων σαφως ειρηται.

We have a further illustration of this point in book ii. c. 25, where Eusebius endeavours to fix the period at which the two leading apostles died, in order to commence his history of the churches from that date. The title of the chapter is, "On that Persecution of the Christian World in Nero's reign, during which Paul and Peter were honoured for their piety with martyrs' monuments at Rome," (καθ' ον επι 'Ρωμης Παυλος και Πετρος ταις υπερ ευσεβειας μαρτυριοις κατεκοσμηθησαν.) And in it Eusebius mentioning an *on-dit* of his day to the effect that Peter's martyrdom, as well as Paul's, took place in Nero's reign, and during this Emperor's persecution of the Christians in the East, expressly avoids saying that Peter's martyrdom was supposed to have taken place in Europe, although he says that it was there that Paul's was supposed to have taken place. After describing Nero's ferocity of disposition and conquest of the Babylonian provinces, he writes thus: "And therefore Paul is said to have been beheaded even in the very city of Rome itself, (επ' αυτης 'Ρωμης,) and Peter to have been crucified likewise in the time of Nero." (Την ανατολην πασαν υποταξας, &c. . . . Ταυτη γουν οντος θεομαχος εν τοις μαλιστα πρωτος ανακηρυχθεις επι τας κατα των Αποστολων εππρθη σφαγας. Παυλος δη ουν επ' αυτης 'Ρωμης την κεφαλην αποτμηθηναι, και Πετρος ωσαυτως ανασκολοπισθηναι κατ' αυτον ιστορουται.) Where the collocation of the words altogether precludes the supposition that Eusebius here meant to say that Peter was crucified where Paul was beheaded,—a suppression on the part of this exact writer which is the more remarkable as it occurs in the very clause in which, if there were even the alleged tradition or rumour on the subject, he would most naturally have made the statement of the one apostle as well as of the other. And that Peter was not put to death at some unknown period, but under the same Emperor as Paul, is, he adds, rendered probable by the association of their names in the most ancient sepulchral records at the Seat of government, (which would not, he supposes, have been likely to have occurred, if the time of Peter's death had been unknown there,) as well as by the distinct statement of Dionysius Corinthus, to the effect that they died "ABOUT THE SAME TIME." In another passage, also, (iii.31,) in which Eusebius professes to recapitulate all the information which he was able to communicate in the chapter ii. 25, respecting Peter's martyrdom, he does not pretend to say that he told the place in which it occurred, or that there was any tradition about its being in Europe. His words there are,—"The time and manner of the death of Paul and Peter, and even the place where their relics were deposited after death, I have already shown."

Some have been led to overlook the structure of the passage in ii. 25, from a mistaken impression that the Greek word "μαρτυριον," in the title, denoted a martyr's death, as the Latin word "martyrium" often does; but this Greek word never has that signification, either in Eusebius or in any other ancient writer. It sometimes signifies a martyr's attestation,—the testimony afforded by a martyr, whether that be attended with his death or not; but ordinarily it signifies the monument or trophy placed over any little stone, bit of chain, or other relic that had ever been connected with the martyr and his sufferings. These monuments at Rome were at first erected under ground in the catacombs, between the Ostian and Appian roads, and subsequently above ground on the hill Bactisanus, now called the Vatican. On this use of the term in Eusebius, the Roman-catholic commentator, Valesius, says: "Μαρτυριον is properly the name applied to the place in which a martyr's relics are deposited," (proprié dicitur locus in quo, &c.) Accordingly we find that Eusebius, as has been seen in his account of the apostolic martyrium at Constantinople, uses the term in this, its ordinary sense, as constantly as any other writer; and in his " Panegyric upon Constantine," ch. ix., he calls our Saviour's monument by the two names here applied to Peter's, a "martyrium" and a " trophy." Suicer in his Lexicon says: " Μαρτυριον means a temple, or any little oratory erected to the honour and memory of a martyr," (Templum sive sacellum in Martyris alicujus honorem et memoriam ædificatum) and cites from Can. ix., Concil. Laodiceni. " To visit the cemeteries, or what were called Martyria" (εις τα κοιμητηρια η εις τα λεγομενα μαρτυρια απιεναι). Henry Stephens, in his Thesaurus, says of this word: " It signifies testimony—sometimes even the witness himself—also the place in which a martyr's relics are kept." Scaliger, in Chronicon Eusebii, says: " It properly means the altar which is placed over the relics of a martyr."—(Martyrium proprie est altare impositum Martyris cineribus.) Arndius, in his " Lexicon of Ecclesiastical Antiquities," says: "τα Μαρτυρια is the name applied to the places and monuments sacred to the martyrs" (loca et monumenta sacra martyribus.) Father Janning says in Acta Sanctorum (vol. vi. Jun. p. 111.) " In various places there were churches (and are still) which kept the bodies or other relics of their saints deposited in crypts beneath the ground, with an altar erected over them. These repositories (conditoria) were called *martyrium* by the Greeks, and *confessio* by the Latins, even in the most ancient times, and were, in most cases, situated underneath the principal altar of the church." Baronius, on the Roman martyrology, says: " The place in which a martyr is buried, is called a martyrium;" and, again; " What we call *confessio* in Latin, is what is called *martyrium* in Greek." He also remarks upon this very chapter: " Precisely the same monuments which we call *confessiones* in Latin, are called *trophies* by Caius in Eusebius ii. 25." The

Roman-catholic annotator, in Caillau's edition of the
Fathers, published in Paris (A.D. 1836) says in Chrysostom, vol. ii.: "Martyrium means a church consecrated in the name of a martyr, or in which the bones
of a martyr are deposited. The word is frequently to be
met with in the ecclesiastical writers" (vox frequens
apud scriptores ecclesiasticos.) For Peter's martyrium
in the catacombs, and the aperture at the top of it, the
reader is referred to Father Aringhi, in his Roma Subterranea B. iii. ch. 3., &c. Thus there is nothing in the
title of the chapter ii. 25 to justify the supposition that
anything in that chapter alludes to the conjecture in iii. 1.

2. On the *second* point to be illustrated it is enough to
quote the memorable words of Cardinal Baronius, as
there is no one perhaps who has laboured with more
zeal, or with more success, than he has, to throw an air
of plausibility around this isolated and original conjecture of Eusebius, or who better knew the utter insuffi-
ciency of the authorities by which it is supposed to be
supported. "As to the history of the apostles," says
Baronius (A.D. 44, paragraph 42), "after they once separated, WE ARE UTTERLY IN THE DARK (res perobscura est).
For as (with the exception of our canonical scriptures) the
actions and the writings that pass under the names of the
apostles, are known to be mere fictions; and as nothing
whatever that has been related about the apostles by
real and trustworthy writers, is now to be found in its
original and uncorrupted form, we are compelled to
despair of being ever able to KNOW FOR CERTAIN anything
that really and truly took place in the lives of these holy
men."—(Quod vero pertinet ad res ab ipsis apostolis
gestas postquam ab invicem semel separati sunt, res quidem æque perobscura est. Cum enim apostolorum nomine
tam facta quam scripta reperiantur esse supposititia, nec,
si quid de illis a veris sincerisque scriptoribus narratum
sit, integrum et incorruptum omnino remanserit, in despe-
rationem plane quandam animum dejiciunt posse unquam
assequi quod verum certumque subsistat.) This very
just and remarkable admission of Baronius neither
Bellarmine nor any other Roman-catholic writer of the

least note, has ever pretended to contradict, although most of them have joined with Baronius in endeavouring to substantiate the conjecture of Eusebius.

That the conjecture, therefore, then and thus first hazarded was purely a conjecture, and neither a tradition nor even an *on dit*, much less a historical fact, is evident both from the terms in which the bishop of Cæsarea expresses it, from his silence respecting it on all other occasions, and from the admissions of those who have most narrowly and indulgently examined the grounds of it. It was, moreover, a conjecture for which there was in his day some excuse, as the epistle in which Peter says he was about to die at Babylon, was not then universally acknowledged to be Peter's. And that Eusebius did not pretend to allege any other grounds for his conjecture except the supposed relics, is abundantly proved by the confession of Cardinal Bellarmine, that cannot be too often repeated: "Eusebius suggests," says he, "no other reason but the relics for supposing Peter to have died in Europe."

As to whether the relics at Rome which gave rise to the conjecture, were really those of the apostle or not, does not require to be here examined, for we have already seen, in the section upon Caius, that the presence of a martyr's relics in a city was but a very slight reason indeed for suspecting that the martyr had been put to death there, and such as cannot be allowed for a moment to stand against the plain indication of the Scriptures. But that the general reader may not be uninformed as to the localities in which the Roman clergy state these relics to be now, and to have been anciently deposited, I give the following from Butler's Lives of the Saints (June 29), "St. Gregory (A.D. 604) writes, that the bodies of the two apostles were buried in the Catacombs two miles out of Rome (near the Ostian Road). The most ancient Roman Calendar published by Bucherius, marks their festival at the Catacombs on the 20th of June. . . . At present, the heads of the two apostles are kept in silver bustoes in the church of St. John Lateran (near the beginning of the Ostian Road). But one half of the body of each apostle is deposited together in a rich vault in the great church of St. Paul, on the Ostian Road, and the other half of both bodies in a more stately vault in the Vatican church." And again (18 Nov., in a note): " St. Paul's Church stands on the Ostian Road. In a subterraneous vault under the patriarchial altar, lie half the relics of St. Peter and St. Paul." The following account of this division of the relics is from the *Acta Petri*, by Paulus Æmilius Sanctorius, Archbishop of Urbino (in Italy), which work was published at Rome A.D. 1597, and may be seen in the Acta Sanctorum (vol. 6, for June): " Peter's bones," says Sanctorius, " were mixed with Paul's in the Catacombs, either because it was the will of Heaven that they who had lived in affection and brotherhood should be enclosed in the same busto, or because the Asiatics did it out of malignity. For certain people from the east came over, out of affection for the apostles, who had lived so much among them, and because they envied the Italians the good fortune that resulted from the possession of the relics, and made an attempt to carry off the bodies ; but being discovered and frightened by the Roman Christians who had arms in their hands, they threw the bodies into a well there (in puteum quendam ad Catacumbas). This was about two, or rather less than two, miles outside the Capine Gate (between the Appian and the Ostian Road). At a subsequent period, there was a voice from heaven declaring that the larger bones were the preacher's, the smaller bones the fisherman's; and immediately St. Sylvester, the high priest of Rome, when Constantine was leaving Rome to live at Byzantium, weighed out these relics in equal quantities (A.D. 319), after having first separated them upon a slab of porphyry; and one half of each body was placed in the church now called the Vatican, the other half of each body in St. Paul's, and the two heads in the church of St. John Lateran." Father Aringhi gives a similar account of this transaction in his *Roma Subterranea*, book iii. chap. iii. Father Janning (*Acta Sanc-*

torum, vol. vi., for June, p. 123), to whom the reader is referred for many interesting particulars upon this subject, makes a very just distinction when he says that the weighing was only necessary to divide Peter's relics into two equal parts, as the voice had already enabled Sylvester to distinguish Peter's relics from those of the other apostle. This writer mentions that at St. Paul's Basilica on the Ostian Road, there is the following inscription over the principal altar:—" Sub hoc altari requiescunt gloriosa corpora Apostolorum Petri et Pauli pro medietate; reliqua autem medictas reposita est in S. Petro; capita vero in S. Joanne Laterano." (Under this altar lie halves of the bodies of the Apostles Peter and Paul; the other halves of them are deposited at St. Peter's, and the two heads are in the Church of St. John Lateran.) He also mentions that the slab of porphyry upon which the division was effected by the Bishop Sylvester, is to be still seen in the Vatican, with the following inscription:—" Super isto lapide porfiretico fuerunt divisa ossa Sanctorum Apostolorum Petri et Pauli et Ponderata per Beatum Silvestrum Papam sub Anno Domini 319, quando facta fuit ista Ecclesia." (Upon this stone of porphyry, the bones of the holy Apostles Peter and Paul were divided and weighed by St. Sylvester, the Pope, A.D. 319, when this church was built.) The Lateran Church, of which many readers may not have often heard, is regarded by the Roman clergy as the most important church at Rome. It contains a martyrium of John the Baptist, and another of St. John the Evangelist, built, as well as the whole Church, by Constantine. Butler, in his *Lives of the Saints*, says, " The popes usually resided at this church, till Gregory IX., returning from Avignon, began to reside at St. Peter's, or the Vatican. This church, nevertheless, retains the pre-eminence above all other churches in Rome. . . . The Lateran Church is styled the head, the mother, and the mistress of all churches, as an inscription on its walls imports."

St. Gregory the Great (A.D. 604) thus alludes to the foregoing history of St. Peter's relics in a letter to the

Empress Constantina, in which he refused to send her St. Paul's head, which she wrote from Constantinople to ask him for:—" In the earliest days of our church, people came from the east to take back the relics of the apostles, upon the ground that both the apostles belonged to them, which relics had been taken as far as the second milestone from the gate, and were deposited there, in a place called the Catacombs. When, however, these people, although there was a great number of them, attempted to carry them off, a storm of thunder and lightning so completely terrified and dispersed them, that they never again presumed to attempt anything of the kind. At a subsequent period, however, the Christians of Rome went out and removed those relics, and placed them where they are now."— 30 Epist. book iii. This original interment of Peter's relics in the Catacombs is thus adverted to by the Dominican Fathers in the Bibliothèque Sacrée: "The body of St. Peter was, we are told (*on dit*) first interred in the Catacombs two miles from Rome." And Father Calmet writes to the same effect: "On dit que le corps de St. Pierre fut d'abord enterré aux Catacombes à deux milles de Rome."—(*Dict.*)

The only earlier authority to which the Roman clergy refer us on this point is Eusebius, the historian of Cæsarea, who alludes (ii. 25) to the relics found in his day, and to the foregoing distribution of them between the two Christian cemeteries of Rome—" This story (viz., Peter's being put to death as well as Paul in Nero's reign) is corroborated by the junction of their names in the appellation still given to the earliest Christian cemeteries in that city, which are called the cemeteries of Peter and Paul. Caius, also, speaks thus of those parts of Rome where the sacred relics of these two apostles have been just deposited" (αυτα δη ταυτα περι των τοπων ενθα των ειρημενων αποστολων τα ιερα σκηνωματα κατατεθειται). Here follow the words of Caius, who, as has been already seen, mentions the Ostian Road, and the Vatican Hill, as the sites of the earliest Christian cemeteries.

Of the foregoing points, then, respecting these relics,

the main outline to be remembered is this: That in the time of Caius (A.D. 250) the remains of the two apostles are supposed to have been lying together in the catacombs, near the Ostian Road, and no portion of them whatever on the Vatican Hill, although there was even then a trophy there of both apostles—that no writer earlier than the historian of Cæsarea ever mentions these relics—that more than a small portion of Peter's body is not supposed, even by the Roman clergy, to be now at the Vatican—that they suppose one half of it to be at St. Paul's on the Ostian Road—that they suppose his head to be at the Lateran church—that St. Gregory the Great said, that no more than half of Peter had ever been placed upon the Vatican Hill, and that there was an interval of, at least, two centuries and a half, during which Peter's relics are supposed to have been in the Catacombs, although not known to be there, nor mentioned by any writer of that period, viz., from his martyrdom at Babylon (about A.D. 67) to the ecclesiastical miracle of the voice in the air, that was heard by St. Sylvester (A.D. 319.). On some of the foregoing points, however, it ought to be stated, that there is rather a controversy among the Roman clergy, a few of whom contradict St. Gregory the Great, and say that he knew nothing at all about it, and that Peter's relics were removed several times from the catacombs to the Vatican, and from the Vatican to the catacombs. Some also acknowledge that they cannot be very certain that any part of the apostle, but his head, had ever at any time been sent to Rome from the East. "We undoubtedly consider," says Father Hardouin on this point, "that Peter's head, at all events, was conveyed by the Christians from Jerusalem to Rome after the siege, and that it ought to be held there in great veneration. But there is no necessity for supposing that Peter himself ever came to Rome." (Petri saltem caput Romam postea fuisse delatum a Christianis ex Hierosolymis omnino credimus, ibique religiose illud coli oportere. At Romam venisse Petrum necesse non est.)

Thus much for the information of the general reader.

It will be seen, however, that these controverted particulars about the relics are all unimportant in the present question.

II.

ALL the other passages in Eusebius (except the foregoing conjecture) that are supposed to bear upon the point now in question, have been so notoriously mistranslated, or have been made the grounds for conclusions which they so notoriously do not warrant, that they have no weight now-a-days, except with such persons as have not access to the original. I shall, nevertheless, lay a thorough analysis of each before the reader, as these passages (such as they are) constitute all, or almost all, that remains in the Fathers to be examined upon the subject. There are five of them. In one passage Eusebius is supposed to say that Peter came into Europe in person, against the impostor of Samaria, in the reign of Claudius; in another, that Peter wrote his first epistle at Rome; in a third, that he was there with Mark, when Mark wrote his Gospel; in a fourth, that he was bishop there; and in a fifth, that Philo, the Jewish writer of Alexandria, saw him there. It will be found that the historian says none of these things.

The first of these five passages occurs in the 14th chapter of the second book. It is brought forward by Father M'Corry, and the Correspondent in the *Times*, as affording the most satisfactory evidence to every serious and enlightened mind, of the apostle's having come into Europe five and twenty years, or thereabouts, before he was put to death at Babylon. It will be seen, however, that the Greek text does not bear the interpretation these parties seek to give it, and that even if it had done so, even if it had borne them out in their views, it is admitted by Baluze, Ceillier, and the Roman clergy in general, that such an interpretation of the passage would have clashed with all history, sacred and profane. Besides, everybody acknowledges that a statement made, for the first time, three hundred years after the event stated, would be inadmissible as evidence of it. But, as I have said, Eusebius does not make it. After adverting to the existence of a Christian Church at Rome, in the reigns of Tiberius, Caligula, and Claudius, (in the preceding chapters ii. iii. and xiii.) the bishop of Cæsarea writes as follows: "The sorcerer of Samaria being struck with the lightning of the mind, when formerly in Judæa, he was detected in his wickedness by the Apostle Peter (Acts viii.), escaped immediately a great way westward across the seas, thinking that thus alone he could have any hope of getting on in his bad career. Beginning at Rome, he was greatly assisted by the spirit of evil that brooded above that city; and had, in a short space of time, so far succeeded in his projects that after his death the inhabitants set up his image, and worshipped it. His triumph, however, did not long continue. Immediately afterwards, in the self-same reign of Claudius, the benign and all-gracious Providence of Heaven directs against Rome (ἐπὶ τὴν Ῥώμην) as against this pest of man, that great and active apostle, who, on account of his ability, was the leader of the rest; and he, as some gallant captain in the service of his Maker—yes, as one equipped in celestial panoply, succeeded in transporting to the inhabitants of the west the precious freight of spiritual light out of the east, light at once and a soul-saving word by promulgating among them his joyful Proclamation (τὸ Κήρυγμα) of the heavenly kingdom: and the divine word having, in this form, sojourned among the Romans, the influence of the sorcerer was foiled—ay, perished almost as rapidly as the man."

The only modern Roman Catholics who interpret these words of Peter's having left the east, are Father M'Corry, and the writer in the *Times*. As these, however, have published their mistaken interpretation of them, the reader is reminded that the Greek preposition ἐπὶ with the name of a city in the accusative, as in this place, does not denote "going to the city," as these writers here translate, but "acting with reference to it" whether that be *for* or *against*; and that this Greek preposition, in order to denote "going to a city," has always a genitive, as every Greek scholar knows, and as Eusebius himself expresses this idea in the neighbouring chapters, when he says that Philo was "sent to Rome" (στειλαμενος επι της 'Ρωμαιων πολεως, ii. 5), and that Philo "came to Rome" (επι της 'Ρωμης αφικομενος, ii. 18), and that Paul was led in bonds to Rome (δεσμιος επι 'Ρωμης αγεται, ii. 22), as well as elsewhere throughout all his writings. The reader is also reminded, that this chapter does not profess to treat of St. Peter's arrival at Rome, but of the success of the Κηρυγμα Πετρου in that city, when it was sent there against the heresy of the Gnostics; the title of the chapter being "On the Κηρυγμα Πετρου (the Apostle Peter's 'Message' or 'Proclamation') at Rome." Of this document Eusebius elsewhere (iii. 3) says: "As to that work, however, which is ascribed to Peter, called his 'Preaching' or 'Proclamation' (το βιβλιον το λεγομενον αυτου Κηρυγμα), we do not by any means know of its having been universally received in all the churches." Valesius, the Roman-catholic commentator, says upon these words: "This book, which was called the Κηρυγμα or *Prædicatio Petri*, is cited by Clemens Alexandrinus, &c., and, finally, by Lactantius, who mentions this document in the 20th chapter of his fourth book." Valesius, also, says on Eusebius vi. 14: "In the extracts from Theodotus, Peter's *Apocalypse* is cited, and also his Κηρυγμα or *Prædicatio*." Lactantius expressly informs us that this "Preaching" or "Message," called the Κηρυγμα, was published at Rome *before* the destruction of Jerusalem (A.D. 70), and that IN IT the Apostles proclaimed and predicted many things to the Gentiles there. (See the section of the present work on the Κηρυγησ Πετρου, also the section on Lactantius.) Clemens, the archbishop of Alexandria, in his treatise against the Gnostics (Stromat. lib. vi. c. 5, &c.) long before the time of Eusebius, often quotes the Κηρυγμα Πετρου as a work of the highest authority, and, as Le Clerc justly remarks, evidently looked upon it as having the sanction of the apostles. This archbishop's manner of quoting the document is as follows: "In the Κηρυγμα Πετρου you will find," &c.—"Peter says in the Κηρυγμα that," &c.

—" Paul shows this in the Κηρυγμα Πετρου, when he says," &c. (or, perhaps, more properly translated, " in addition to it")—" In the early part of the Κηρυγμα Πετρου, our Lord says to his disciples," &c. &c. Origen, who also preceded Eusebius, informs us that Heracleon, one of the Samaritan's immediate successors in the Gnostic school, quoted from it as authentic. " It would be tedious," says Origen in his Commentary on St. John, " to produce here what Heracleon has quoted from what is called the Κηρυγμα Πετρου, or to stay to inquire respecting that book whether it is to be regarded as genuine, or spurious, or interpolated." The reality of the work is thus clearly proved, although the work itself is now lost. No evidence, then, could be more complete of Eusebius's meaning, if the text were not clear enough, than the title of this chapter; for the titles of the chapters are proved to have been written by Eusebius himself, and are admitted on all hands to have been so. It has been shown, however, that the text is abundantly explicit.

But even if this chapter had been about Peter's having left the east in the reign of Claudius, the Roman clergy have long since acknowledged that no testimony to that effect could have been accepted, as such a statement would have contradicted both the Scriptures and the Fathers, and was in itself altogether improbable. Even Bishop Pearson and Mr. Baratier, Father Ceillier, and Baluze, the very authorities to whom the Correspondent in the *Times* refers us, acknowledge this. It is therefore truly remarkable that Father McCorry and this correspondent should have thus not only asserted an inaccurate interpretation of Eusebius, but also reasserted the long since exploded hypothesis of the learned Cardinal Baronius, that Peter might have come into Europe in the reign of Claudius, twenty-five years before he was supposed to have been put to death. As, however, these writers consider the hypothesis such conclusive evidence of Peter's having left the East, and as the errors into which they have fallen on this point might mislead others if allowed to remain uncontradicted,

M

I must trespass upon the patience of the reader with a few quotations, to show that these writers are alone in their strange views, and that the Roman clergy have long since seen the necessity of abandoning this most extravagant hypothesis about the reign of Claudius and the Five-and-Twenty years.

This theory was first promulgated by Baronius (A.D. 1607) some ten or twenty years before his death. He began by making the statement already quoted: "As to the history of the apostles, after they once separated from each other, the whole matter is overhung with extreme obscurity. . . . We cannot now hope to be ever able to know with anything like historical certainty what really took place in the subsequent lives of the apostles."—(Annal. A.D. 44, paragraph 42.) The annalist then puts it forward, as a not improbable supposition, that Peter may have passed from the East to Europe in the reign of Claudius, twenty-five years before he was put to death, deriving the suggestion, as he himself acknowledges, not from anything in the "Ecclesiastical History" by Eusebius, nor from anything in any writer previous to Eusebius, but from what all now admit to be a most inaccurate translation by Jerome, nearly a century afterwards, of another Greek work by Eusebius, the original of which is now lost. As, however, we learn from the Acts of the Apostles that Peter was subsequently at Jerusalem, the Cardinal seeks to make his first hypothesis harmonize with this fact and with other passages of history, by a further hypothesis, to the effect that Peter might have gone back again from Europe to Jerusalem, though no ancient writer ever said he did, and that he might have come a second time from the East into Europe, in the reign of Nero. These two suppositions once made, Baronius in his Annals, and naturally enough, deals with them (as Father Parsons did with Peter's residence in England) as facts that are no longer to be discussed or disputed; a circumstance which has misled many, for it was thence imagined that he must have had evidence for them in authentic records, and that he did not regard them as suppositions.

Fleury, Bossuet, Petau, Calmet, Bellarmine, Valesius, Ceillier, and all the Roman-catholic writers, without exception, acknowledge that if the first supposition is allowed to stand, the second becomes indispensable;—that if Peter came from the East in the reign of Claudius, he must have made more than one journey from there; in fact, so many are supposed necessary by some, that they are no longer called "journey" but "excursions," by the writers who speak of them.

These two extraordinary suppositions, however, were not long unopposed by the Roman clergy, as being, (however well intended by Baronius) calculated to bring their church into disrepute with all the educated portion of the Christian world. The celebrated Father Antonio Pagi (A.D. 1699), a Franciscan monk, and the most learned as well as partial of Baronius's commentators, candidly declares, that the first of these suppositions is contrary to Scripture,—"a point," he says, "to which Baronius had not sufficiently attended,"—and that the second of them is "absurd."—(See his Index). He informs us that Father Papebroche, the Jesuit, and the Abbé de Longuerue, both names that command the highest respect in the Roman church, told him that they agreed with him on these points, and he refers us to the opinions of Baluze and Valesius, as exactly representing his own.—(See Baronii Annales, vol. i. A.D. 45, notes.)

Father Calmet (A.D. 1757) says, that even before his time, the suppositions of Baronius had been abandoned by the Roman clergy as untenable. "As to saying that Peter lived twenty-five years at Rome as bishop, that is a notion that people do not now pretend to justify; besides, it is but very partially entertained."—(Quand on dit que St. Pierre a siegé à Rome pendant vingt-cinq ans, c'est déjà une chose que l'on ne pretend pas soutenir avec opiniâtreté et qui n'est point avoué de tout le monde.—Preliminary Dissertation on 1 Peter.)

Nicholas Thoynard, a very distinguished Roman-catholic writer, and friend of Cardinal Noris, admits this also, and hints pretty plainly that their inconsistency with Scripture is against them. "Many of our church," says he, in his Notes upon Lactantius, "assert two journeys of Peter's to Rome, one under Claudius, and one under Nero. Others acknowledge only one, under Nero." And again: " But if that excursion of Peter's (ista Petri excursio) is condemned on account of its inconsistency with the Scriptural account of events as far as the 12th chapter of the Acts, then his first visit to Europe was in the reign of Nero."

The Roman-catholic commentator on Petau's "Abrégé Chronologique," says that the supposition of Baronius is attended with a good deal of difficulty (ce qui souffre de très-grandes difficultés) and refers to Baluze, as entertaining a more rational view of matters. Father Tillemont (A.D. 1698) admits this also: "There is something," says he, in his Notes on Peter's History, " not easy to believe (Il y a quelque chose de difficile a croire) in what is said about Peter's going to Rome in 42, according to Eusebius and Jerome (*i.e.* Jerome's translation of Eusebius), and being put in prison at Jerusalem in 44."

Father Dupin (A.D. 1719) looks upon the story as so utterly without foundation, that he nowhere takes the least notice of it.

Valesius (A.D. 1676) writes as follows on the subject: " Eusebius, indeed, in his Chronicon (i.e. in Jerome's translation of it), mentions a visit of Peter's to Rome in the second year of Claudius, which was the notion adopted by Baronius, Petau, and several others. But this notion is found to be refuted by the Acts of the Apostles, for in them it is clear that Peter remained constantly in Judæa and Syria until the last year of Agrippa's reign, and Agrippa died at Cæsarea, after having imprisoned Peter at Jerusalem, as is recorded by St. Luke. Since, therefore, Agrippa died, as we are all agreed, in the fourth year of Claudius, Peter could not have gone to Rome prior to that year. This view is strongly corroborated by Apollonius, an ancient writer, who composed an able work against the heresy of Montanus. He says that there was a tradition in his time that the dispersion of the apostles took place after the twelfth year from the Ascension, our Lord himself having so commanded them. Bede also mentions this in his Commentary on the 13th Chapter of the Acts. But the author of the Alexandrian Chronicle makes Peter's visit to Rome still later." (Val. in Euseb. ii. 16).

Stephen Baluze (A.D. 1718), writes thus on this point:—" There are several very great difficulties (tot tantasque difficultates) connected with the notion of his having gone to Europe in the reign of Claudius, inasmuch as it obliges us to suppose that he went there twice, and had two contests there with the Samaritan heretic, once under Claudius and again under Nero. How preposterous such a supposition as this is (Quæ res quam absurda sit) when no ancient writer states it, those well know who are acquainted with this subject; for as Cardinal Baronius himself justly observes elsewhere, every one disregards as untrue, or worse (contemnitur) what a later writer states without the authority of some one preceding him." (Baluze in Lactant.)

Father Ceillier endeavours to transfer the responsibility of these absurd suppositions from Baronius to Jerome and the old Roman catalogue, as well as to the lost work of Eusebius, translated by Jerome. It will be seen, however, in a future page, that these writings are exempt from all such responsibility, and afford not the slightest pretext for these singular suppositions of Cardinal Baronius. "I know that several able men," says Ceillier, "suppose two voyages of St. Peter to Rome, and that they place the first of these in the second year of the reign of the Emperor Claudius. *They depend for the truth of this statement upon Eusebius and St. Jerome* (*i.e. Jerome's translation of Eusebius*), *and upon an ancient catalogue of the Roman Pontiffs, published by Father Boucher.* But it is not perhaps very difficult to show that upon that point Eusebius and St. Jerome have (*i.e.* Jerome's translation of Eusebius has) deviated from the truth of history, to which they (*i.e.* the translator) did not sufficiently attend." He here points out some of the inconsistencies of the story, and then proceeds thus: "A learned member of our church of the last century (Stephen Baluze), conjectures, with much appearance of truth, that the notion which has been entertained for some time about St. Peter's having governed the Church of Rome during twenty-five years, has arisen from mistaking the twenty-five years employed by the apostles separately in proclaiming the gospel throughout the world, for the time that St. Peter governed the Church of Rome by himself; and this writer has no hesitation in abandoning, upon this point, Eusebius and St. Jerome (*i.e.* Jerome's translation of Eusebius), to adopt the opinion of Lactantius, who admitted but one of the voyages to Rome, and who places that, not under Claudius but under Nero; and this also is the view of the matter that I adopt."—(Ceill. vol. i. c. 9.)

The Dominican Fathers in their "Bibliothèque Sacrée" (A.D. 1822), are very short and explicit as to the hypothesis of Baronius about the reign of Claudius and the Five-and-Twenty years: "What is certain is, that Peter did not go to Rome until the reign of Nero." (Ce qu'il y a de certain c'est qu'il n'alla à Rome que sous l'empire de Neron.—*Art.* Antioch.)

Bishop Pearson, and Mr. Baratier, to whom we are referred by the writer in the *Times* as the very best authorities upon the subject of Peter's having left the East, are equally explicit upon this point. "I do not see any reason for thinking," says Bishop Pearson, "that Peter came into Europe in the reign of Claudius."—(Dissert. i. c. 8.) "This notion," says Mr. Baratier, "the learned have long since shown to be untrue, and contrary alike to the facts of history and to the testimony of the ancients." (Sententiam hanc falsam esse et contra historiæ fidem, antiquorumque testimonia peccare, jamdudum ostenderunt Eruditi. c. i.)

Thus it is clear that the hypothesis about the reign of Claudius has long ago fallen to the ground, and that even the Roman clergy themselves do not now pretend to say that Peter came at that time into Europe. But besides this, it has been seen that the Greek passage we have been considering (Euseb. ii. 14) does not bear the sense which Father M'Corry and the Correspondent in the *Times* seek to force upon it, nor afford the slightest evidence of St. Peter's having ever at any time abandoned his mission to the lost sheep of the house of Israel. (See also, on Jerome's passages, p. 243 and Addenda.)

III.

The next passage to be considered occurs ii. 15, and is that upon which most stress is laid; yet in it the historian of Cæsarea merely tells us that the Jewish notion about Babylon meaning Rome in Isaiah and the ancient prophets, was extended by some of the Jewish converts in his day, to Peter's First Epistle—that "Babylon" was supposed by these parties to stand for "Rome" in that Epistle as well as in Isaiah—and that there was therefore a supposition among them that Peter must have been in Europe when he wrote it. The language of Eusebius distinctly implies that this was but an *on-dit*, and a partial one,—that no one could be sure it was true,—that he could not vouch for it,—nor was himself at all inclined to credit it. He thus expresses himself: "We hear it said (φασι) that this is the Mark whom Peter mentions in his First Epistle as with him at Babylon; which it is also the *on-dit* (φασι, again) that he composed at Rome, and that he himself shows this—but the metaphor is too bold (τροπικωτερον)—by designating that city 'Babylon,' when he says, 'the church at Babylon where I am, which was founded on the same occasion as you were, salutes you, as does also my son Mark, who is here with me.'" Nothing can be more evident than it is that Eusebius does not here state that Peter wrote his Epistle at Rome, but only speaks of the supposition as an improbable *on-dit* of the fourth century; nor do I now find any writer who pretends to say he does. Since, however, this passage, occurring in an historian of the highest credit, and being greatly misunderstood, has, no doubt, had much weight with those Roman Catholics who entertain the conjecture of Euse-

bius, about Peter's not having been put to death at
Babylon, it will not perhaps be uninteresting or unin-
structive to examine thoroughly the circumstances of
the *on-dit* which it records.

St. Jerome in his "Commentary upon Isaiah," distinctly mentions it as a Jewish saying that "Babylon"
meant "Rome" in Scripture; and mentions it moreover as
a saying that existed exclusively among the more carnal-
minded of the Jews (not assuredly such of them as our
Lord's apostles), and as being without a shadow of foundation in fact,—nay, as a nonsensical supposition which no
one could entertain. "The Jews," says Jerome, "understand Isaiah xiv. 2 in a carnal and worldly sense, because
after they returned from Babylon, they could not say
that that which is here mentioned had taken place. The
Babylonians who had enslaved them had not been in
their turn enslaved by them. The Jews had not beaten
the Babylonians in battle, nor taken possession of their
houses, nor employed them as menials. They are therefore reduced to think in their own foolish way (juxta
fabulas suas) that the prediction must have reference to
the Roman empire; and that when they conquer the
Romans, it will then be true that nations to whom the
Jews were slaves will have become slaves to the Jews.
But though they deceive themselves with these literal
interpretations of prophetic language, and the false hopes
they give rise to, WHO, AFTER ALL, WILL BELIEVE THEM
THAT ROME IS CALLED BABYLON (Quis eis concedet ut
Roma vocetur Babylon?) and Nebuchadnezzar a Roman
King?"—(St. Jerome on Isaiah, chap. xiv. 2.) It is
unnecessary to repeat that St. Peter and the apostles
were of all men the most unlikely to have in any of their
writings afforded the least countenance to such a worldly-
minded interpretation of the Scriptures.

The report which applies this Jewish saying to the
apostle's language, and of which we have not the slightest
trace in all antiquity except in this passage of Eusebius
and its translations, was looked upon by two writers of the
middle ages, and subsequently by Baronius, Bellarmine,
and some others, as not improbable under two mistaken

impressions: 1, that it was stated by Eusebius, on the authority of Papias, as existing in the earliest days of the church; and 2, that it was the opinion of Eusebius himself and of all the Fathers who succeeded him. It is, however, now in every one's power to see that both these suppositions are, as happily every one now admits, utterly groundless. Eusebius does not give the report as existing in the earlier days of the church, nor on the authority of Papias (see the section on Papias), he only says that it existed in his own day (*i.e.* in the fourth century). He also says that he did not believe it—that the Jewish metaphor upon which it depended appeared to him to be too far-fetched to leave the story any probability. Nor does any one of the Fathers repeat this *on-dit,* or say one word in vindication of it, although almost every one of them comment upon this First Epistle of St. Peter. This is what Father Tillemont adverts to when he says: "Bishop Pearson attributes this notion to many of the Fathers. It is to be regretted that he has not mentioned who they were. He did not, however, himself entertain it." (Pearson attribue ce sentiment en général à beaucoup de Pères. Je voudrais qu'il les eût marqués. Il ne les suit pas néanmoins.—Tillem., *art.* Peter.) Jerome, indeed, who was a Latin writer, fell into the error of supposing that Eusebius, who wrote in Greek, stated the fact in question upon his own authority, and accordingly where Jerome professes to give a translation of the passage from Eusebius, the statement is that Peter did use this Jewish metaphor, and not that there was a rumour of his having done so. But everyone admits that Jerome was (as he himself acknowledges) very inexpert in translating Greek, and that he in this place only made one of his not unusual blunders respecting the Greek text of Eusebius. In common fairness, then, we cannot cite Jerome as authority on the subject, since the evidence of his mistake is before us, unless it be to prove that the rumour was so very partial when it did exist, that it did not reach Jerome in the next generation except through this incidental solitary statement of Eusebius, a writer in Palestine, wholly unconnected with the Church of Rome. We have, however, abundant evidence that Jerome himself gave no countenance to the story even when he supposed he had it upon the authority of Eusebius; for in none of his original writings, not even in his criticisms upon this very Epistle of St. Peter, does he so much as make the slightest allusion to its existence; and in his commentary on the prophet Haggai (ch. ii.), in a passage already quoted in the section on Irenæus, when speaking of the cities in which there were churches in Peter's day, he mentions Babylon as a matter of course, and as being the city where Peter lived, without the least allusion to the Jewish saying which some of the less spiritual-minded of the Jewish converts connected with that name.

An Englishman in the eighth century—our own Bede —is the first after Eusebius who adverts to this story, but he only repeats the erroneous Latin translation of St. Jerome, not the *on-dit* of Eusebius. About two or three centuries after Bede, an obscure writer named Œcumenius, is supposed by some to have written a book, in which he alluded to it; and no one has been able to discover any other mention of it in the writings of the ancients. Scarcely any one now, therefore, seeks to justify this interpretation of the apostle's language, except some of the Roman clergy who are still deceived as to its having had the sanction of the Fathers, and as to its having been adopted in the days of Papias. It is almost needless to add that in the countries adjoining Babylonia the Christian commentators never understood "Babylon" to mean Rome. "The Syriac and Arabic writers," says Adam Clarke, "understood it literally as denoting a town in the East; and if we are to be guided by opinion, an oriental writer is surely as good authority on the present question as a European."— (Clarke on 1 Peter.)

The groundlessness of the suppositions about Papias and the Fathers having been discovered, and the importance of maintaining the *on-dit* in connexion with the present controversy having been felt by some of the writers in communion with the Church of Rome, two new suggestions were offered by Baronius and others of them, for the purpose of investing the story with something like probability. *First*, it was said that Rome is called "Babylon" in the Revelations of St. John; and *secondly*, that Babylon itself was a very unlikely place for Peter, the most active of the apostles for the circumcision, to have gone to.

With regard to the first of these suggestions, it is to be observed that St. John does not do what is imputed to him. He nowhere uses the mere term "Babylon" to designate Rome. The expression he employs is invariably "Babylon the Great" (Βαβυλων ἡ μεγαλη) and this obviously for the purpose of distinction; the invariableness of the expression being rendered the more remarkable by the frequency of its recurrence—almost in successive verses. The English version does not always exhibit the fact I now speak of, but every one who reads the original is aware of it. It is, therefore, a mistake to suppose that St. John expected Rome to be understood by the mere name "Babylon" in the Revelations. He does not. The passages clearly prove the contrary—clearly prove that he did not consider that name alone sufficient to designate it,—clearly prove that for that purpose St. Peter must have written at least "The church at Babylon the Great salutes you." But that is not all. Even if St. John had attached this mystical sense to the mere name of Babylon in that mystical book of Revelations, how could we have thence inferred, without absurdity, that the word must bear the same mystical sense in all the other books of the New Testament? By "Egypt," St. John understood Jerusalem in this mystical sense in the same book, and tells us that others also used that name "Egypt" to designate "the city where our Lord was crucified."—(Rev. xi. 8.) But how can the Roman clergy hence pretend with any show of reason, that "Egypt" stands for Jerusalem in the gospels and epistles? Surely there is neither critical accuracy nor common sense, to say nothing of piety, in this mode of dealing with the Scriptures. But, as has been stated, St. John nowhere calls Rome merely "Babylon," nor considered that this term would have sufficiently designated the Capital of the Gentiles.

As to the second suggestion, so far was Babylon from being a very unlikely place for Peter to have gone to, that it can easily be shown to have been by a great deal the most likely—nay, that it is in the last degree unlikely that he should not have gone there, even if we had not his own express and solemn record of his having gone. *In the first place,* there was no quarter of the then known world, except Judæa, in which there were so many Jews and so many synagogues in Peter's time as in Babylon and the surrounding provinces. Josephus, who was Peter's contemporary, and a Jew, speaking of the Jews that were at Babylon about his own time, says in one place that they were there "in great numbers," (ενδα και πληθος ην Ιουδαιων—Antiq. xv. 2.) And in another, that there were several myriads of them permanently settled there as emigrants, (ου γαρ ολιγαι μυριαδες τουδε λαου περι την βαβυλωνι ανατψεισθησαν—Antiq. xv. 3.) The "myriad" was ten thousand. He also relates that there was upon one occasion, about half a century before he wrote, such an immense population of Jews together in Seleucia alone, which was the new capital of that country, about forty miles from Babylon, that although nearly fifty thousand of them were then slaughtered in that city by the factions there, yet such of them as escaped through the compassion of the neutral Seleucians, and such of the other Jews of Babylonia as had rendered themselves obnoxious, were still able to hold out the strong cities of Neerda and Nisibis against the united force of those Seleucians and Babylonians that were opposed to them.—(Josephus, Antiquit. xviii. 9.) In another passage, when speaking of the few Jews who returned with Ezra from Babylon in the olden time, he says: "But the whole people of the Israelites remained where they were. Whence it has happened, that there are but two tribes subject to the Romans in Asia and Europe. The ten tribes still exist beyond the Euphrates to this day,—

infinite myriads, whose numbers it is no longer possible for us to calculate," (μυριαδες απειροι και αριθμῳ γνωσθηναι μη δυναμεναι—Antiq. xi. 5.) Philo, another Jew, and also a contemporary of St. Peter, describes the Jews at Babylon in his own days as appearing to constitute almost one-half of the inhabitants. (ὡς των αυθιγενων μη πολλῳ τινι δοκειν ἑλαττουσθαι—Phil. de Virtutibus.) On another occasion, this writer speaks of them as the chief occupants of Babylon and its neighbourhood, and as being so numerous that Petronius the Syrian Prefect was deterred by their numbers from withdrawing, as Caligula had ordered him, one half of the Roman forces from the Euphrates to Judæa, to insist on the Emperor's statue being placed in the temple at Jerusalem (ibid.); and in another passage he says, that the Jews were, in his own day, "in very great numbers" (παμπληθεις—ibid.) in that as well as in all the rest of the cities in that part of Asia. "If we except Palestine," says Adam Clarke, "there was no country in the world where the Jews were so numerous and so powerful as in the province of Babylonia, in which they had their two celebrated seats of learning, Nehardea and Sura." With these accounts of the Jews in the Babylonian district during the apostolic times, the other numerous indications that we have perfectly agree. Of all the Jewish records, for instance, the two Talmuds—that of Babylon and that of Jerusalem—are looked upon by the Jews themselves as the most important; and of those the Talmud of Jerusalem is contained in one volume while the Talmud of Babylon, supposed to have been a work of the second century, and considered by the Jews as of higher authority than the other, extends to no less than fourteen thick folio volumes. Surely such a fact alone is evidence of the importance of the Jewish colony at Babylon, even as late as the second century. But further: Babylon was always considered the metropolis of the Jews that did not live in Judæa. This fact is not only recognised by all the learned, but is distinctly stated in the Talmud of Babylon: "The Babylonians," says Joseph Scaliger, "were the head of the Asiatic Dispersion, as is

clear from innumerable passages of the Talmud." And
we cannot wonder that it was so. The Jews here were
the original "lost sheep of the house of Israel," mentioned by the ancient prophets and our Saviour,—the
nucleus, as it were, around which all the rest of the
Dispersion formed; and what can be more natural than
that the metropolis of the dispersed Jews should have
been in Jews the most populous of their cities. One
other illustration will suffice. The mere Jewish escort that
accompanied the sacred treasures which were annually
sent from Babylon to Jerusalem, amounted in the time of
Peter and Josephus to forty, fifty, sixty thousand men,
and upwards (πολλαι μυριαδες ανθρωπων—Josephus, Antiq.
xviii. 9). Whereas, on the other hand, the highest number of Jews that we ever hear of at the Gentile capital
in the apostolic times, or indeed at any other period,
does not appear to have much exceeded eight thousand (Josephus, Antiq. xvii. 11); so few, that they were
all easily banished from the city whenever their conduct
made this necessary. For one instance of this consult
Suetonius (Tib. 36), Tacitus (Ann. ii. 85), and Josephus (Antiq. xviii. 3). Another instance occurs in
Suetonius (Claud. 25), and in the Acts of the Apostles
(xviii. 2). How then can any one pretend to say that
in this particular Babylon was not a much more likely
place for Peter to have gone to than Rome? All that
Baronius and Bellarmine say in reply to these historical
facts is, that after the massacre at Seleucia of the Jews
that had rendered themselves obnoxious to the factions
of that city, about forty or fifty years before Philo or
Josephus wrote, it was not likely that there should have
been Jews enough left alive afterwards in any part of
Babylonia, during Peter's life, to have made it at
all reasonable to suppose that "Babylon" could have
meant Babylon in his epistle! "As Peter speaks of the
church at Babylon," says Baronius, "and as this cannot
possibly be understood of Babylon in Assyria, inasmuch
as it is clear from Josephus that the Jews who lived in
the Assyrian Babylon were expelled and slaughtered in
the reign of Caligula, we cannot possibly avoid the

conclusion, that Peter understood Rome when he wrote Babylon." (Bur. in Annal.)

After what has just been stated about the subsequent numbers of the Jews in Babylon, both from Josephus and Philo, another of Peter's contemporaries, this argument requires no answer. As, however, Baronius was mistaken as to the expulsion from Babylon, and as to the total slaughter of the Babylonian or even of the Seleucian Jews, I append Josephus's own account of this transaction, by which it will be seen that he speaks of "*the whole nation of the Jews in that quarter*" as still existing after the massacre of the 50,000, which massacre, moreover, it must not be forgotten, had occurred nearly a quarter of a century before Peter is at all likely to have gone to Babylon,—and occurred in opposition to the wishes of the Parthian government, which always favoured the Jews. "They (the Jews and Gentiles of Babylon) were," says Josephus, "almost always at variance, by reason of the contrariety of their laws; and which party soever grew boldest before the other, they assaulted the other; and at this time in particular it was that the Babylonians attacked the Jews, which made those Jews so vehemently to resent the injuries they received from the Babylonians, that being neither able to fight with them nor bearing to live with them, they went to Seleucia, the principal city of those parts, which was built by Seleucus Nicator. It was inhabited by many of the Macedonians, but by more of the Grecians; not a few of the Syrians also dwelt there; and thither went some of the Jews, and lived there five years without any misfortunes. But in the sixth year, a pestilence came upon those at Babylon, which occasioned new removals of men's habitations out of that city; and because they came to Seleucia, it happened that a still heavier calamity came upon them on that account, which I am going to relate immediately. Now the way of living of the people of Seleucia, who were Greeks and Syrians, was commonly quarrelsome and full of discords, though the Greeks were too hard for the Syrians. When, therefore, the Jews were come thither and dwelt

among them, there arose a sedition, and the Syrians
were too hard for the other by the assistance of the
Jews, who are men that despise dangers, and very ready
to fight upon any occasion. Now when the Greeks had
the worst in this sedition, and saw that they had but
one way of recovering their former authority, and that
was if they could prevent the agreement between the
Jews and the Syrians, they every one discoursed with
such of the Syrians as were formerly their acquaintance, and promised they would be at peace and friendship with them. Accordingly they gladly agreed so to
do; and when this was done by the principal men of
both nations, they soon agreed to a reconciliation; and
when they were so agreed, they both knew that the
great design of such their union would be their common hatred to the Jews. Accordingly they fell upon
them, and slew about fifty thousand of them; yes, the
Jews there were all destroyed, except such as could escape
by the compassion which their friends and neighbours
afforded them in order to let them get away. These
retired to Ctesiphon, a Grecian city, and situated near
to Seleucia, where the king of Parthia lives in winter,
every year, and where the greatest part of his riches
are deposited; but the Jews had here no security, as
the Seleucians had but little respect for their king.
Now the whole nation of the Jews in that quarter (παν
το πρὸς Ιουδαιων ἰθνος) were in fear both of the Babylonians and of the Seleucians, because all the Syrians
that live in those places agreed with the Seleucians in
the war against the Jews; so that the most of them
(ὡς το πολυ) gathered themselves together and went to
Neerda and Nisibis, and obtained security there by the
strength of those cities; besides which, the inhabitants
of those cities, who are a great many, were all warlike
men; and this was the state of the Jews in Babylonia."
(Josephus, Antiq. xviii. 9.) I shall here merely draw
attention to the fact, that *the whole* of the Macedonian
population in Seleucia were favourable to the Jews;
that only *a portion* of the Jewish population were
obliged to take refuge in the two strong cities men-

tioned; and that both then and afterwards the Parthian government, as I have said, afforded all the protection in their power to the Jews.

In the second place, there was as much travelling to and fro between Babylon and Jerusalem in the days of the apostles as there was between any other two neighbouring cities in the then known world, for the provinces of Judæa and Babylonia were separated only by the Euphrates. Between Babylon and Antioch (the capital of Syria, another province adjoining Babylonia) the intercourse of all kinds was absolutely incessant (as may be seen in Diodorus Siculus, Josephus, Quintus Curtius, Strabo, &c.), quite as much so as between Jerusalem and Antioch, the distance in the former case being but little more than that in the latter, and the means of access much easier; for the Euphrates with its navigable current extended the whole way from Syria to Babylon. The distance that the caravans had to travel from Jerusalem to Babylon was only the same as the distance from Jerusalem to Antioch, these three cities, Babylon, Jerusalem, and Antioch, the capitals of three adjoining provinces, being almost equidistant from each other, and occupying, as it were, the three angles of an equilateral triangle, with Palmyra (or Tadmor) in the centre of the triangle. Whoever attends to this, and to the facilities indispensable in the nature of things, for the transmission of the large quantities of merchandize, and of the large bodies of men which, for religious and military, as well as for commercial purposes, we find constantly passing and repassing between Babylon and Jerusalem, and reads at the same time of the constant letters, presents, messengers, and even mere compliments that passed between the authorities of these two cities in or about the time of the apostles, will see at once, without any further argument, that there is not the slightest pretext for supposing that Babylon was so remote or inaccessible as to make it unreasonable to believe the plain statement of the Scriptures when they tell us that Peter went there. But in addition to all this very obvious reasoning, let us hear what St. Chrysostom, who was a native and resident of Antioch, says upon the proximity of Babylon to the Levant, and of the caravan route from that city, in his own day (A.D. 407), which was after Babylon had greatly fallen away even from what it was in Peter's time. We cannot desire a better authority. "The land of Judæa," says St. Chrysostom, "that is, all Palestine from Egypt to the Euphrates, lies on the bank opposite to Babylonia, which was Abraham's native country; and the river flows between the two lands, a mutual boundary to both of them. Since, then, he (Abraham) was not from Palestine, but came from the other side of the river, from Babylonia, his name was derived from the spot and act, and he was called 'The one who passes over,' because he came from the opposite bank of the Euphrates." And again, after speaking of the distance between Babylon and the Levant, St. Chrysostom thus proceeds: "The road is no longer in the same state as it was (in Abraham's time), for now it is divided into a succession of stations, and towns, and villas, and the pedestrian meets several fellow-travellers, which contributes to security quite as much as station, or town, or villa does. And besides this, the local governors of the towns levy men of superior bodily strength, and professionally skilled in the use of the lance and sling, and appoint captains over them, and employ them for no other purpose than that alone of attending to the safety of the highways. Another source of protection is, that there are sheds (οικηματα) built a thousand paces distant from each other along the whole way, in which watchmen are placed at night, whose vigilance and care are the greatest check upon the robbers. But in the days of Abraham there were none of these things to be seen,—no continuous villas, no towns, no stations, no caravansaries, no fellow-travellers," &c. &c. (Chrysos. ad Stagirium, lib. ii. c. 6.)

The following is from Father Calmet's Dictionary to the Bible: "The most extensive dominion of the Hebrews," says Calmet, "was from the river of Egypt, south, to the river Euphrates, north-east. . . . . Northward, the Hebrew power extended not only along the western bank of the Euphrates, but occasionally included towns on the eastern side." (Calmet, Fragment. 589.) Again: "Probably the major part by far of the Israelites who revisited their native land were from Babylon (Ezra, ii. 2; viii. 1); this caravan, however, did not take the northern route, but crossed the desert south of Tadmor." (Fragm. 589.) And again, "Josephus," says Calmet, "places it (Tadmor, or Palmyra) two days' journey from the Upper Syria, one day's journey from the Euphrates, and six days' journey from Babylon." (Calmet. Dict., Palmyra.) With this information before us, and we have much more to the same effect in these and other writers, equally accepted by the Roman Catholics, how can any one pretend to say that Peter might not just as well have gone to Babylon from Jerusalem as to Antioch from Jerusalem, and we read in the New Testament also that he went to Antioch. As to Rome, the distance from Jerusalem to Rome, either by land or sea, in those days, was considerably upwards of two thousand miles,—much more than four times as far as from Jerusalem to Babylon! Not only, therefore, with regard to the Jewish population of Rome, but also as far as its relations of distance and intercourse with Jerusalem are concerned, the scriptural account of Peter's mission is by far more probable than that partial *on-dit* of the fourth century alluded to by Eusebius, which represents this apostle not to have gone to Babylon.

In the third place (as has been already observed in the section on Clemens Romanus), Babylon was plainly and specially indicated to all the twelve apostles by our Lord himself as the post of the more active and enterprising of their party, when He told them to go to the Jewish *rather than* to the Gentile districts of the earth, and to convert the Gentiles, as much as possible, through the Jews. "Go, rather," said our blessed Lord, "to the lost sheep of the house of Israel." (Matt. x.) Now, as there were some Jews almost everywhere, but more of them in some places than in others, no one denies that our Lord here meant that the apostles should bestow most of their personal attention upon those countries and cities in which the Jews resided in the greatest numbers; and since the apostles could not have done this,—could not have been said to go rather to the Jews than to the Gentiles, if they selected the districts in which there were the fewest of the race, and left unvisited the districts in which the Jewish population was the largest,— it therefore clearly follows, that Babylon was specially and distinctly pointed out by our Lord himself to Peter as his peculiar post on this occasion; a consideration of immense importance in this inquiry, and which has been wholly overlooked by Baronius and Bellarmine. Nor was it alone because Babylon, beyond all comparison, exceeded Rome in its Jewish population, that it was pointed out to Peter in our Lord's own words. Babylon was also the capital—the original settlement of "the lost sheep of the house of Israel"—that first colony of the captive Jews to whom the great prophets of old had often and emphatically applied that memorable denomination. They were "the lost sheep"—"the scattered sheep"— "the scattered flock" of Jeremiah, who were to be "brought again to their own folds." (Jer. xxiii. 2; l. 6 & 17; also 1 Peter, ii. 25.) They were what Ezekiel called "the flock that had no shepherd;" "the sheep that were to be sought out;" that were "to be fed;" that were "again to feed upon the high mountains of Israel." (Ezekiel xxxiv. 5, 11, &c.; also, John xxi. 16 & 17.) Nothing, I think, can be more evident than that when our Lord told Peter to go to the lost sheep of the house of Israel rather than to any other people of the earth, he did not mean by those words that he should go to Rome. Thus, in whatever way we look at this question, we see that Babylon was not only not an unlikely place for Peter to have gone to, but that it is in the last degree unlikely that he should not have gone there, even if we had never heard of his having gone.

As some have been led to adopt the rumour of the

fourth century, under the unaccountable impression that in Peter's day Babylon was no longer in existence, or at least was so much dilapidated as to be uninhabitable, I adduce the following authorities on that point, from which it will be seen that Babylon was then (about A.D. 50), very much the same as it ever was, except in the diminished number of its inhabitants, which was now scarce one-half of what it had been—in the ruined state of its public buildings, many of which, however, were in ruins even when Alexander entered it—and in its being no longer the constant residence of a court. There were still, it will be seen, those immense walls, the area of 225 square miles (a little province in itself) that they enclosed, the people necessary to till all the arable portion of that land, which was so extensive that it could maintain the inhabitants of the city when these were at their highest number,—the manufacturers and tradesmen who supplied the agricultural population,—the houses for all these people to live in, which covered eleven or twelve square miles of the whole enclosure, and were being still constantly constructed as there was a demand for them,—the places of worship, the markets, the courts of law,—the royal preserves and parks, still kept up there on account of the great height and sound condition of the city walls,—the establishment of officers and attendants connected with those parks and preserves, as well as with the courts of law and the revenues,—a Parthian garrison constantly kept there, the bridges still spanning that mighty river, the splendid remains of ruined palaces, and one in very good repair, an immemorial temple crumbling to the dust, and gardens with vaulted terraces carried high into the air, a graceful and stupendous structure, that even in these apostolic days overtopped the walls of Babylon with the flowing foliage of a thousand years; and all this within forty miles of the populous and flourishing, though less extensive, city of Seleucia!

Diodorus Siculus, a contemporary of St. Peter's, who flourished throughout the first century, says of Babylon in his own day: " The palaces and other public buildings time has partly obliterated, and partly laid in ruins. For comparatively only a small part of what is called Babylon is taken up with the houses of the inhabitants; the greatest portion of the space within the walls (which are sixty miles in circuit) is employed for agricultural purposes." (Dio. Sic. ii. 9.)

Strabo, another contemporary of Peter's, that died about A.D. 25, describing its condition as he saw it, writes thus: " The bridge across the Caprus is close to Seleucia and Babylon. Babylon itself is in a plain, and has a wall about sixty miles round, thirty-two feet thick, and seventy-five feet high. These walls are reckoned among the seven wonders of the world, as well as the hanging gardens, which form a square, and measure about 400 feet every way. These gardens are constructed with terraces, that are raised with vaults over one another, &c.; they are situated upon the banks of the river. The tomb (by some called 'the tower,' by others 'the temple') of Belus is also situated there, now in ruins. They say that it was pulled down by Xerxes. It was originally a square pyramid, &c. Alexander the Great began to rebuild it, but he had not time to complete the undertaking. None of his successors interested themselves about it. Even the rest of the city (*i. e.* the ancient architecture) was neglected, and reduced to ruins, partly by the Persians, partly by time, and partly by the indifference of the Macedonians to such things, but chiefly when Seleucus Nicator fortified Seleucia, on the Tigris, within forty miles of Babylon. For he, and his successors, bestowed all their care upon this city, and removed the court there, and it is now a greater city than Babylon itself is. (Pliny tells us that Seleucia at this time contained 600,000 inhabitants; and Calmet sets down a million and a quarter as the largest population that had ever occupied the 225 square miles of Babylon.) The greater part of the immense space within the walls is neither occupied with houses nor inhabitants; so that one may say of it what one of the comic poets said of Megalopolis, in Arcadia, ' the great city is a great wilderness.' On account of the scarcity of timber there, they now build their houses with both rafters and posts of the palm-tree wood, and twist bands of reeds around the posts, which bands they then paint with oil-colours. They cover their doors with asphalt, and these are made high, as well as the houses, which are all constructed with arches in consequence of the scarcity of timber; for Babylon has little wood, except brushwood and the palm-tree; and they do not use tiled roofs, as they have not much rain."—(Strabo, book xvi.)

Pliny the elder, another of St. Peter's contemporaries (born A.D. 23, died A.D. 79), says: " Babylon, the capital of the Chaldæan nations, was for a long time famous throughout the whole world, in consequence of which the rest of Mesopotamia and Assyria, in which it occupied a circuit of sixty miles, was called Babylonia. . . . The temple of Jupiter Belus is still to be seen there; but the city has no longer the population it used to have, having been drained of it by the proximity of Seleucia, which was built by Nicator for that very purpose." (Plin. Hist. Nat., lib. vi. c. 30.)

Plutarch, who was a young man when Peter was at Babylon (born A.D. 50, died A.D. 120), speaking of Crassus, who was in those countries only about forty years before that apostle was born, says: " Among the many errors which Crassus committed in this (Parthian) war, the first, and not the least, was his returning so soon into Syria. He ought to have gone forward, and strengthened himself with the accession of Babylon and Seleucia, cities (πολις) always at enmity with the Parthians; instead of which he gave the enemy abundant time to prepare themselves," &c. &c., (Crassus, xvii.) And, again: " In what raptures would the Romans have been if Crassus could have written to them from Babylon that he was victorious; and if he had proceeded from thence through Media, Persia," &c. (Niciæ cum Crass. Compar.)

Quintus Curtius, who is supposed to have lived about the time of the apostles, writes as follows of his own times: " There is room for carriages to pass each other, as we hear, upon these walls in safety. . . . The houses are not built close up to the walls, but with an interval of about an acre of land to each house; and even the whole of the city is not taken up with houses. These cover only about eleven or twelve miles of it, nor do they adjoin each other; because, I suppose, it is thought safer that they should stand in isolated positions. All the rest of the area within the walls, they still plant and cultivate, that in case of siege the land within the city might maintain the inhabitants. There is a stone bridge across the river, &c. &c. Near the castle are those wonders which are so often celebrated by the Greek poets: gardens elevated in the air, consisting of entire groves of trees, growing as high as the tops of the towers (150 feet) marvellously beautiful and pleasant from their height and shade. The whole weight of them is sustained and borne up by huge pillars, upon which there is a floor of square stone that both sustains the earth that lies deep upon the pillar, and also the cisterns with which it is watered. The trees that grow upon this are many of them twelve feet in circumference, and everything is as fruitful as if it grew on the natural ground; and although process of time destroys things made by mortal hands, and also even the works of nature, yet these terraces, although weighed down with so much earth and so many trees, still remain unshaken, held up by seventy broad walls, about eleven feet distant from each other. When we see these trees from a distance, they seem to be a wood growing upon a mountain." (Quintus Curt. v. 1.)

Pausanius (A.D. 170), about a century after Peter was there, says: " The temple of Belus is still to be seen in Babylon, but of Babylon itself—that Babylon which was the most mighty city that the sun ever shone on in his course—there is no longer anything worth mentioning, except its gigantic walls."—(Pausanias, Descrip. Gr., viii. 33.)

When the Emperors Trajan and Severus entered Parthia, they went to Babylon. Trajan had to take it by force of arms from the Parthian garrison, A.D. 111; but when Severus came up, A.D. 200, the garrison had abandoned it, and the gates were opened to him. These facts are recorded by Dio Cassius and Eutropius.

Eutropius (viii. 3) in relating the victories on the Euphrates over the Parthians gained by Trajan, about forty years after Peter's martyrdom, says: " Seleucia, Ctesiphon, and Babylon, he took and garrisoned (vicit ac tenuit); and reduced Armenia, Assyria, and Mesopotamia, to the condition of mere provinces."

Dio Cassius (lxviii. 26, &c.) after saying that Trajan went round by Armenia, Mesopotamia, Nisibis, and Adiabene, (" which country," says he, " is the part of Assyria about Nineveh,") proceeds thus: " Trajan and his army came to Babylon itself, under very little opposition from the enemy; for the Parthian forces had been wasted in civil wars, and were even then in a state of insubordination. There Trajan had an opportunity of seeing the asphalt of which the walls of Babylon are built, &c. &c. . . . Trajan fearing lest the Parthians should rebel against him, resolved to give them a king of their own. So when he came to Ctesiphon (not far from Babylon), he assembled all the Romans and Parthians that were there in an immense plain, and after haranguing them from an elevated platform upon his victories, he appointed Parthamaspides to be their king, and put at the same time the diadem upon his head." And of Severus he says (lib. xxv. c. 9): " When Severus reached Nisibis, the Parthians retired without giving him battle, and went home; and Severus having constructed rafts on the Euphrates, proceeded along the river, partly by water and partly on the banks, and in a very short time took possession of Seleucia and Babylon, which had been both abandoned. He afterwards took Ctesiphon, and allowed his soldiers to pillage it, killing an immense number, and making 100,000 prisoners."

In the Fathers, also, Babylon is constantly mentioned, not only as existing in Peter's day, but for centuries afterwards, and as having a Christian and a Jewish population. St. Chrysostom, for instance, mentions it as one of the cities whose churches were founded by St. Peter and the apostles at Jerusalem immediately after the Ascension. This eminent Father, in his 17th Homily on the Epistle to the Hebrews, says, when speaking of the temple at Jerusalem: "The Jews came there from the most distant places, not only from Babylon, but from Ethiopia also, and this is what Luke means when he says (Acts ii. 5, &c.), there were dwelling at Jerusalem Jews, devout men out of every nation under heaven. . . . Parthians and Medes . . . the dwellers in Egypt," &c.

Jerome (A.D. 420) writes: "I have learned from an Elamite who has just come out of that country, and is now living at Jerusalem, that there are still royal preserves within Babylon, and that wild beasts of every description can be kept in for the chase, in the immense area enclosed by the walls of that city." (Jerom. Commentar. in Isaiæ, c. xiii.)

Theodoret (A.D. 459), one of the bishops on the Euphrates, says, that in his day Babylon was very thinly inhabited, but wholly by Jews. "Even still," says he, "it has a few inhabitants, who are, however, neither Assyrians nor Chaldeans, but Jews only." (Theod. Comment. on Isaiah, c. xiii.)

As the point to be illustrated is not only the existence of Babylon as a Parthian city in Peter's day, but its existence as a considerable Jewish colony at that time, the following passage from Josephus, relating to an event that occurred in Peter's lifetime, is to the purpose: "And when Hyrcanus (the high priest, a captive from Judæa) was brought into Parthia, the king Phraates treated him after a very gentle manner, as having already learned of what an illustrious family he was, on which account he set him free from his bonds, and gave him a habitation at Babylon, where there were Jews in great numbers. These Jews honoured Hyrcanus as their high priest and king, as did all the Jewish nation that dwelt as far as the Euphrates; which respect was very much to his satisfaction. But when he was informed that Herod had received the kingdom, new hopes came upon him. . . . Accordingly he talked of that matter with the Jews that came often to him with great affection; but they endeavoured to retain him among them, (at Babylon,) . . . . yet did Hyrcanus still desire to depart. Herod also wrote to him, and persuaded him to desire of Phraates and the Jews that were there that they should not grudge him the royal authority. . . . . And as he wrote thus to Hyrcanus, so did he also send Saramallas, his ambassador, to Phraates, and many presents with him, and desired him in the most obliging way, &c. . . . Accordingly, when Hyrcanus came to Judæa full of assurance, by the permission of the king of Parthia, and at the expense of the Jews, who supplied him with money, Herod received him with all possible respect, &c. . . . yet being cautious how he made any illustrious person the high priest of God, he sent for an obscure priest out of Babylon, whose name was Ananelus, and bestowed the high priesthood upon him." (Jos. Ant. xv. 2, &c. Whiston's Translation.)

Josephus also (in his Wars) frequently speaks of Silas of Babylon as one of the most distinguished leaders of the war party at Babylon in Peter's time, and as having taken a very active part among the generals of that city in the campaigns which began in Nero's reign, and terminated in the destruction of Jerusalem.

The life of Apollonius of Tyana, in Cappadocia, a contemporary of Peter's, (who was born about the beginning, and died about the end of the first century,) affords much illustration respecting the condition of Babylon at that time. Flavius Philostratus, in his account of this person, tells of his having set off from Antioch to Babylon with two attendants about the same time as St. Peter went to Babylon; of his passing through a town called Ninus, and into Mesopotamia, by Zeugma, which had a bridge then across the Euphrates; of his entertainment on the frontiers of Babylonia by one of King Vardanes' ten satraps, when the guards of the satrap brought the three travellers before him; of his reception subsequently in the palace at Babylon by the king, who happened to be there hunting at the time; of the decorations and paintings of this ancient palace; of his journey thence to India; of his return to Babylon by ship along the Euphrates from the Persian gulf; and of his return from Babylon to Antioch by the same route as he had gone. The passages are too long for quotation here, but are highly illustrative of the place and time in question. (See Berwick's translation of Philostratus.)

But enough has been said to satisfy every sincere and conscientious inquirer, that Babylon did exist and flourish in Peter's time, and that there is no pretext, therefore, (as far as that point is concerned,) for preferring a partial Jewish rumour of the fourth century to the plain and natural language of the Epistles. Accordingly, the learned of both churches are now pretty well agreed about it. The following quotations and authorities will show, 1, that many of the most enlightened of the Roman clergy have expressly denied the supposition altogether; 2, that even those of them who have not done so in express terms, have abandoned subsequently all the grounds upon which they originally professed to adopt it; and, 3, that as to father M'Corry's having, as some Roman Catholics think, the support of Protestant writers in thus still preferring what was rumoured in the fourth century to what is written in the Bible, there never was a more complete delusion, inasmuch as scarcely a single modern Protestant writer can be found who adopts the *on-dit* in question; and any who have ever done so, have done it under the avowed impression, created by Papal writers, that Babylon did not exist as a flourishing city of Parthia, with a large Jewish population, in St. Peter's time.

1. Even the Correspondent in the *Times* does not feel justified in putting forward this perversion of the Holy Scriptures. I find so many matters in his statement to condemn, that I the more willingly now acknowledge, that this is not one of his arguments for supposing that Peter left the East. This argument is also abandoned by Father Hardouin, Father Caron, (both Jesuits,) and

others of the Roman clergy, who, although they considered that "Babylon" could not be literally interpreted in Peter's Epistles, from the mistaken impression that there was no such city in his day, yet acknowledge that whatever place it meant, it did not, and could not mean Rome, or any other Gentile city. For instance, Hardouin supposes that it meant Jerusalem, and Caron that it meant Antioch. Father Dupin admits that there is not only no reason for supposing it to mean Rome, but that there is no room whatever for doubting that it means the Parthian Babylon; and this, although he supposes that Eusebius and some of the other fathers had understood it to mean Rome. "The First Epistle," says he, "was written from Babylon. Some of the ancients were of opinion that Rome was meant by this name, but this would not be a natural interpretation, (mais ce sens n'est pas naturel). . . . . We cannot precisely assign the time when it was written; but we may consider that it was written at Babylon, A.D. 45." (Prelim. Diss., sec. 4.) And again: "Eusebius says that it is Rome that is meant, though, after all, this interpretation is false, and it is more natural to say that it was written from Babylon." (Toutefois ce sens parait faux, et il est plus naturel de dire qu'il a écrit cette lettre de Babylone. *Ibid.*) Father Calmet mentions several members of his church as having abandoned this interpretation of the carnal-minded Jews. "Some (Roman) Catholic writers," says he, "for instance, Peter de Marca, John Baptist Mantuan, Michael de Ceza, Marsile de Padua, John Aventin, John Leland, Charles du Moulin, and perhaps some others, have expressed their misgivings as to the truth of this interpretation." (Calmet's Comment., Prelimin. Diss. on 1 Peter.) But it is not misgivings that they express—it is unqualified denial, as any one may see by reference to their works. For instance: "St. Peter went to Antioch," says Peter de Marca, archbishop of Paris, a writer of extreme celebrity and favour in the Roman church, "and from there to Babylon, where the hereditary Patriarch of the first Dispersion of the Jews resided. When established in that city, he wrote his first Epistle, as is clear from the words, 'The church at Babylon salutes you.' For although the ancients (?) supposed Peter to have here meant Rome, Scaliger can be shown to be right when he says, that this letter was written by the apostle from Babylon itself, to those dispersed Jews whose provincial synagogues depended upon the Patriarch of Babylon." (De Marca de Concordia Sacerdotii et Imperii, lib. vi. c. 1.) It is not misgivings, then, that these writers have expressed.

2. Cardinal Baronius betrays how little faith he reposed in this *on-dit*, by having abandoned, on different occasions, the different arguments alleged in favour of it. For instance, on one occasion the cardinal not only acknowledges that Babylon did exist as a city full of Jews in Peter's day, and that it was thought a very likely place for Peter to have gone to, but he even suggests that the apostle availed himself of these very circumstances to practise a pious fraud upon his persecutors. Peter might, we are told, have wished to conceal from the Jews where he really was, and could not have put them more astray than by dating from Babylon, though he lived in Europe. "I may here add," says Baronius, "without any disadvantage to our cause, that Peter's reason for not calling Rome "Rome," was his not wishing it to be publicly known where he went to live after his escape from prison at Jerusalem." (Nec me imprudenter dicturum existimo si his addiderim, Petrum non esse usum proprio Urbis nomine, quòd Hierosolymis fugâ lapsus e carcere, ubi ageret, non ab omnibus percipi vellet. Annals, A.D. 45. par. 17.) It is evident, *first*, that the only chance of the success of such a fraud lay in the extreme unlikelihood that the apostle should have written Babylon for Rome; *secondly*, in the well known reality of the Parthian city in that day; and, *thirdly*, in the great probability that there was of Peter's having gone into Parthia. If Baronius believed these three things, which his hypothesis implies he did, is it too much to say that he must have looked upon the *on-dit* in question as rather improbable, and that he was only endeavouring to make out a mere *possibility* in its

favour? And Father Calmet follows him in this singular hypothesis, mentioning it as one of the opinions of his church. "It is thought," says Calmet, "that he did so to prevent its being known where he was when he wrote it, for the apostles had a great many enemies everywhere, and it was but prudent not to expose themselves inconsiderately to persecution." (Pour ne pas decouvrir le lieu où il était. Prelim. Diss. on 1 Peter.) Father Ceillier also mentions this hypothesis of Baronius with approbation. "The apostle is believed to have written in this figurative manner," says Ceillier, "to prevent its being known where he was." (Pour ne pas faire connaitre le lieu où il était. Ceill. vol. i. art. Pierre.) Father Tillemont says that he found the question attended with some difficulty. After speaking of the language in which Peter wrote, he says: "There is more difficulty with regard to Babylon, from which St. Peter says he wrote it." (Il y a plus de difficulté sur Babylone d'où S. Pierre dit qu'il l'a ecrite. Eccl. Hist. vol. i.) Finally, a large class of Roman-catholic writers enrol themselves at once as recognising the improbability of the *on-dit* in question. All the Roman clergy admit that Peter's First Epistle was written in the reign of Claudius, for they agree in assigning it to A.D. 45. All those of them, therefore, (and as I have shown, they are almost all,) who consider that the supposed journey to Europe did not take place until Nero's reign, are of course compelled to abandon this *on-dit*, although many of them still continue to express themselves but vaguely as to the impossibility of its being true. So far are the Roman clergy from agreeing with Father M'Corry in his contradiction of one of the plainest passages in Scripture.

3. Nor is he supported in it by any of the Protestant writers. Bishop Pearson and Mr. Baratier, to whom we are so confidently referred as affording the most satisfactory evidence upon Peter's supposed journey into Europe, saw no reason whatever for supposing that he meant Rome when he wrote Babylon, or that this supposed journey preceded the Epistle.

"We may, indeed, justly regard it," says Dr. Bloomfield, "as a mere notion, first originating in error, and afterwards caught up by the Romanists, for the purpose of supporting their assertion, that Peter was the first bishop of Rome. The best founded supposition is, I apprehend, that of Erasmus, Calvin, Beza, Lightfoot, Scaliger, Salmasius, Le Clerc, Beausobre, Wetstein, Bengel, Bishop Conybeare, Benson, Rosenmuller, and Adam Clarke, that it means Babylon in Assyria." (Bloomfield on the Gr. Test.)

"St. Peter," says Matthew Henry, "being at Babylon, in Assyria, when he wrote this Epistle, (whither he travelled as the apostle of the circumcision, to visit that church which was the chief of the Dispersion) sends the salutation of that church to the other churches to whom he wrote. In this salutation he particularly joins Mark, the evangelist, who was then with him." (Old and New Test.)

"No satisfactory reason can be assigned for supposing, as many have done, that Babylon signifies Rome." (Thomas Scott on the Old and New Test.)

"By some," says Dr. Kitto, "an attempt has been made to obtain the support of the apostle's own testimony, in favour of his having at one period resided at Rome, by interpreting the words, 'the church that is at Babylon,' as applying to the church at Rome; an attempt which Dr. Campbell justly stigmatizes as poor, not to call it ridiculous." (Kitto's Cyclop. of Biblical Literature.)

"The word 'Babylon,' without something to give it a different application, would," says Barnes, "have been understood anywhere to denote the well-known place on the Euphrates. Babylon had been an important place; and its history was such, and its relations to the Jews such, as to make it probable that the attention of the apostles would be turned to it. Nothing would be more natural than that they should visit Babylon. There were many Jews of the captivity remaining in that region, and it would be in the highest degree probable that they would seek to carry the gospel to their own countrymen there. .... It should be added here, however, that upon the supposition that the word Babylon refers to Rome, rests nearly all the evidence which the Roman Catholics can adduce that the apostle Peter was ever at Rome at all. There is nothing else in the New Testament that furnishes the slightest proof that he ever was there. The only passage on which Bellarmine relies to show that Peter was at Rome is the very passage now under consideration." (Barnes on the New Testament.)

"Among the advocates for the latter sense (the figurative), have been men of such learning and abilities," says Adam Clarke, "that I was misled by their authority in the younger part of my life to subscribe to it; but at present, as I have more impartially examined the question, it appears to me very extraordinary that when an apostle dates his epistle from Babylon, it should ever occur to any commentator to ascribe to this word a mystical meaning, instead of taking it in its literal and proper sense. For in the first century the ancient Babylon on the Euphrates was still in existence, ... but through some mistake it has been supposed that it was not. ... It is true that, in comparison of its original splendour, it might be called in the first century a desolated city; but it was not wholly a heap of ruins, nor wholly destitute of inhabitants. .... Babylon was at that time so far from being literally destitute of inhabitants, that Strabo draws a parallel between this city and Seleucia, saying, at present Babylon is not so great as Seleucia, which was then the capital of the Parthian empire, and, according to Pliny, contained 600,000 inhabitants." (Adam Clarke on 1 Peter.)

Calvin says, in his Commentaries on the Epistles: "I see no reason whatever to doubt that Peter was at Babylon at that time, for he distinctly tells us that he was." Again: "It is a great deal more likely to be true that Peter, as his mission required, (ut ferebat apostolatus ratio,) travelled in the districts in which there was the greatest proportion of Jews; and we know that there were great multitudes of them at Babylon, and in the countries round it." And again: "It also accorded with his mission, (ejus vocationi fuit consentaneum,) for we know that he was specially given to the Jews as their apostle; and, for this reason, his travels were mainly confined to those countries in which there were the greatest numbers of his own nation." And, in another place: "For as to the Roman Catholics calling themselves 'Babylonians,' and Rome 'Babylon,' merely to make it appear that they have Peter's relics, the absurdity of this shall be elsewhere exposed." But this is enough of such illustration. There are, as I have said, no Protestant commentators, with our modern knowledge of history, who would choose so far to trifle with the sacred text of the inspired writings, as to set aside the plain and natural meaning, in order to adopt this or any other rumour that might have been afloat in the fourth century.

There are other arguments on this subject which it is unnecessary to unfold here. The Greek scholar will himself see at once in the παρα of Peter's expression παρεπιδημοις, that the parties to whom that letter was addressed lived in provinces adjoining that in which the writer was at the time. The reader of Jewish history will remember that Babylon had other claims to the care of the great apostle of the circumcision beside our Lord's command. The land of Babylon was the native land of Abraham. It was there he was married, and thence that he emigrated to Canaan. It was to that, his father's native country, that Isaac went to seek his wife, Rebecca, and from there that Jacob took his wives, Leah and Rachel. The country of Babylon was, in short, the parent country of the whole Jewish nation, and to which, even in its hostility to them, they ever turned with affection. The general critic will see that the letter written from the capital of the Dispersion, would be naturally expected to have on that account the more authority, and that Peter's not having mentioned the province of Babylon, the capital of the Dispersion, among the names of the provinces to which he addressed his Epistle, could only be because he wrote it from that province. Such arguments will occur to every one. It may, however, be observed, in conclusion, that Baronius, and all the Roman clergy, acknowledge that the Chair of St. Peter was established in great splendour upon the Euphrates in St. Peter's time, that it had its martyrs as well as the other churches, and that the bishop of Babylon was at the Nicene Council. Of this church on the Euphrates, in Mesopotamia, Baronius says: "The church of this province was not only one of the earliest of all the churches, but also one of the most steadfast and most numerous." (Sicut enim antiquissima ita et florentissima erat ejus provinciæ ecclesia. Annals, A.D. 311, paragraph 28.) "There was an episcopal chair at Babylon," says Father Richard, in the Bibliothèque Sacrée, "from the very first." (Il y eut un siège épiscopal à Babylone dès les premiers temps de l'église.) This work also mentions four or five of the bishops that sat in Peter's Chair at Babylon, of whom the first appears to have been that Abdias to whom one of the absurd works got up in the thirteenth century was attributed. Another of them, Polychronius, is mentioned by Baronius (A.D. 254, paragraph 27), also at considerable length in The Acts of the Saints (Acta Sanctorum, Feb. 17), as having been crucified before the time of the Nicene Council. De Marca, archbishop of Paris, has also several important remarks upon the archbishopric of Babylon, in his Dissertation, De Primatibus (vol. iv. p. 26), from which, as well as from Baronius, it appears to have been one of the most illustrious of Peter's Chairs. For the bishops who were present at the Nicene Council, the reader is referred to Eusebius (Vit. Const. iii. 7), to Theodoret (i. 7), and to Baronius's Annals (A.D. 325, paragraphs 25 and 26). It ought to be borne in mind, that in Peter's time and until the year 229, Babylon belonged to the Parthians, and that it was subsequently within the territorial possessions of the king of Persia, its bishop being then called a Persian bishop, and the Jews inhabiting it, Persian Jews.

IV.

The next passage to be considered is also at ii. 15, and is the tradition about Mark's Gospel over again. After saying, in the preceding chapter, that Peter had extended his care even to the Gentiles of Rome, who had never heard him, by sending them an abstract of his doctrine through the church already there, the historian of Cæsarea tells us, that the Jewish disciples of this apostle, who had been his hearers in the East, of whom some were, as we have seen, Alexandrians, some Romans, but, of course, the major part Asiatics, were so delighted with his doctrine, as he delivered it *virâ voce* to them, that they also wished for some permanent record of it for themselves;—that as Mark had travelled with him a good deal they implored this evangelist to commit it to writing;—that this was the origin of the Gospel according to St. Mark;—and that when Peter came to hear of the existence of that document, he gave his consent that it should be read, not only in the churches of Babylon, Jerusalem, and Alexandria, but even at Rome, and in all the other churches of the Christian world. Eusebius adds, that what he states on this point is also stated by Clemens Alexandrinus and Papias, for whose words the reader is referred to the sections of this work that bear their names. The Bishop of Cæsarea's own words are as follows. They occur immediately after the chapter on the Κηρυγμα Πετρου:—

"Hist. B. II. Ch. XV.

"*On the Gospel according to St. Mark.*

"The splendour of Peter's piety so enlightened the understanding of all his personal disciples, that they were not satisfied with merely hearing him, or with the unwritten teaching of his divine Proclamation, but earnestly implored Mark, (whose gospel we have,) as he was so much Peter's associate, to leave them a record in writing of the teaching which they had received by word of mouth, and never desisted until they had prevailed upon this person to do so, and thus gave rise to the document which is called the Gospel according to St. Mark. It is also said, that when the apostle came to know of what was done, which he did by divine revelation, he was pleased with the enthusiasm of the parties, and allowed the document to be read in all the churches, (Clemens gives this account in the 6th book of his 'Institutions,' and Papias, the bishop of Hierapolis, corroborates it,) and that this is the Mark whom Peter mentions in his First Epistle," &c.

It is evident that this passage has not one word about Mark's Gospel not having been written in Egypt, as St. Chrysostom says it was, nor one word about Peter's being with him, wherever he was, when he wrote it. Nor does Nicephorus, (A.D. 1320,) who wrote in the same language as Eusebius, and who was very credulous in all such matters, introduce in his paraphrase of this passage the slightest allusion to these suppositions, which only date, like the rest, from the Reformation. As to the first of them, that it was not at Alexandria but at Rome that Mark wrote his Gospel, neither Papias, nor Irenæus, nor Clemens Alexandrinus, nor Eusebius, nor Jerome, nor Epiphanius, afford the least countenance to this contradiction of what St. Chrysostom so positively states. This has been already shown in the section upon Clemens Alexandrinus. And as to the second of these suppositions, that Peter was with him when he wrote his gospel, the four first of these six earliest authorities upon the subject attest the exact contrary, and the two last say nothing. "Papias," I repeat my own words out of that section, "says plainly, that Mark had to write from memory; Irenæus, that Mark did not write until after Peter's death; Clemens Alexandrinus repeats what Papias said, adding, that the existence of Mark's Gospel did not come to Peter's knowledge for some time after it was written; Eusebius repeats this addition of Clemens, and says, that it was by divine revelation the thing came to Peter's knowledge; all which expressions are inconsistent with the supposition that Peter was then with Mark; and neither Jerome, nor Epiphanius, nor any subsequent Father, has ever pretended to say he was."

The main source of the modern misconception as to what Eusebius writes in the passage we are now considering seems to be, that some of the earliest Roman-catholic editors have inadvertently made the 15th chapter to begin with the last words of the chapter preceding it, which relate to the success of the Κηρυγμα Πιτρου at Rome, and that this oversight naturally led people to suppose that the 15th chapter itself related to something in that city, which it does not. On this point I can do no more here than invite the reader's attention to the arrangement of the text in the additions alluded to. Robert Stephens's Paris edition, which was one of the first, and carefully taken from the most ancient MSS., is free from this mistake. Dr. Burton, in his edition of Eusebius, printed at Oxford in 1838, gives the vulgar error in his text, but acknowledges in his notes that he considers it an error, and that several very early MSS. are expressly opposed to it. That Eusebius himself intended it to stand as Stephens has placed it, is clear from the title he gave the 14th chapter, "On the Κηρυγμα Πιτρου at Rome;" the *effects* of which work there, one naturally expects to find in this 14th chapter, and not in the chapter about Mark's Gospel; whereas the editors we speak of transferred to the following chapter about Mark's Gospel the passage of two lines in which these effects are stated, making this short chapter of a dozen lines, about Mark's Gospel, to begin thus: "And the divine word having in this form sojourned among the Romans, the influence of the sorcerer was foiled, and perished almost as rapidly as the man. The splendour of Peter's piety," &c., an incongruity so glaring as to require only to have the attention drawn to it. Finally, Nicephorus, in his paraphrase of Eusebius, divides the chapters as Stephens does, and not one of the MSS. warrants any other division. Thus we see, that in the most approved and natural division of the chapters, there is no ground for supposing that what is related in chapter xv. took place at Rome; that in the chapter itself there is no allusion to that city as being the place where the Gospel was written; and none in either of the two passages referred to by Eusebius as his sources of information on the subject; that St. Chrysostom assured us it was written in Egypt; and that all the early authorities agree in acknowledging, that wherever Mark composed his Gospel, Peter was not with him when he did so. To this we may add, that even modern writers of the highest standing both for learning and piety in the church of Rome, admit, after the closest search for evidence of the affirmative, that there is no good reason to believe that Mark wrote in Italy. "Some persons mentioned by St. Chrysostom were of opinion," says Father Calmet, "that Mark wrote in Egypt. Others affirm that he wrote after St. Peter's death. These different sentiments are *enough to prove* that the circumstances of time and *place* are *uncertain*, when and where St. Mark composed his Gospel." (Calmet, Dict. of the Bible, *art.* Mark.) Those who follow the Fathers, will here find no uncertainty.

V.

THE next passage in Eusebius is as follows: "And Linus, whom Paul has mentioned in his Second Epistle to Timothy, as being with him at Rome, I have already just now stated to have been the first elected bishop of the Roman church after Peter's time; and Clement also, who was appointed the third bishop of that church, is declared by Paul to have been his fellow-labourer and fellow-soldier." (Euseb. iii. 4.) Although this was not written at Rome, but in a part of the East much frequented by Peter, and where everything connected with the management of the churches would naturally have had its duration reckoned from his death, yet from the introduction of his name here, it is supposed that Eusebius meant to imply that Peter was the first bishop of Rome, and that therefore he must have lived in that city.

One brief and conclusive answer to these suppositions is, that Roman-catholic writers themselves, when at all acquainted with Greek, frankly and instantly confess that such passages do not imply that the parties *from* whom, or *after* whom, bishops are reckoned, were themselves bishops. Carminus Fiminnus, for instance, already cited upon this point, an extremely zealous Roman Catholic, the royal Neapolitan professor who edited the works of De Marca, archbishop of Paris, says, in his preface to the fourth volume, (Naples, 1773,) "When Eusebius says that any one was third or sixth bishop of Rome *after* Peter and Paul, or *from* the apostles, he does not mean that these apostles, or that all the apostles, were bishops of Rome." And again, on Jerome's saying that James was the first bishop of Jerusalem after the apostles, the learned Neapolitan at once remarks,— "Neither the expression '*from* the apostles,' nor the other expression, '*after* the apostles,' implies that the apostles were bishops of Jerusalem. In like manner when Eusebius says that any one was third bishop of Rome," &c., (pp. 14 and 15,) where he adds much more to the same effect.

Another brief and conclusive answer to the above suppositions is, that we have the candid and unequivocal confession of Cardinal Bellarmine, as well as of other enlightened Roman Catholics, that Peter's being shown to have been bishop of Rome, would be no indication whatever of his having ever been in that city, "because," says the Cardinal, "several other Roman pontiffs never were in Rome in their lives." (Bell. de Summ. Pontif. lib. ii. c. 1.)

After two such conclusive answers, it will, perhaps, to many appear superfluous that I should adduce the six following further illustrations of the present passage; but, as I have already remarked, it is important to show not only that the statements of the Roman clergy about Peter's having left the East are groundless, but that they are so utterly—one may even say, so ridiculously groundless, as to render it matter of speculation how it has ever been possible for the human intellect to entertain them.

In the first place the Greek word denoting "after the time of," ($\mu\epsilon\tau\acute{\alpha}$,) in this passage, although sometimes used to speak of things or persons of the same sort, succeeding one another, is nevertheless the most usual expression in the Greek language to denote " after the time of," even with regard to things or persons of the most different kinds. Eusebius himself adopts it in countless instances, from which I select the following: " The last siege of the Jews after the time of Christ," (iii. 5.) " After Nero and Domitian it is reported that there was a partial persecution, in consequence of a popular insurrection in the reign of the emperor whose times we are now recording," (iii. 32.) " Stephen was the first after our Lord who was stoned to death by our Lord's own murderers," (ii. 1.) " Dionysius, of whom Luke writes in the Acts that he was the first who believed after St. Paul's address to the Athenians in the Areopagus," (iii. 4.) " James, who was the first elected bishop of Jerusalem after the ascension of our Saviour," (iii. 5.) Thucydides writes, " On the sixtieth day after the battle," (Thucyd. i. 108;) and Polybius " On the third day after the death of the king," (Polyb. xxxvii. 3;) but examples of this are almost in every page of every work, for it was the most usual way of expressing, " after the time of."

In the second place, Eusebius, writing from the East where the apostles lived, always dates the series of the bishops, and other ecclesiastical matters, in the European churches as well as in those of Asia, *from* the apostles, or *after* the apostles, (as has been already shown in the section on " The Anonymous Author," in Euseb. v. 28;) and he does this even respecting those churches in which it is known and acknowledged, on all hands, that " the apostles" were not bishops, such as Antioch, Jerusalem, and Alexandria; when, therefore, he does this in the case of Rome, it cannot fairly be inferred that he thereby means to imply that the apostles, or any of them, were bishops of that church. He says, for instance, " Theophilus was distinguished in the church at Antioch as the sixth bishop from the apostles," (iv. 20,) although no writer of any description pretends that there were apostles bishops of that church. Even those Roman-catholic writers who, contrary to Eusebius and all previous historical evidence, suppose that Peter resided seven years at Antioch, as local bishop there, do not pretend to say that any other apostle did so beside Peter; or that, dating the episcopal series at Antioch from "the apostles," implies that these apostles were bishops of that church. Eusebius has also: "Maximinus succeeded Theophilus, and was the seventh bishop from the apostles of the church at Antioch," (iv. 24.) And again: "Serapion was the eighth bishop of the church at Antioch after the apostles," (v. 22.) In the same way Ignatius, in his Twelfth Epistle, addressed to the people of Antioch, says: "Remember your holy bishop Evodius, to whom first was allotted the helm of your church after the apostles." Of Jerusalem, Eusebius writes: "These are the bishops of Jerusalem from the apostles until the above-mentioned period," (iv. 5,) although there is no writer whatever who says that any other of the apostles besides St. James was regarded as bishop of that church. Eusebius also says, in the same chapter: "For the church at Jerusalem consisted solely of converted Jews from the apostles to the siege;" and again: "Narcissus was the fifteenth bishop of Jerusalem in succession from the siege of the Jews under Adrian, and the thirtieth in regular succession from the apostles," (v. 12.) Then, of Alexandria, no one alleges that even any single one of the apostles was ever bishop of Alexandria, yet Eusebius writes thus: "About the twelfth year of the reign of Trajan, the bishop of the church of Alexandria, who was mentioned by us a little before, departed this life; and Primus was the fourth from the apostles who was elected to fulfil the episcopal functions of that city," (iv. 1.) Thus also, in the case of Rome, Eusebius says that "Eleutherus was the twelfth bishop of Rome from the apostles," (v. Procem,) and that "Telesphorus was the seventh bishop of the Roman church from the apostles," (iv. 5,) although the Roman-catholic writers consider that only one of the apostles was bishop there; and although Eusebius and all the ecclesiastical writers, from the earliest period, considered that (as was determined at the Nicene Council) there could not be more than one bishop at the same time in the same city, (Euseb.

vi. 43.) In the one passage that we are now considering, Eusebius names Peter alone as being the leader and representative of all our Lord's apostles, which in another place (ii. 14,) he distinctly says that, on account of his ability, Peter was. On two or three occasions of this sort he names Paul and Peter, instead of the apostles generally; because, although Peter's name sufficiently represented the rest of the apostles (both those of the Jews and those of the Gentiles) in such expressions, yet as Paul, the Gentile apostle, was more closely connected with Rome, the capital of the Gentiles, than the Jewish apostles were, his name obtains thus occasionally a special mention in reference to Rome which it does not in reference to any of the Jewish cities. Thus, we read in Eusebius: " Clement was the third of the bishops after Paul and Peter," (iii. 21,) and " Alexander was the fifth bishop of Rome after Peter and Paul," (iv. 1;) and that such expressions have nothing to do with either a residence or a bishopric in Rome is further clearly proved by the fact, that we even find the name of St. James, whom no Roman Catholic ever supposed to have been at Rome or bishop of its church, prefixed to those of Peter and Paul in the enumeration of the Roman bishops. Thus: " Cerdon lived in the time of Hyginus, who was the ninth bishop of Rome after James and Peter and Paul," (Epiphanius, Hæres. iv. 1.) Nothing can more clearly show how arbitrarily the names of apostles were selected on such occasions. " Whoever," says Valesius, the Roman-catholic commentator, " would infer from this that St. James was bishop of Rome, would only make himself ridiculous." (Val. in Euseb. iii. 21.)

In the third place, Eusebius never in any one case dates the episcopal series from the first bishop of the series. He always makes use of the apostles generally for this purpose, or at least of the apostolic times, which he supposes to terminate with the martyrdom of St. Peter, whom, as he tells us, (ii. 14,) on account of his superior ability, he considered as the leader of the twelve, and therefore as their representative. Even when he speaks of the episcopal series at Jerusalem, where St.

James, one of the apostles, was regarded as first bishop, he never on any occasion speaks of the third or fourth bishop after James, but always the third or fourth after the apostles, and even reckons James as the first of the series after them; which may be seen by reference to the passages about the church of Jerusalem in the last paragraph. In a catalogue of the bishops of this church, Eusebius thus expresses himself: "The first then was James, called the brother of our Lord; after whom the second was Symeon, the third Justus," &c. (iv. 5.) He does not say after whom the *first* was Symeon, but the *second* was Symeon. According to this method of expression, if Peter had been first bishop of Rome, Eusebius would have described Linus in the text, as after Peter the second bishop, instead of (as he has done) the first, and also as the second, instead of the first bishop from the apostles, just as he has described Symeon. To the attentive reader of Eusebius's text—to the sincere and conscientious inquirer after truth—this argument will, I think, when duly considered, supersede all others upon this point.

Fourthly. Another consideration, which will prove conclusive to the classical Roman Catholic as to the import of the passage in question, is that if Linus's being said to be the first bishop after Peter, implies Peter's being bishop, then Linus's being the first bishop elected by lot after Peter, as it is in the text, would mean, not that Peter constituted himself bishop of Rome, (which is what Roman Catholics think he did do,) but that the office was assigned to him by lot, and that he was elected to that episcopate by the *sortilegium* of the Roman Christians, a supposition which no Roman Catholic would, I think, choose to entertain, but which is involved in the interpretation that some have endeavoured to force upon this passage.

Fifthly. Eusebius plainly tells us in the text that he is there only repeating in a brief form what he had just previously explained more at length; thus referring us to his fuller and only previous statement respecting the first bishop of the Roman church (book iii., chap. ii.), where we find not one word about Peter's having been in that capacity, but only that it was not until after Paul and he (the two great apostolic leaders) had closed their career, the one in Italy, the other in the East, that St. Paul's friend Linus, who had been at Rome with him, was elected by lot first bishop of that church. The words to which Eusebius in the text refers us are: "After the martyrdom of Paul and Peter, Linus was elected by lot, first bishop of the see of Rome." (Euseb. iii. 2.) When, therefore, we find him in the next page professing to recapitulate this statement in an abbreviated form, giving Peter's name the preference in the second statement, as he had given Paul's the preference in the first, it is as unfair as it is contrary to common sense, to attribute to the second statement a sense which is evidently excluded from the first.

Sixthly. That Eusebius does not mean to say here or anywhere else that Peter was bishop of Rome, is clearly proved from numberless places in which he distinctly says that Peter never was bishop of Rome. I select the following: In the very chapter (iii. 2) to which he refers us in the text that we are now considering, we have an instance of this. Over that chapter as its title he places the words—"Who first presided over the church of Rome;" and the whole short chapter is as follows: "After this martyrdom of Paul and Peter, Linus was first elected by lot to the see of Rome. It is he whom Paul mentions in his Epistle to Timothy from Rome, in the salutation towards the close of the Epistle, when he says, 'Eubulus, and Pudens, and Linus, and Claudia salute you.'" (iii. 2.) Is not this distinctly saying that it was not Peter who was so?—Again, over the thirteenth chapter of the same book the title is "That Anencletus was second bishop of Rome;" and the chapter begins thus: "After Vespasian had reigned about ten years, he is succeeded by his son Titus,—in the second year of whose reign Linus, bishop of the church of Rome, who had held the office about twelve years, hands it down to Anencletus." (ii. 13.) Is not this, I again ask,—is not this distinctly saying that it was not Peter who was first bishop of Rome? And if he was not bishop before any one else, is it not true that he was never so? Is that man in earnest who gainsays this conclusion? Again, the title of the fifteenth chapter is "That Clement was the third bishop of the Roman church." The chapter itself is as follows: "In the twelfth year of the same reign, after Anencletus had been bishop of Rome twelve years, he was succeeded by Clement, who, the apostle, in his Epistle to the Philippians, shows had been his fellow-labourer, in these words: "With Clement and the rest of my fellow-labourers, whose names are in the Book of Life." Let the reader here also pause. Is it not quite certain that the historian, when he wrote this title and these words, considered that Peter had never been bishop of Rome? "That Evarestus was the fourth who presided over the church of Rome," is the title of chapter thirty-four of this book. The chapter itself is as follows: "In the third year of the above reign, Clement, bishop of Rome, transmitting the episcopal charge to Evarestus, departed this life, after having superintended the teaching of the divine word for nine years with great diligence." The question is, was Evarestus the fifth or the fourth of the Roman bishops? It is useless to extend these illustrations. I need only add that Henry de Valois (Valesius), the Roman-catholic commentator upon Eusebius, acknowledges that neither Irenæus nor Eusebius (our only two authorities on that point) ever speak of Peter as a bishop anywhere, and that it is a great mistake to suppose they do. "The apostles," says de Valois, "had a rank peculiar to themselves, nor were they ever reckoned among the bishops of the churches." (On Euseb. iii. 14.) And again: "It must not be forgotten that Eusebius never reckons the apostles among the bishops of the churches, as I have already remarked.... Irenæus, as well as Eusebius, says that Peter and Paul laid the first foundations of the church which was in Rome, but these writers nowhere reckon them among the bishops of that church." (Val. on Euseb. iii. 21.) Thus, in all that Eusebius has written—in all the records that we have of the early church up to his time, there is nothing more clear than that neither he nor any one else ever thought Peter had been bishop of Rome;—a fact which, as far as Eusebius is concerned, I have been induced to set forth in a clearer light than others have thought necessary, because the Correspondent in the *Times*, and a few serious Roman Catholics of modern times, appear to be so utterly misinformed upon this point as to suppose that Eusebius says that St. Peter held the See of Rome for five-and-twenty years!—and because this historian himself tells us that he gives us in his history all the information that had reached his times respecting the apostles. (iii. 31.)

VI.

The last passage that we have to examine is that in which Eusebius is supposed to say that Philo, the Jew, saw Peter at Rome: it occurs book ii. ch. xvii., where this eastern historian tells us, that there was another rumour in the East, in the fourth century, to the effect that Philo, who had been sent into Europe by the Jews of Alexandria, on an embassy to Caligula, went there again in the reign of Claudius, when he was nearly a hundred years old, and that on that occasion he had some correspondence with Peter, who was still then engaged at Jerusalem in the promulgation of the gospel throughout the European cities; an occupation which of course ceased as soon as the apostle went to Babylon; and that this rumour about Philo's correspondence with the apostles, vague as it was, derived a sort of credibility from the fact, that one of Philo's works evidently alludes to some customs and practices that existed in all the Christian churches in the days of Eusebius. The bishop of Cæsarea writes thus: "Philo, of whom there is a rumour afloat (λογος εχει) that when he was at Rome in the reign of Claudius, he entered into communications with Peter, who was at that time transmitting evangelical tidings to the inhabitants of that city;

and this is not improbable, for the work I now speak of evidently contains allusions to the practices of the church that have come down to our days." (ii. 17.) Greek scholars will see at once, not only that Eusebius does not say that Peter was then at Rome with Philo, but that (as we so often find to be the case in these passages) he says the exact contrary; for such readers know that ὁμιλια does not mean only verbal communication, but also such as is carried on between parties in different cities, in which way we find it used to express the communications by letter of Dionysius, bishop of Corinth, to the church of Rome, as may be seen in the section on this bishop's alleged testimony upon this subject; and they also know that *ικησι* unequivocally indicates Peter's absence from the place in favour of which he was then and thus engaged, a peculiarity connected with words terminating in the syllable *σι*, which may be seen explained in any grammar. Jerome, who (as has been already said) did not seek to conceal his defective knowledge of Greek, understood ὁμιλια to mean only intimate friendship and personal interviews, and so translated it in this passage, which seems to have led Baronius, and one or two others, into their mistake. But none of the Roman clergy now-a-days pretend, either that Philo saw Peter in Europe, or even had any communications with him of any kind. On this point the Abbé Labouderie, who was vicar of Notre Dame in 1815, until Napoleon's return from Elba, writes thus in the "Biographie Universelle," which (as we have so often said) had some of the most learned of the Roman clergy among its contributors: "All that story is without foundation, and the critics had an easy task to prove that it was false. It is even doubtful whether Philo had any knowledge of the Messiah. So unreal are those indications of Christian truth which some have fancied that they detected in his writings," Biogr. Univ., *art.* Philon.) And in this opinion the Abbé is fully supported by Mangey and Pfeiffer, the most exact and learned of all Philo's editors. Accordingly, we find that even Fathers Richard and Giraud, in the "Bibliothèque Sacrée," omit the *on-dit* altogether. Besides which, it is unnecessary to remind the reader, that all those Roman-catholic writers who consider that Peter did not come into Europe, at all events, until the reign of Nero, are compelled to admit that Philo could not have seen him at Rome in the reign of Claudius; and that, therefore, if there were any truth in this other rumour of the fourth century, the communication could only have been in writing, and must have been carried on between Jerusalem and Rome. Among these writers we find (the reader will remember) such men as Father Ceillier, Father Baluze, Father Papebroche, Father Pagi, the Abbé de Longuerue, Archbishop de Marca, Father Dupin, and a host of other distinguished men of that period, as well as almost all who have written since their time. In conclusion I may observe, that there is not a word about Peter, or this alleged interview, in all Philo's voluminous writings; nor one word, except this passage, in any ancient writer about Philo's being in Europe in the reign of Claudius; and that every one can judge how very slight a rumour that must have been, which could derive the smallest accession of probability from the mere circumstance mentioned by Eusebius,—a circumstance which most people will think quite as likely to have occurred if Philo had had no communications with Peter as if he had, and which some have been disposed to think Eusebius placed here for the express purpose of showing how devoid of foundation the rumour appeared to him to be. "Of a conversation with Peter," says Cyprian, in his commentary on Jerome's translation of 'Ομιλια, "there is not the slightest trace in Philo's works;" and again, "In all Philo's works there is not one word about Christ, or Mark, or anything whatever connected with the Christian faith. . . . . But there can be no doubt that Eusebius himself considered that the rumour he was mentioning was not true." (Ernest Salomon Cyprian, in Hieronym. Catal., art. Philo.)

The main point here to be attended to is, that the rumour, as Eusebius reports it, does not say that Philo's communications with Peter were verbal; but, on the contrary, that Peter had not yet relinquished his central position at Jerusalem, and his general proclamation of the Gospel from that city, when these took place, as is plainly expressed by the Greek word employed in the passage. According to the Roman clergy, however, there not only is no reason to believe that Philo went to Italy in the reign of Claudius, as this rumour states, but they acknowledge that, even if he did, he could not have found Peter there; and that, as far as his writings are concerned, there are no grounds in them for supposing that he had had any communication with any of the apostles, or that he had ever even heard of our Lord. From all which we learn how little reliance can be placed, or indeed is placed, even by the Roman clergy, upon what Eusebius gives us under the name of rumours. It is but fair, however, to state, that no modern writer adduces this rumour as a reason for thinking that Peter ever left the East. Even Father M'Corry does not do so.

VII.

EUSEBIUS's CHRONICON (a chronological synopsis, written before his History, and in Greek, as all his works were) is supposed by a few of the less informed of the Roman clergy to have stated that Peter went to Rome to become local bishop of the church there, in the second year of Claudius, and that he was for the greater part of five-and-twenty years resident at Rome in that capacity. I have already shown in Section II. of this Part, that the Roman clergy and all the learned in communion with that church, have for centuries admitted that Peter could not have gone to Rome in the reign of Claudius at all; and that it is their opinion that the writer who states he did, is in no case to be depended on. This is abundant answer to the supposition in question. But that the reader may see the whole of the absurdity of supposing that we have the alleged statement upon the authority of Eusebius's Chronicon, his attention is invited to the following facts, all admitted by the Roman clergy, as may be seen in the subjoined testimonies:—

1. The Greek text of this Chronicon is admitted by the Roman clergy to be lost.

2. Jerome's Latin Chronicon, called by some a "Translation" of the foregoing, is admitted, both by Jerome himself and by all the Roman clergy, to be so only in a very vague sense, and to have been rather an abridgment condensed by him from Eusebius and other writers.

3. Jerome's Latin Chronicon is admitted by the Roman clergy to be, as it was discovered at the Reformation, full of errors and interpolations. Baronius called it at that time a "Labyrinth of Error."

4. Jerome's difficulty in translating from the Greek language (in which Eusebius wrote) was, he tells us himself, very great; and Scaliger says that it amounted to the most unaccountable ignorance of the simplest expressions of the language.

5. Scaliger collected from two Greek works professedly compiled in the twelfth or thirteenth century from works a few centuries earlier, certain passages which appeared to him to represent, more or less exactly, some of the lost Greek text of Eusebius. But the Roman clergy roundly dissent upon this point from Scaliger. They consider that it is very doubtful whether any of these passages originated with Eusebius, and perfectly certain that a great many of them did not.

6. One of the Greek works referred to by Scaliger is an abridgment of Cedrenus's "Synopsis." The Synopsis is now lost. It was originally written by Cedrenus, a monk of the eleventh century, who professed to have compiled it from various writings extant in his time, (one of which was a work on the same subject by Syncellus.) Soon after the death of Cedrenus, it was re-written in a form further condensed; and it is this second abridgment, which is still extant, to which Scaliger had recourse on this occasion.

7. The other work of the middle ages is a collection of extracts from Syncellus's "Compilation of Chronology." Syncellus was a monk of the eighth century,

who also professed to have compiled his work from various writings extant in his time; one of which Scaliger thinks was the Chronicon of Eusebius; but Syncellus scruples not to say that he does not follow Eusebius, and frequently acknowledges that their works do not agree. As Syncellus's work existed complete in the eleventh century, the extracts or abridgment of it that Scaliger used, and that we now have, may have probably been drawn up about that period.

8. Even the Greek work thus compiled by Scaliger is admitted by the Roman clergy not to contain the alleged statement about the second year of Claudius and the Five-and-Twenty years.

The following testimonies will be sufficient:—

Father Ceillier, after saying that the Chronicon of Eusebius consisted of two parts or books, proceeds thus (vol. iv. p. 221): "The Greek text is lost, except some fragments scattered here and there, without order or connexion, in the writings of Syncellus and Cedrenus. Joseph Scaliger is the first who collected these; and to make his work of more importance, he has connected these fragments by the aid of a great number of other passages derived, not only from these two authors, but from the Chronicon of Alexandria, insisting that although they are not cited as taken from Eusebius, they are nevertheless to be regarded as his. It is from all these different passages that the first book of the Chronicon is composed, which he has given us in Greek under the name of Eusebius. But no one has been deceived about it, and the learned have found several paragraphs which could not have been written by Eusebius. . . . . Besides, how could Scaliger be sure that the passages which he took from Cedrenus, Syncellus, and the Alexandrian chronicle, were really written by Eusebius? . . . . Scaliger has also given us in Greek the second part of this work of Eusebius, in which he assures us that he has inserted nothing but what he found in books. If this be so, we have through him recovered the Greek text of Eusebius which had been so long lost. But he ought to have told us in what books he found these things. . . . . St. Jerome translated into Latin the whole of the two books of this Greek Chronicon, but took at the same time the liberty of adding whatever he thought necessary; so that he made, as we may say, a new work of it. (En sorte qu'il en fit pour ainsi dire un nouvel ouvrage.) He inserted several things in it taken from Suetonius and various other writers, especially in the Roman history, which Eusebius had not much treated of, as not being interesting to his own (Eastern) nation. It also seems that he introduced much fresh matter into the history of the church. . . . . All the Latin writers who succeeded Jerome made use of his labours; but confining themselves only to the second part, the first part of this Latin work was so much neglected that it no longer exists but in a very imperfect state. Even in the second there are several errors (beaucoup de fautes); whether they originated with Eusebius himself, or with those who transcribed his MSS., or with his translator Jerome. The first had its errors also," &c.

Dr. Cave in his " Ecclesiastical Writers," says: " The Greek text is lost; and Scaliger, to supply this deficiency, collected what could be found of it in Syncellus, Cedrenus, and the Alexandrian Chronicle; but there is good reason to doubt whether these fragments are to be considered as having been written by Eusebius."

In Butler's " Lives of the Saints," (Edition 1838. Note, vol. ii. p. 80,) we read " The Chronicle of Eusebius was a work of immense labour. . . . . Scaliger gathered the scattered fragments from Syncellus, Cedrenus, and the Alexandrian Chronicle; but Scaliger ought to have pointed out his sources, and has inserted many things which certainly belong not to Eusebius."

Scaliger, in one of the prefaces to his " Thesaurus Temporum," after saying that Syncellus's original work was called a " Compilation (εκλογη) of Chronology," and that that which we now have is called " Selections (παρεκβολαι—excerpta) from Syncellus," then proceeds thus: " This MS. was written about 600 years ago. I drew from it all that I was able to detect as likely to have been derived from Eusebius; which is not, however, the hundredth part of what Eusebius wrote. But just in the same manner as Eusebius used to censure Africanus and others who wrote in this department before his time, for mis-stating dates and facts, so also this Syncellus reprimands Eusebius whenever he considers him deviating from the truth; and this to such an extent, that whenever he has an opportunity, he rarely lets Eusebius off without some severe and even abusive language. Cedrenus had, it seems, taken verbatim the whole of Syncellus's original work, and compiled from it and other such works, a very large volume, which he called a 'Synopsis.' But even that did not escape the hands of the condensers,—that most certain poison of the libraries. Nay, more; these were guilty not only of condensing, but of mutilating the work. For what we now have is not a fair abridgment of that Synopsis, but rather selections from it without any regard to dates or the succession of events, and without any discrimination as to what was taken, or as to what was suppressed. Cedrenus himself was bad enough. His writings show him to have been little better than a fool; but those who tore his book to pieces in this cruel way are still worse. In short, Cedrenus's work, as we now have it, is a mass of sweepings,—a mere piece of patchwork, in which there is both what is false and what is true. In this hodge-podge (faragine) I have found many things which I consider to be from Eusebius; some of which Cedrenus took from Syncellus, and gave as if the latter had taken them from Eusebius; and some of which, although not given by Cedrenus as if taken from Eusebius, are nevertheless evidently derived from him, as we may infer from what we see in Syncellus and other writers. The Synopsis of Cedrenus was, I consider, reduced by the book-butchers to its present condition not long after the writer's death. But even what the condensers had selected, has not come down to us quite in the state they left it."

Jerome, in his preface to what is called "his Translation" of Eusebius's Chronicon, says, after alluding to the general difficulties which he experienced in translating Greek: "Is there a peculiar propriety in the use of some one word, I cannot find one to express it, and when I seek to complete the sense by a long circumlocution, I scarcely hit the meaning of the single word. Then come the abrupt transitions—the differences of cases in the two languages—the varieties of metaphors employed; and, in short, the mode of expression peculiar to each tongue. If I attempt a literal translation it has a stupid sound. If I am obliged to alter anything in the order or the language, I shall be considered to have neglected the duty of translator. I must therefore beg of you to read as friends, and not as critics, whatever inaccuracies you find, especially as I have dictated the work to an amanuensis, and, as you know, with very great rapidity." And again: "The fresh matter that I have introduced I have taken from other highly approved writers. For I wish it to be known, that I am to some extent both author and translator in this work. I have not only been most careful to give all that is in the Greek, but I have also added things of myself which it appeared to me that Eusebius had passed over, especially about Roman affairs, which he seems, I do not say to have been unacquainted with, for he was an extremely well-informed writer, but to have only slightly alluded to, as being unimportant to the eastern nations for whom he wrote. . . . . From the Trojan war, for instance, to the twentieth year of Constantine, I have appended and interpolated many things (nunc addita nunc mixta sunt plurima), which I took from Tranquillus and the rest of the historians of distinction." Scaliger confirms one portion of this statement, when he indulgently says, in his Prolegomena, prefixed to this work of Jerome's: "It seems that when Jerome was dictating the translation of Eusebius's Chronicon, his attention was divided at the same moment between his amanuensis and the writing of other things, so that this distinguished man necessarily made blunders, as any one else would have done in such a case, and blunders, moreover, which now-a-days would be considered inexcusable in any one with the humblest pretensions to classical knowledge, and which would be regarded not as accidental mistakes, but as culpable acts of ignorance or negligence. Of the infinite instances of this I select a few of the more important, and it is truly wonderful how such a thing could happen in such an age, when the Greek language was more or less used almost everywhere." And again: "Never did any work come to our hands blotted over with so many extensive corrections, overspread with so many inaccuracies, and so marvellously corrupt as are the MSS. of this Latin Chronicon of Jerome's."

Father Tillemont makes the same remarks as Ceillier: "St. Jerome translated Eusebius's Chronicon into Latin," (says he, *art.* Eusebius) "or rather, he has converted it into a new work." And again: "Every one acknowledges that there are a great many errors in what we have now-a-days as Eusebius's Chronicon by Jerome, whether through the negligence of Eusebius himself, or through that of his copyists, to whom Dodwell attributes all the discrepancies that we find between this Latin work and the history."

Cardinal Baronius, in his Annals, (A.D. 325, paragraph 215,) is foremost in acknowledging that the errors and corruptions of this Latin work are incalculably great—that they occasioned him a greater amount of labour than almost any other ecclesiastical record, and that the whole work, a "Labyrinth of Error," (Labyrinthus erroris) as he calls it, was altered even in form from what it originally must have been.

It is now a century and a half ago since Dr. Cave challenged the Roman clergy to produce, even from Scaliger's fragmentary and hypothetical copy of the Greek Chronicon, the alleged statement about the second year of Claudius and the Five-and-Twenty years, "no such thing," he truly says, "being to be found in this Greek copy of Eusebius," (Cave, Antiquit. Apost., *art.* Peter;) since which time no one has ever pretended to produce Greek words to the effect in question.

Thus, it has been seen that we neither have the original Greek text of Eusebius's Chronicon, nor any document by which we can know what was or what was not stated in that original Greek text. Another consideration, however, connected with this point, shows that there could have been no such statement in the Chronicon, or that even if there had been, Eusebius considered it inaccurate. It is admitted on all hands, that the Chronicon was written by Eusebius *before* the History—that the History is of the two the more copious and more correct record, and that it was subsequently drawn from the materials set down by date in the Chronicon. Even if the Chronicon, therefore, had contained the statement in question, its not being repeated in the History would alone show that it was not to be depended on, and either that Eusebius had discovered it to be false after having written it in the Chronicon, or that it was the mere interpolation of some copyists. On this point Father Ceillier, in speaking of the History by Eusebius, says: " Eusebius had already written a history of the church in his Chronicon, but it was too short in that work. . . . . He therefore undertook the task again, to make a more copious and more accurate one (plus ample et plus correcte). . . . Eusebius has incorporated in one work all those detached statements of the Chronicon, and has left us a complete history of all that occurred most important in the church (ce qui s'était passé de plus considérable dans l'église) during nearly 325 years. . . . Socrates, Sozomen, and Theodoret, who wrote the history of the church after Eusebius, saw that there was nothing more to add to what he had written, and so began where he left off." (Vol. iv. p. 256-7.) The later and completerwork is thus evident. But, as I have said, no such Greek passage of the Chronicon exists, nor even the slightest reason for supposing that it ever did, the words in Jerome's translation supposed to refer to a journey, being evidently derived from Euseb. ii. 14.

The Correspondent in the *Times* and Father M'Corry were not aware, it is to be supposed, of all the facts now stated, when they last year cited a passage from Jerome's Latin Chronicon, and represented it as a passage from either some Greek or Latin Chronicon of Eusebius; and there can be no doubt that they will consider it incumbent upon them to take an early opportunity, without waiting to be called upon, of publicly undeceiving those whom, in this most important particular, they have inadvertently so grossly deceived.

To revert then to the main subject of our iniquiry. I have said, that as Eusebius lived *nine or ten* generations after the event in question, his merely asserting it, without having the testimony of any previous writer in support of his assertion, would have constituted no evidence of it. I have now shown that he not only adduces no testimony in support of it, but that he nowhere asserts it. And I beg the special attention of the reader to this point. In Part I. it has been seen that none of the writers that now remain to us from the centuries preceding Eusebius mention Peter's having left the East. In Part II. every passage has been analysed in which the Greek historian is said to have asserted that he did; and it has been seen not only that there is no such assertion contained in any one of them, but that the Roman clergy themselves admit that there is not; which fact, together with the silence of Eusebius as to any prior testimony, affords the strongest possible corroboration to the whole of Part I. It now remains to see what allusions subsequent writers have made to the isolated conjecture—the unhistorical and untraditional EOIKE,—that Eusebius alone has suggested on the subject.

PART III.

THE POSTNICENE RECORDS.

I.

THE EMPEROR JULIAN THE APOSTATE (A.D. 361) is represented in the works of St. Cyril, archbishop of Alexandria, (A.D. 440,) nearly a century after Julian's time, as having said that Peter's monumental urn *was in the habit of being carried about from city to city by the Christians* while St. John the Evangelist was alive, and that St. John did not begin to write his gospel until he heard of this. This statement not only has nothing in it about Rome, but, if we may rely upon it, indicates quite a new solution of those allusions which we find in Eusebius, and two or three other later Fathers, to the supposed existence of Peter's relics in that city. "It was, I suppose," says Julian, "after receiving information, privately no doubt, but still after receiving information, that Paul's and Peter's monumental records were being carried about from city to city, (τᾶ μνηματα Πετρου και Παυλου περιφερομενα,) that St John first began to write his gospel." (Cyril Alex. adv. Jul. lib. 10, in init.) There is not the least imaginable pretext for supposing that this passage could have more reference to Rome than to Constantinople where Julian lived, or to Jerusalem, or to any other Christian city; but far from it. It is, as I say, one of the passages in the patristic records that might (if attentively considered) most effectually undeceive those who imagine that, as Peter's relics were sometimes said to have been in Europe, it was therefore evident that Peter himself had not been put to death at Babylon.

II.

EUTROPIUS, (before A.D. 400,) a Roman historian, says of Nero that it was at his instigation, and in consequence of the persecution which he had set on foot, that St. Peter was put to death at Babylon, as is indicated in Scripture, and Paul at Rome, as we learn from other sources. "At length," says Eutropius, "to all his other crimes, he added this, that he butchered the holy apostles Peter and Paul." (Eutrop. Hist. lib. 7.) It is not easy to see upon what principle such words as these are supposed to refer to the conjecture of Eusebius, that Peter might have been put to death in Europe. For though it is true that Nero was not then with the army on the Euphrates, yet it is not pretended that the Emperor used his own hands in the butcheries of this persecution on these occasions, nor that his emissaries did not find their way into Babylon while it was going on. We learn from the younger Pliny and Tertullian, that he caused THE CHRISTIANS TO BE LOOKED FOR wherever they could be found; and this fact is now fully admitted by the Roman clergy. Father Palma, for instance, as has been already mentioned, says, that "this notion (of Nero's persecution being confined to Rome) is manifestly false, and utterly at variance with the history of those times." And, accordingly, Father Dufresnoy admits, (as may be seen in the section on Lactantius,) that an expression of the kind here used by Eutropius does not indicate where either Paul or Peter was put to death, and that we must depend for these points upon other sources.

III.

ATHANASIUS (A.D. 373) was not thought, even by Baronius, to afford evidence of Peter's having been in Europe. Yet in "The Apology for evading his Persecutors," this distinguished Father is supposed by Bishop Pearson, though by him only, to hint at that most improbable conjecture of Eusebius, about Peter's having been put to death in Europe; but any one can see that Athanasius does not make any allusion that could be so interpreted. He merely refers to the account given of Paul and Peter in the New Testament, (and says he does so,) where the one is commissioned to bear witness of the Saviour in the Jewish cities of the earth, which all agree were not in Europe, (Matt. x. 6, 23, also xxviii. 19; John xxi. 15, &c.; Gal. ii. 7, &c.) and the other at Rome, (Acts xxiii. 11.) Athanasius's words are: "Peter, although he concealed himself through fear of the Jews, (Acts xii.,) and Paul, although he escaped from Damascus in a basket, (2 Cor. xi. 32 and 33,) yet, when they heard *such words as* 'You must bear witness of me at Rome,' did not look upon a residence in foreign lands as a thing too terrible. On the contrary, when they did leave Judæa, it was in the greatest spirits; and the one hastening to the Jews, (*in some* MSS. 'to his own people,') anticipated his predicted martyrdom among them with delight, (2 Peter, i. 14,) while the other, when the occasion came, did not recoil from it, but rejoiced, saying: 'I am now ready to be offered, and the time of my departure is at hand,'" (2 Tim. iv. 6.) Surely it cannot be pretended that it is here said that Peter ever came into Europe, nor even that he left Jerusalem for the purpose of going there. Is it not here said, on the contrary, that he did not?—that he went, as directed by his master, to the lost sheep of the house of Israel, to some Jewish district,—some city such as Babylon, filled with his own people, and with the associations of his ancestors,—in which he himself says, that he was about to suffer the kind of crucifixion which our Lord had predicted for him at the hands of the Jews. We know that Athanasius, notwithstanding the construction of his sentence, does not mean to say that the very summons above quoted was addressed to Peter as well as to Paul. That we know from the New Testament, and we cannot suffer anything to contradict such knowledge. Luke's words (Acts xxiii. 11) are addressed exclusively to Paul; but as may be seen in the texts above referred to, words of similar import about the East were addressed to Peter; to the one—"Thou must bear witness of me at Rome;" to the other—"Thou must bear witness of me in the cities of Israel, among the lost sheep that have no shepherd." This is the Scripture account. There is here, therefore, no allusion to the conjecture of Eusebius, or to any other account of Peter than that given in the New Testament, as Athanasius himself will be found to intimate in those very paragraphs. We cannot wonder, therefore, to find that even Baronius does not pretend to say that this Father thought the apostle was in Europe.

VI.

PHILASTRIUS, (A.D. 380,) an obscure bishop, not known of what place, in a little tract upon "The Heresies," alludes to the story about the Fiery Chariot of the Gnostics, of which Arnobius tells us, "It was seen by the Romans to have been scattered by the breath of Peter;" but he seems to have inferred from this circumstance that Rome itself was the scene of the phenomenon, and to have supposed that there were neither Roman soldiers nor Romans of any description in any other part of the empire except at Rome. It is unnecessary to discuss such an extravagant supposition as this, as I know of none of the Roman clergy who entertain it. But even Philastrius does not say that Peter was personally present. He only mentions his prayers: "When the impostor left Samaria, to escape from Simon Peter, and came to Rome, and had there to wrestle in Nero's very presence with the apostle, he was overpowered on all sides by the apostle's PRAYERS, and was struck by an angel, and perished as he deserved to perish." (De Hæres. c. xxx.) It will be seen at once that we have here (if there be any who still require it) a large accession of evidence that the story about the fiery chariot was an allegory among the ancients, and not, as some think, an ecclesiastical miracle. For he mentions it as having occurred in the reign of Nero, as well as upon the occasion mentioned by Arnobius, in the reign of Claudius; and if (as Father M‘Corry and the Correspondent in the *Times* pretend) there had really been a flaming chariot and four wild horses, with wings of fire, passing on this occasion over the highest pinnacles of the imperial city, is it to be believed that the most insignificant writer—even Philastrius—would speak of it in such terms as these—as a mere wrestling in the presence of Nero? Is it not quite evident that he would not? Is it not quite evident that he would advert to the very unusual phenomena of a fiery phaeton and flying horses, and the wings of these aerial horses supporting all that mass, to raise which even for ten minutes into the air would have been much more of a miracle than to make it fall. Besides, as I have said before, even if it had been one of these ecclesiastical miracles, why suppose that Peter's prayers at Babylon, or at Jerusalem, would not have taken effect at Rome? Why suppose the necessity of his presence in order to have had the advantage of his prayers? Is there not something, to say the least of it, most uncalled for in such a supposition? But, independently of this consideration, and still assuming the reality of the phenomenon in question, Peter's part is—as was shown in the section on Arnobius—abundantly explained by the doctrines of the apostle, disseminated among the Gentiles at Rome in the Κήρυγμα Πέτρου, which was published against the Gnostic heresy, during the reign of Claudius, and in the Christian church—the Chair of Peter—that had been estab-

lished there during the lifetime of Tiberius, even before
this heresy had ever been heard of, and whose prayers
might very appropriately have been spoken of as "Peter's
prayers." That the story, however, was considered as
a mere allegory by Philastrius and the writers of his
time, is further confirmed by Epiphanius, the celebrated contemporary of this very obscure writer. For
Epiphanius also wrote a work upon the Heresies, a much
longer one than that of Philastrius, and he gives in it a
long narrative about the Gnostic chief at Rome,—a narrative covering some folio pages,—yet he never once
alludes to a chariot in the air, nor to Peter's being in
Europe at the time, nor to its being supposed by any
one that he was.

V.

St. Cyril, archbishop of Jerusalem, (A.D. 386,) is relied
upon by Father M'Corry, as affording very distinct and
positive evidence that Peter must have left the East:
because Cyril, in mentioning the fiery chariot of the
Gnostics, not only says that it was overthrown by the
prayers of Peter, as Arnobius and Philastrius had said
before him, but states positively (which they had not)
that Peter was present at the time, and on his knees at
prayer while the fiery chariot was careering in mid air
above his head. Over and above the fact which seems
to have escaped Father M'Corry, that Cyril (like the
one or two other Fathers who mention it) does not make
Europe the scene of this narrative at all, the narrative itself proves at once, with overwhelming evidence,
that the whole story is, as has been already shown, a
mere allegory; for the archbishop alters the details in
three most important particulars, and apparently under
the impression that he was at full liberty to do so to any
extent he pleased. He tells us that Paul was present
on the occasion as well as Peter; that the impostor was
a dragon, instead of a man; and that his aerial chariot

was drawn by devils instead of horses. Now, there can
be no doubt that if these were the facts of an ecclesiastical miracle, and not of a mere allegory, the archbishop
of Jerusalem would have considered it incumbent on him
to state his authority for deviating so widely from all
preceding writers on so remarkable a subject. His statement, after mentioning the occurrence related in the
Acts (chap. viii.) and the statue erected at Rome, thus
proceeds: "But when this heresy first began to spread,
Peter and Paul, the presidents of the Christian church,
came forward and showed that this worshipped Samaritan was a mortal. For he having announced that he
would rise to heaven, and having been borne aloft in a
chariot of devils, the apostles upon their knees, and exhibiting that unity of spirit which renders prayer available, shot at the enchanter with the arrow of concord
through that prayer, and struck him to the earth. This
was the first dragon of the heresy; but, as soon as one
head was cut off," &c. &c. I repeat that we have here
the most conclusive evidence possible that the story is
an allegory. But even if we had not this, even if it
were all a literal fact, the archbishop of Jerusalem is
not (we see) one of the writers who say that it was in
Europe it took place; a point strangely overlooked by
Father M'Corry, who would otherwise have seen that
this statement, in whatever way we view it, does not (as
he supposes) make it appear that Peter left the East.

VI.

St. Ambrose, bishop of Milan, (a.d. 397,) does not say
anywhere one word about Peter's having been at Rome.
Baronius and Bellarmine thought he did, and refer us
to two sermons attributed in their day to Ambrose, one
on the Nativity of the Apostles, and the other against
Auxentius; but all the Roman-catholic writers are now
agreed, that the bishop of Milan did not write these
sermons. On this point Fathers Richard and Giraud

say: "With regard to the sermons attributed to St. Ambrose, there is not, according to the Benedictine Fathers, a single one of them that was written by him," (Biblioth. Sacr., *art.* Ambrose;) and Father Ceillier makes the same remark. But, in addition to this, it is to be observed, that in the sermon against Auxentius there is not one word at all about Peter's having been at Rome. The Benedictine monks themselves, who closely examined the text and its MSS., acknowledge that there is not; and have even gone so far as to confess that the name of "Rome" had been dishonestly interpolated, so as to connect it with the absurd incidents mentioned in that sermon; but that, even if the writer of the sermon, whoever he was, had so written, the statement was wholly unauthenticated by any previous writer, and ought not, therefore, to be believed. The passage in question refers to a scene supposed to have taken place at the walls of Babylon, on the eve of Peter's crucifixion there, and tells us, that although anxious to die, yet yielding to the tears of his disciples, he escaped from prison, and endeavoured to hide himself. "He was," says the writer of the sermon, "just getting outside the walls at night, when, seeing his Divine Master appear to him at the gate, as if he was going into the city, he said, 'Lord, whither goest thou?' The Saviour's answer was, 'I am coming to my second crucifixion,' (venio iterum crucifigi,) which words Peter understood to allude to his own death, as predicted by our Lord; for Christ could not be crucified a second time." At the words, "venio iterum crucifigi," the Benedictine monks have written in their Paris edition of Ambrose, A.D. 1790: "The old editions have it thus, and all the MSS., except very few, in which the word 'Romam' is interpolated in a modern hand, (posterior aliqua manus 'Romam' addidit;) and this word has also found its way into the text of the Roman edition. As to the apparition, however, of our Lord to Peter, you will not find it mentioned by any ancient writer except Hegesippus the Spurious, (lib. iii.,) and Gregory, (in Psal. Pœnit.)"

VII.

St. Optatus, bishop of Milevis, in Numidia (at the end of the fourth century), merely reiterates what had been said upwards of a century before by Cyprian, another African bishop, about Peter's Chair being in the Church at Rome, as well as in all the other orthodox churches of the earth; for the orthodoxy of the Roman church was a constant subject of dispute upon the other side of the Mediterranean. All the addition that Optatus makes is, that in order to enforce the expression, he once or twice speaks of it as "the Chair in which Peter sat," instead of merely "Peter's Chair;" and some of the Roman clergy think (or shall I not rather say, endeavour to think) that this marks with more certainty than Cyprian's words did, that the apostle must have come into Europe; that the "Chair" in question was something in Europe, which was not in the East; and that as Peter occupied it he must have been in Europe. But this is an argument of which (as may be seen in the section upon Cyprian) the Roman clergy have for centuries acknowledged the unsoundness and the absurdity. It will be there seen that the "Chair" in which the apostle sat was, as St. Jerome states, a mere figurative expression, to denote either the doctrine which Peter and the apostles taught, or the authority with which they were invested to teach it; and that, as St. Gregory the Great distinctly tells us, Peter filled no capacity in this respect with regard to Rome, or, as Father M'Corry terms it, "sat in" nothing there, that he did not equally "sit in," and equally fill, and moreover at the same time, at Alexandria; yet we know that Peter never was at Alexandria any more than he was at Rome; and with this authority, or in this "Chair," Baronius admits that Peter "sat" in all the churches in the world. (Cum negari non possit Petrum suâ auctoritate, quâ universi gregis pastorem agit, omnibus Christiani orbis ecclesiis PRÆSIDERE. Annals, A.D. 39, paragraph 20.) This was also the doctrine of Cyprian and Optatus, and in general of the African and the Roman bishops, as the Roman-catholic bishop Aubespine explains in his Commentary upon Optatus. They considered that Peter's Chair was in every orthodox church in Christendom, and, of course, in the church of Alexandria, of Carthage, and of Rome, as well as in that at Jerusalem and elsewhere; in other words, that the chairs in all the churches, from the Euphrates to the Thames, had been conferred upon Peter by our Lord before they had been occupied by their respective bishops, and, therefore, that he had "sat in" every one of them. They considered, for instance, as did Cardinal Baronius and the Roman-catholic bishop Aubespine, that the episcopal chair in England had been conferred upon Peter before it had been occupied by any of the English bishops; that therefore Peter was the first who sat in it, and that the first English bishop was his immediate successor. And this is the doctrine to which we find St. Gildas alluding, soon after the time of Optatus, when he speaks of the chair in England as one in which Peter sat.

The passage from Optatus is addressed to the leader of a refractory African sect, that were called the Donatists, and is as follows:—" You cannot deny that you know that the chair in which the bishops sit, in the city of Rome, was conferred upon Peter before it belonged to any one else;—that in that chair therefore Peter was the first who sat, and that in that chair Linus succeeded him," (lib. ii. c. 2 and 3.) The learned Aubespine, who was bishop of Orleans, in 1600, and who enjoyed the highest reputation in his church, says in his commentary upon this passage, that the chair here meant by Optatus was "that which our Lord himself occupied, which was given by him to Peter, and which Peter imparted to every bishop in the world, ay, and still imparts to them." (Christi Cathedra—quam Petrus accepit a Christo—

quam singulis episcopis communicavit Petrus, et singulis etiam nunc diebus communicat.)

Father Dupin also, in his commentary upon the same passage of Optatus, explains this African doctrine of Peter's being said to have sat in all the chairs of Christendom before the various bishops occupied them, by observing that the chair in which Peter sat consisted of all the different chairs in all the different cities, just as we say that the church of Christ consists of all the different local churches. (Singulæ cathedræ inter se dici possunt una cathedra, sicut plures ecclesiæ sunt una ecclesia. In Opt. ii. 2.)

Such, then, is the chair in which Eulogius sat at Alexandria, while St. Gregory the Great was sitting in it at Rome, and in which Damasus was sitting at Rome, while St. Optatus sat in it at Milevis, in Numidia—Peter having first sat in all these chairs. I do not here stay to canvass this doctrine of the African and Roman Fathers; but is it, I ask, common sense to say that it is a proof that Peter must have left the East?

VIII.

THE OLD ROMAN CALENDAR, (assigned to the beginning of the 5th century,) published first by Father Boucher (Latinè, Bucherius) A.D. 1600, and half a century afterwards by Father Henschenius, the Bollandist, states that immediately upon our Lord's ascension, and while Tiberius was still emperor, Peter took upon himself to act at Jerusalem as general bishop of all the Christian churches wherever they were planted; that he acted in this capacity with reference to the capital of the empire, for twenty-five years, one month, and nine days—(*i. e.*, until Paul went there upon his appeal to Nero, and Paul's friend Linus was made local bishop of the church there;) that it was not until about ten years after Linus's local episcopate began, that Peter was crucified by the Jews at Babylon, and that this occurred in Nero's reign upon the same occasion as St. Paul was put to death at Rome. On this statement Father M'Corry and the Correspondent in the *Times* rely as one of the most remarkable proofs of Peter's having left the East in the reign of Claudius, and of his having been a resident local European bishop for five-and-twenty years.

It has been already shown in Part II., section ii., that the Roman clergy have acknowledged for centuries that this old hypothesis of Cardinal Baronius, about the reign of Claudius and the Five-and-Twenty years, was utterly untenable and preposterous. That fact, therefore, is a sufficient answer to the supposition that this exploded theory is contained in the foregoing statement, if the foregoing statement could possibly have contained it. But what such a statement can have to do with proving that Europe was Peter's head-quarters for five-and-twenty years, it is no very easy matter to imagine; for no one pretends or ever has pretended, that the apostle appeared in Europe in the reign of Tiberius, upon the ascension of our Lord, at which time he is said to have had the episcopate of Rome; and Father Henschenius, who was a Jesuit of great learning and celebrity in his church, even takes pains to guard the reader against supposing that the general episcopate, described in this old Roman Calendar, has anything whatever to do with the local episcopate of Rome, although Roman consulships, and the reigns of Roman emperors are employed as dates to indicate the duration of it.

The Calendar in question is entitled "A list of the high-priests of Rome," and begins with the three following paragraphs:—

"Our Lord was put to death in the reign of Tiberius, on the 8th of the Calends of April, during the consulship of the two Gemini; and immediately after His ascension, the most blessed Peter undertook the episcopate. From which time it is here set down in regular succession, who was bishop of Rome, how many years each presided over that church, and under whose reign each did so.

"Peter, twenty-five years, one month, nine days. His episcopate was in the reigns of Tiberius, Caligula,

Claudius, and Nero; from the consulship of Vinicius and Longinus (A.D. 30) until that of Nerva and Vestinus, (A.D. 65.) He was put to death (on the same occasion as Paul) on the 3rd of the Calends of July, during this latter consulship, in the reign of Nero.

"Linus, twelve years, four months, ten days. His episcopate was in the time of Nero, from the consulship of Saturninus and Scipio (A.D. 56) to that of Capito and Rufus," (A.D. 67.)

The only commentary required here is that of Father Henschenius, who remarks on the first of these three paragraphs: "As is mentioned in this preamble, St. Peter undertook the episcopate after Christ's Ascension; but WITHOUT ITS BEING LIMITED TO ANY GIVEN CITY," (sed nulli certo loco adstrictum,) than which nothing could be more pointed or explicit; and that afforded by a passage in Eusebius (ii. 22), from which we learn that the year in which Linus's local episcopate began (*i. e.* in which Peter's general episcopate ended) at Rome, was that in which St. Paul arrived there from the East. It is thus translated by Jerome: "In the twenty-fifth year after our Lord's Passion, that is, in the second year of Nero's reign, Paul is sent bound to Rome." (Scrip. Eccles., *art.* Paul.) The old Roman Calendar, then, (which, with copious notes, is inserted in the Acta Sanctorum, in the beginning of the first volume for April,) affords not the slightest ground for supposing that Peter left the East for a single hour, much less for the episcopate of five-and-twenty years. Upon this point it says the exact contrary of what Father M'Corry and the Correspondent in the *Times* imagine, and was always known to have said the exact contrary. For it says that the episcopate which Peter held was a general one—was, for instance, that of the English and Grecian churches, of Antioch and Babylon, of Ephesus, of Alexandria, and of Ancona, as well as of Rome; that it lasted for thirty-five years after the Ascension, *i.e.*, as long as he lived, but that it terminated in the case of each church upon the establishment there of the first local bishop; that this occurred, in the case of Rome, on St. Paul's arrival there, twenty-five years after the Ascension, and ten years before Peter's martyrdom at Babylon; that his Roman episcopate therefore was nearly half over before the second year of Claudius; that after the second year of Claudius it lasted but fifteen years; and that, not being of a local character, the apostle was able to fulfil its functions while he was living at Jerusalem and Babylon. Thus, I repeat, the old Roman Calendar, published by Bucherius, flatly contradicts Father M'Corry and the Correspondent in the *Times* upon the very point which they brought it forward to prove; and yields not in any other respect the shadow of a pretext for supposing that Peter ever left the East; but, on the contrary, shows very clearly that whoever drew up that document in the fifth century had never heard of such a supposition.

IX.

EPIPHANIUS, (A.D. 403,) bishop of Constantia, in Cyprus, is the earliest writer who applies the term "bishop" to St. Peter. Upon the faith of the old Roman Calendar he says that this apostle was considered a bishop at Rome before Linus; and from this expression Bishop Pearson thought it probable that Epiphanius supposed Peter had left the East. Bishop Pearson it is true does not much press this inference, and none of the Roman-catholic writers cite the passage as affording any evidence respecting Peter's movements. Nevertheless, as this is one of the expressions which are liable to mislead the general reader, I shall seek to obviate this effect of it by suggesting the following reflections:—

1. According to the old Roman Calendar, which existed in his day, and was then the highest authority respecting the annals of the Roman church, Epiphanius considered that Peter was bishop at Rome during the ten or twelve first years after the Ascension, a period during which, it is admitted on all hands that Peter was in the East. How then does his being considered bishop at Rome afterwards show that he must have left the

East afterwards, or make it at all probable that Epiphanius thought he did? But that this writer did not mean to imply this in the expression that he uses is further evident from the fact (already alluded to) that he wrote at considerable length about the Gnostic contest with the church at Rome, which occurred in Peter's lifetime, and which is the great alleged occasion of the apostle's having been bishop of that church, yet does not in that very, minute account of Roman matters, give the least hint that Peter ever left the East.

2. Even the being considered as the local bishop of any given city does not imply (and never did) the being resident there, as the Roman clergy themselves are foremost in admitting, and as all who are conversant with ecclesiastical language well know. There are, for instance, everybody is aware, several bishops in the Roman church—the titular bishops—who never in their lives went near the places of which they are said to be bishops. No one, for instance would think it a very rational conclusion to infer that the Bishop of Melipotamus ever made a single excursion to that Eastern see from the mere fact of his being spoken of and considered as the bishop there. Is the Correspondent in the *Times* not aware of this? And it is the same with regard to Rome and the apostle. Cardinal Bellarmine says, honestly, that the being bishop at Rome does not imply one's having ever been in one's life in that city. "It is evident," says the discerning Cardinal, "that Peter's having been at Rome is not essential to his having been bishop there; for many who were bishops at Rome, never resided at Rome, such as Clement V., John XXII., Benedict XII., Clement VI., and Innocent VI., who were ordained in France, and in France lived all their lives," (Bellar. de Summo Pontif. lib. ii. c. 1,)—a just and ingenuous avowal, which proves this eminent controversialist to have considered that his church was independent of all the evanescent reasons suggested by its clergy for supposing that St. Peter made a journey into Europe. Father Hardouin, and several others of the Roman clergy were, it will be remem-

bered, of the same opinion as Cardinal Bellarmine. "We need not try to make out that Peter went to Rome," says the learned Jesuit, Hardouin, "in order to show that the Pope is his successor." (Romam venisse Petrum necesse non est, ut sit summus Pontifex Petri successor. Quippe qui proprie Episcopus Romanus sive solius urbis Romæ non sit.) On this principle also all the Roman-catholic historians construct their catalogues of the Roman bishops. They speak of Peter as succeeding Christ, and Linus as succeeding Peter, where there is as much reason for inferring that our Lord was at Rome, and local bishop there, like Linus, as that Peter was; and these historians always mention in their catalogues, with the rest, the five bishops of Rome, who, from A.D. 1305 to A.D. 1367, resided constantly in France, at Avignon, and were never able to go to Rome at all. All this may be seen illustrated in the "Chronologia Reformata," by Riccioli, the learned Jesuit of the 17th century. In the ninth book of this distinguished work, he gives his "Catalogus Pontificum Romanorum," which begins with the statement, "Peter succeeded Christ immediately after the Ascension." (Petrus successit Christo statim ab ascensione.) Then follows Linus, and in due order among the rest the five bishops of Rome that never even saw that city. Thus even if the apostle has been considered as local bishop of Rome, this does not show that he had ever left the East.

3. But the apostle never was considered, and never was, a local bishop of Rome. By those Fathers who most frequently speak of him as an Italian bishop, he was also considered to be at the same time bishop of all the Eastern and of the remotest European churches. None of them ever speak of him as bishop of the church in Italy, in any other sense than as they speak of him as bishop of the church in these Islands and of the church in Egypt. The reader ought not to allow his attention to be diverted from this point, as a good deal of the misapprehension he may have laboured under respecting such expressions as that of Epiphanius arises from con-

founding a general episcopate, such as that attributed to St. Peter, with a local one, such as that of Eulogius, at Alexandria, or that of Gregory the Great at Rome. The whole world, we are told by the Fathers of the fifth century, was Peter's diocese. That is the common language of that period, although language not heard of until then. This is what Epiphanius says when he speaks of Rome as having no other bishops but the apostles until Paul's friend Linus was appointed by Paul five-and-twenty years after the Ascension (p. 56, 231.) St. Augustin says the same thing, when he remarks that "Peter received the whole world for his diocese." (Totum mundum Petrus accepit. August., vol. iv. p. 1161.) Theodoret, in the passage where he says that "Paul's Chair" (Θρονος) was at Rome, yet that Paul was looked upon "as a general founder of all the churches, and as a universal teacher of the truth in all," says that Peter likewise stood in this general relation to ALL the churches. (Κοινοι Πατερες και διδασκαλοι της αληθειας. Theodoret's Epistle to Pope Leo, the 113th Epistle.) The same thing is stated, as has been seen, in the old Roman Calendar, and is to be found in various other writings after the commencement of the fifth century. Thus, then, Peter was at this time considered as bishop of the whole world. He was bishop, therefore, of every part of the world, as well as of the whole of it. He was called so, and was considered so. But this does not prove that he was personally present in every part of it—and therefore it does not prove that he was personally present in any one given part of it (say, England, Egypt, or Italy), however much that one given part of it may be found, from the difficulties of its position, to surpass other parts in the vehemence and reiteration with which it declared him to be its bishop.

The words of Epiphanius occur where he mentions the order in which the earlier bishops were considered to have succeeded one another in the ancient capital of the Empire: "At Rome, Peter and Paul were the first— bishops and apostles at the same time—then Linus,"&c.

And again: "The succession of the bishops at Rome is in this order—Peter and Paul, Linus," &c. (Epiph. adv. Hæres., lib. i. Hæres. 27.)

X.

PRUDENTIUS, a Spanish poet (about A.D. 406), is supposed by Baronius to allude, in one of his Latin poems, to the conjecture hazarded by Eusebius, upon the discovery in the Catacombs, during the fourth century, of some mixed and broken relics, supposed by Sylvester the then bishop of Rome, to have been those of Peter. But it is very doubtful whether the poet ever heard of this conjecture, or whether he meant anything more by his poetical allusion than that some of Peter's relics were thought to be deposited in his *Martyrium* at Rome, although there were none in his *Martyrium* at Constantinople. The words of Prudentius may be thus translated: "One day saw them both die (*i.e.* Peter and Paul), but with the interval of one whole year. The marsh of the Tiber knows the ground dedicated to their two trophies, and is a witness thus both of the cross and of the sword; for the two showers of blood that sprinkled these, found their way through the herbage of the self-same marsh. . . . Yes, the Tiber divides their bones." (Pruden. Peristeph. 12.) The poet's somewhat fantastic object seems to be to combine a sort of unity with separation, which leads him to make two statements that the church of Rome denies. One day, says he, saw them die, but with the interval of a year; one spot received their relics (or their showers of blood), but with the Tiber flowing between the two. The church of Rome considers that they died on the same day, and that after death their relics were always united. Whether the poet here means their martyrdom, or merely the interment of their relics, depends upon the sense that we give to the "two showers of blood" (bis imber sanguinis), which, applied to Peter, is in any sense as far-fetched as anything can well be; and will, therefore, quite as appropriately represent his relics as it would his bloodless crucifixion. But it is of little importance which sense we give these words. The conjecture of Eusebius, in the fourth century, would gain no credit from its having been seized upon as a *fact* by a Spanish poet in the fifth. We know that the idlest fictions of mythology are mentioned as facts by the Greek and Latin poets, and are allowed to be so mentioned, without its being thought by any one necessary to contradict or to believe them. I know of no one, except Baronius and Bellarmine, who has adduced this poet as a competent witness—a witness sufficiently early, sufficiently well-informed, and sufficiently exact, to give credibility to the conjecture, that Peter was *not* put to death at Babylon, although he himself says that he was living there in daily expectation of that event. Yet that we must not look for historical accuracy in the poems of Prudentius, is proved even by Cardinal Baronius himself, who tells us that we must not implicitly rely upon this poet for anything, and least of all for the particulars of Peter's crucifixion; that the poet's notion of the period of this event, for instance, is quite wrong (see Annals, A.D. 69, paragraph 3), and (to omit numberless other instances of inaccuracy or ignorance), that in the poem on the martyrdom of St. Hypolitus, Prudentius, with a more than ordinary amount of poetic licence, unites in one person the stories of three very different individuals—a priest, a soldier, and a bishop (see the section of this work on Hypolitus). I appeal to any conscientious reader in communion with the church of Rome, whether he accepts such evidence as this of St. Peter's having left the East? and whether he is not rather shocked than otherwise, that his church should be obliged to have recourse to such a justification of its pretensions?

The verse of Prudentius, which Bellarmine calls proof, is still wider from the mark. It occurs in a hymn upon St. Lawrence:—

> "Avaunt, vile Jupiter!
> Leave Rome her freedom,—leave Christ's people free!
> Paul bids thee hence, the blood of Peter, hence,—
> Yes, Nero's act and thine is now against thee!"

IX.

CHRYSOSTOM (A.D. 407) is cited only by Baronius and Father M'Corry. The former says, "that in the homily upon the martyrdoms of Peter and Paul," this Father says that Peter was residing at Rome, as well as superintending its church. But all the Roman-catholic writers, without exception, are now agreed that this homily was not written by St. Chrysostom. Bernard de Montfaucon, the Benedictine monk, to whose learning and care we are indebted for the last and most splendid edition of this Father's works, says of this homily: "It is the universal opinion of the learned that it is spurious and unworthy the pen of Chrysostom; that the style of it, and everything else belonging to it, makes this manifest—so manifest, in fact, that it is not worth while to lose any more time in proving it." "It is unanimously agreed," says Ceillier, "that the homily on St. Peter's martyrdom is not by St. Chrysostom." (Ceillier on Chrysost. vol. ix.) The fact is, there have been so many documents discovered to be spurious since the times of Cardinal Baronius, that there can be no doubt, if he lived now, he would at once acknowledge that the porposition he defended is untenable.

Father M'Corry acknowledges the spuriousness of this homily, but says that Chrysostom speaks of Peter's *Martyria* at Rome, and speaks as if Peter's relics were there within them. This is true. But Chrysostom speaks also of Peter's *Martyria* at Constantinople, and speaks also as if the apostle inhabited his tombs there as well as those at Rome. This may be seen in the section of this work upon Caius. It is, however, of little moment in this inquiry, whether Chrysostom is here alluding to Peter's relics at all. And if we are to suppose he is, it is equally of little moment whether he only alludes to the popular notion mentioned by St. Augustine, ("Men speak as if Peter's relics were at Rome,") or whether he thought as Father Hardouin and others, that it was only Peter's head that had been sent there from the East, (Petri saltem caput Romam fuisse delatum a Christianis ex Hierosolymis omnino credimus ibique religiose illud coli. Hardouin,) or whether he supposed, with Eusebius, that the complete, though broken skeleton, found in the catacombs by Sylvester, in the reign of Constantine, and supposed to have lain there unnoticed and un-identified for nearly three centuries, was really that of the apostle. Whatever Chrysostom may have thought upon this point, he says nothing that could be laid hold of as denoting that he, like Eusebius, hesitated about the authenticity of Peter's Second Epistle; or that, like him, he inferred from the relics found at Rome, that Peter was not put to death at Babylon, where it is indicated in that Epistle that his death was about to take place.

XII.

St. Jerome, (A.D. 420,) a Latin writer, made some Latin translations from the Greek language, which Father M'Corry and the Correspondent in the *Times* regard as very tolerable evidence of the old exploded hypothesis of Baronius about the reign of Claudius and the Five-and-Twenty Years. For, as I have had occasion already to observe, these two modern writers do not seem to be aware that their church has, for centuries past, been compelled to forego this notion altogether, on account of its extreme absurdity, and on account of the discovery that, notwithstanding the most diligent search, there was not the slightest trace of such a notion in any of the Fathers, nor even anything that could be brought to prop up the hypothesis.

Nor do these writers seem, with regard to Jerome, to be aware of the fact, that in his own works, which are very voluminous, there is not one word to make it appear that he thought Peter had at any period abandoned the East, and his special mission to the lost sheep of the house of Israel. This is quite as extraordinary an inadvertence on the part of these two writers as the former; for they cannot mean to pretend, that although Jerome did not assert the thing in his own writings, he should be thought to assert whatever was mentioned in the works that he translated, or even whatever he supposed to have been mentioned in them; and that, in general, what is stated, or supposed to be stated, in a translation, is to be regarded as the statement of the translator! Surely there is no one who will not admit the necessity of *some* distinction here; no one who will not see at once, that if we would examine this question earnestly and honestly, we are bound to distinguish what Jerome sets down as his own words and his own opinion from what he considers that he sets down as the words and opinion of another.

Nor are these their only oversights. They appear to have neglected, also, to examine into the circumstances connected with the Latin text of the works they quote from, either with regard to their accuracy as translations, or with regard to the precise import of the words employed in the Latin passages they have selected. For if they had done so, they would have found that their own church teaches (and most properly so too) that the accuracy of these works is in no case to be depended on; and that, even if it were, yet the expressions employed did not, in Jerome's day, imply the sense that is attributed to them by these two modern writers, nor are even now considered by the educated clergy of Rome to involve any meaning of this kind.

As all these points have unaccountably escaped the attention of these two writers, it is not impossible that others also may be deceived about them; for which reason it is important that, in a treatise of this description, they should not wholly be passed over. As to the first of them, however, viz., that the Roman clergy now reject *in toto* their old hypothesis about the reign of Claudius and the Five-and-Twenty years, this has been so fully shown in Part II. section ii., that it is unnecessary to enlarge further upon it here. Yet, as evidence of the extent to which these writers have taken information second-hand upon this subject, and of the insufficient study which they have bestowed upon the authorities they have cited, I may here advert to the remarkable fact there exhibited, that all the principal authorities in this matter mentioned by these writers, flatly contradict them upon the hypothesis in question. Take, for instance, the four following:—Father Ceillier says, he does not consider that Peter left the East until the reign of Nero; *i. e.*, until after he had been to Babylon. Baluze, that to suppose him to have left the East earlier, is perfectly preposterous. "Quæ res quam absurda sit," is the unceremonious censure which this learned Roman Catholic addresses to these two writers. Bishop Pearson said he saw no pretext whatever in the Fathers for the hypothesis; and Mr. Barntier, that the learned of all creeds had long ago determined that the thing was utterly false, and utterly at variance with all history, sacred and profane; and these Father M'Corry and the Correspondent in the *Times* refer us to, as four of the ablest authorities on this subject!

The two points which require a brief illustration here are these: 1, That Jerome's original works have nothing in them that in the slightest degree warrants the supposition that he thought Peter ever left the East, BUT THE REVERSE; 2, That the passages quoted from his translations, only mention Peter as being considered bishop at Rome for twenty-five years, and not his having resided there for that time, as is alleged by these two mistaken writers of last year.

1. Almost the only illustration that the first point admits of, is to be found in the fact that no Roman-catholic writer has been able to produce any such passage from his original works, the two which they cite being in his translations; viz., in the *Chronicon*, which he says, in his preface to it, he condensed from various writings, as

R

well as from the Greek text of a Chronicon by Eusebius; and in his *Catalogue* of Ecclesiastical Writers, which he also says, in a preface, was mainly translated from the "Ecclesiastical History" written by this same Greek Father. From each of these two works the Roman clergy, in the days of Baronius, (*i. e.*, literally, *centuries ago*,) used to quote one passage, which they have since withdrawn, on account of the absurdity of the interpretation which, to make these two passages of use, would have been necessary; and, from all the rest of his works, not one single word has at any time been put forward by any writer as a reason for supposing this alleged journey from the East; which blank, it will be granted, could not well have happened if Jerome thought that nearly half of the apostle's life had been spent in Italy. Another consideration, illustrative of this point, is, that Jerome considered Peter to have been put to death at Babylon; a fact in Peter's history which is only recognised by such writers as admit the other fact of Peter's never having left the East; no writers, of any description or of any period, having imagined that the apostle came into Europe in the reign of Claudius, unless they likewise imagined that he had been put to death there. From this also, therefore, we may see that Jerome did not consider that Peter had left the East. It is true that he does not expressly name Babylon as the place where the apostle was put to death, but we know that Jerome did not reject Peter's Second Epistle, in which the apostle mentions his crucifixion as imminent at Babylon; and we know, also, that he did not think the conjecture of Eusebius on the subject worth translating in the memoir of Peter, contained in the Catalogue of Ecclesiastical Writers taken out of the History of Eusebius; which omission is the more remarkable, as he there mentions Peter's relics, found at Rome by St. Sylvester, and Constantine's Church upon the Vatican Hill as one of the repositories in which some of these relics were preserved. He says: "Peter has a tomb upon the Vatican Hill, near the road of Triumph," (sepultus est in Vaticano juxta viam Triumphalem,) and no more;

just as in the memoir of Luke, in the same Catalogue, he says: "Luke was buried at Constantinople," (sepultus est Constantinopoli,) although it is well known that it was not at Constantinople that Luke was put to death, and that his tomb and Peter's were both built by Constantine. He plainly says, however, (as is seen in Part I. section xiv., and Part II. section iii.,) that Peter lived at Babylon; and in one of his letters to Marcella, he distinctly speaks of Peter's martyrdom as not having occurred at the same place as Paul's. Jerome there says: "Why call Jerusalem accursed on account of our Lord's blood having been shed there, while THOSE PARTS OF THE EARTH are considered blessed in which Peter and Paul, the generals of the Christian army, poured forth their blood?" (Benedicta LOCA putant in quibus, &c.) As Jerome, therefore, did not deny that Peter had been put to death at Babylon, we have, from this fact alone, almost as clear an indication that he did not imagine him to have lived five-and-twenty years in Europe, as we have in the other fact of his never having said one word in his own writings on the subject. The attentive and conscientious student will see in what is here said, proof as clear as the distinctest statement on the part of Jerome would have been, that he knew nothing about Peter's having ever left the East.

2. I now proceed to the two passages called "translations." All Roman Catholic scholars are agreed that these passages afford no reason whatever for supposing that Peter left Asia either for twenty-five years, as Cardinal Wiseman and Father M'Corry suppose, or even for a short time in the second year of Claudius, as some of the words used have sometimes been interpreted; and they assign as their reason for this opinion, *first*, that the statement clashed with all history sacred and profane; and *secondly*, that Jerome, who names no authority for the statement, was too late a writer to be himself accepted as authority for it; and all the learned of every creed, even our Bishop Pearson and the German youth Baratier (whose acquaintance with this subject Cardinal Wiseman highly extols) agree upon these

points with the Roman Catholic clergy. This clashing however of the statement with history, and this latencss of Jerome do not constitute the whole truth. The fact is that the passages do not contain the supposed statement at all, and that any reflecting reader can easily see that we have not the smallest ground for saying that they do. They merely tell us that for twenty-five years there was no other Bishop of the Roman Church but Peter, (230, &c.) that his general proclamation of the gospel at Jerusalem extended to the Gentile cities, although his appointed business was with Jewish cities only, [64] that his martyrdom at Babylon took place in Nero's persecution, [42-5] and that it was in the second year of Claudius that the book called "Peter's Preaching" was sent to Rome by the apostle, against the heresy of the Gnostics, (23, 135, 158, &c.)

The only words in these two passages that could in any case be supposed to imply the alleged journey from Babylon, are those respecting his conduct against the Gnostic heresy in the second year of Claudius; and the whole question respecting this portion of these passages is as to whether the Latin terms employed by Jerome—"mittitur" in the one, and "pergit" in the other—are to have the literal sense of "proficiscitur," which Jerome's ignorance of Greek, (p. 215, &c.) might easily have led him to give to the Greek words in Euseb. ii. 14, about the book called "Peter's Preaching," which words it is admitted that he is here translating, or whether they are to bear the ecclesiastical sense of such terms, in which Eusebius himself has there employed the corresponding term χειραγωγει; which will, I think, appear upon reflection to every student of the Fathers the only true interpretation of these words here; for although Jerome's ignorance of Greek was great, he could have known, even from the translations which he used, that the whole passage in Eusebius is a metaphorical one, and he knew that it was in metaphor always that the Fathers spoke of the Gnostic heresy at Rome. That he even intended this sense himself to be placed upon his own words in this passage is clearly proved by his employment of the term "expugnandum." Besides all this, the above and similar words are constantly used in the old Ecclesiastical Historians, both Greek and Latin, in this figurative sense. Nicephorus, for instance, says also of St. Peter's relations with Alexandria in Egypt, that the apostle past on to that church: ἐπὶ τὴν Ἀλεξάνδρου πόλιν μεταβαίνει (xiv. 39) which the Roman Catholic version renders "Alexandriam TRANSIT Petrus," although neither this nor any writer ever pretended to say that Peter went in person to Alexandria.

The passages are, from the "Ecclesiastical Writers:" "Simon Peter, after his Episcopate of the Church of Antioch, and after his proclamation to the Jewish Christians of the Dispersion in Pontus, Galatia, Cappadocia, Asia and Bithynia (see this proclamation, 1 Peter i. 1,) passed on (pergit) to Rome to the storming of Simon Magus in the second year of Claudius, and he also held the sacerdotal chair of that city twenty-five years, until the fourteenth year of Nero, by whom it was that he was crowned with martyrdom," &c. From the "Latin Chronicon:" "In the second year of Claudius, Peter, as soon as he had founded the church of Antioch, is given the mission of Rome (literally 'is sent' to Rome —'*Mittitur*' in all the *MSS.*) and he continues bishop of the same church for twenty-five years, promulgating the gospel there."

Respecting the authority of this "Latin Chronicon," see page 216 of this work. On Jerome's Catalogue of Ecclesiastical Writers, Father Ceillier remarks: "What is certain is that the History of Eusebius afforded Jerome the chief materials for his Catalogue, in which he often merely translated the History, with too much freedom however it must be admitted, and sometimes with too little truth." (A la verité avec trop de liberté et quelquefois même peu fidèlement. Vol. iv. p. 257.)

We see then from what has been said above, that we have no other ground whatever except this undoubted ignorance of Greek on Jerome's part, for supposing him to attribute here to Eusebius the having said that Peter was in Europe in the reign of Claudius. It is true that

we have this single ground for the supposition. But
the conscientious student will consider it more just and
more natural that, of the two interpretations which
Jerome's words admit of, we should suppose him to have
intended that one which the writer intended, whom it is
admitted on all hands that he is here translating.

For the passage from Jerome's List of Ecclesiastical
Writers (*art.* Mark) cited by Bellarmine, respecting
1 Peter, v. 13, see Part II. section iii., where it is seen
that this was merely one of Jerome's many mistranslations from Eusebius, who never said the thing imputed
to him, and that Jerome himself distinctly says that
Rome was not to be understood by " Babylon."

For the other passage from the same article, cited
also by Bellarmine, to make it appear that Mark's gospel
was written at Rome, and that Peter was there at the
time, see Part I., in the section on Clemens Alexandrinus,
(p. 83) where it will be seen that Jerome alludes to
nothing of the kind.

XIII.

SULPITIUS SEVERUS, (A.D. 420 or 429,) a Spanish priest,
merely makes the same special application to Italy of
the statement in the old Roman Calendar, as had been
made before by Epiphanius and Jerome. He says,
"while Rome had no other bishop yet but Peter," or
"while Peter was still bishop of Rome," a form of expression from which, as has been already fully shown, it
cannot be inferred that the apostle ever left the East.
This writer also repeats the allegory about the fiery
chariot mentioned by Arnobius, imitating Cyril of Jerusalem in the additions which that bishop introduced into
the story. He says, for instance, that it was by two
devils that the chariot and four was mainly held up in
its progress through the air above the heads of the
astonished multitude, and not only by the eight wings
of fire of the four wild horses, as in Arnobius's account
of it; and further, that its fall was occasioned not only

by the prayers of St. Peter, but by those of St. Paul also. He does not say, however, that Europe was represented as the scene of this story, nor give us the least reason to suppose that, if it was, he considered the apostle's prayers could not have had effect there, without the apostle's having come himself from Babylon to offer them upon the spot. He also gives us the same proof as Philastrius does, of his not looking upon it as a real event; for he likewise supposes it to have occurred not only at the foundation of the Roman church, as mentioned by Arnobius, but again in the early part of Nero's reign, after the arrival of St. Paul in Italy.

Neither, therefore, in what he says of Peter's universal episcopate, still extending to Rome in the early part of Nero's reign, nor in what he says of the fiery chariot that was supported by the two devils, and dashed to pieces by the prayers of the two apostles, Paul's in the West and Peter's in East, have we the slightest indication of the latter apostle's having come to Europe. His words are: " For in Nero's reign the divine religion had acquired strength at Rome, Peter acting as the bishop there, and Paul having been brought to that city (when he appealed to Cæsar), which eminent apostle many came there to hear, and all these were converted under the influence of the truth and of the apostolic miracles which were then frequently performed. For it was in those days that that celebrated engagement took place of Peter and Paul against the impostor of Samaria, who, by magic art, to prove himself a god, soared aloft in a fiery equipage, supported by two devils, (duobus suffultus demoniis,) and when the devils were put to flight through the prayers of the apostles, fell down, and was dashed to pieces in the sight of all the people." (Sulpit. Lev. Hist. ii. 40 and 41.)

This writer also mentions the general laws of the empire which were passed against the Christians in Nero's time, and that it was during the persecution thus promoted by the Romans in all parts of the world, that Peter was crucified by the Jews, as the Scriptures intimate, in the capital of the Lost Sheep of the House of

Israel, and that Paul was beheaded in the capital of the Gentiles. After describing the commencement of this persecution as at Rome, he says: "Afterwards even laws were passed to prohibit the religion, and proclamations were issued forbidding any one to be a Christian. It was at that period of the persecution that Paul and Peter were put to death, of whom one had his head cut off, and the other was fastened to the cross."—*Ibid.*

XIV.

ST. AUGUSTINE, or ST. AUSTEN, bishop of Hippo, in Africa, (A.D. 430,) says nothing whatever even from which we *might infer* that he thought Peter had ever left the East. In one of the places referred to by Baronius, he states that there was a saying in his day that Peter's body was deposited in Rome; which not only is no sign of Peter's having been there when he was alive, but shows how doubtful it was whether even his relics were deposited there at all. His words are: "Peter's body, PEOPLE SAY, lies at Rome; Paul's body lies there; the body of Laurentius lies there; the bodies of all the holy martyrs lie at Rome, and yet Rome is unfortunate! .... Is there all this destruction where monuments are erected to the apostles?" (Augus. Sermo in *Natali Apostolorum*.) Would he have introduced the words "people say" if he was speaking of a fact well ascertained? In the other place cited by Baronius, Augustine says that the Roman church laid claim to having the Chair of Peter, quite as much as Jerusalem or any other catholic church. But Augustine does not hereby mean that Peter had been at Rome. This he shows by his illustration; for in it he says, that the Roman church was the Cathedra Christi, although, as has been already remarked, our Lord never went to Rome; that the Roman church was Peter's Chair in the same way as the Synagogue at Jerusalem was Moses' Chair, although Moses never was at Jerusalem; and that even Hippo, Augustine's own little diocese, was Peter's Chair, without its being even a sign of the Apostle's having been at Hippo. The passage is as follows: Petilianus had said to this bishop, "If you lay claim to a chair it is that which David calls the chair of the scorner, for the righteous do not sit in it." Whereupon Augustine replies: "What has the Chair of the Roman church done to you, in which Peter sat and in which Anastatius sits to-day? Or what has the Chair of the Church of Jerusalem done to you, in which James sat and in which John sits now, with whom we are associated in Catholic unity, (*i.e.*, which is one and the same chair as ours,) and from whom you have madly separated, in separating from us? Why do you call the apostolic chair the chair of the scorner? If it is on account of the men who, you think, speak the law and do it not, did our Lord on account of the Pharisees, of whom he says, they say and do not, offer any insult to the chair in which they were sitting? Did He not uphold that chair of Moses, and condemn them without dishonouring the chair? For, He says, they sit in the chair of Moses," &c.; and, again, a page or two afterwards: "And yet not even on account of those Pharisees, to whom you unjustly compare us (who sit in Peter's chair) did our Lord declare the chair of Moses vacant, which therefore He meant as a type of His own, inasmuch as He says, that it was while they were still sitting in the chair of Moses that they professed what they did not practise," &c. (August. lib. ii. contra literas Petiliani. cap. 51 and 61.) This passage not only does not prove Peter to have been in Europe, as the Correspondent in the *Times* supposes, but even explains in a very clear and useful manner the fallacy of inferring the apostle's residence in a city from the mere circumstance of its boasting that it possessed his chair; a fallacy already exposed in the sections upon Cyprian and Optatus.

The passage cited by Pearson is that in which, without speaking of Rome at all, Augustine, who lived in Africa, says, that the most eminent emperors paid their homage at the "Fisherman's tomb." But even if this means his monument that was at Rome, his having a monument there does not prove he died there. His brother Andrew had one at Constantinople, and even Andrew's body was deposited there; but it is well known that Andrew was not put to death at Constantinople. St. Chrysostom, however, as has been seen, speaks of the Fisherman's tomb that was at Constantinople, and of the homage paid to it by the emperors, whom he frequently calls "the door-keepers of the Fisherman," because they were interred in the vestibule of Peter's martyrium, or martyr's tomb, in that city.

XV.

PAULINUS NOLANUS, bishop of Nola, in Campania, (A.D. 431,) wrote some letters and poems, and in one of the latter—the third of the fifteen poems upon the nativity of St. Felix, he says that Peter had a monument erected to his memory at Rome, as well as that which we know of at Constantinople. It is thence inferred by Bellarmine that some of the relics must have been connected with it; and thence again, that the martyrdom could not have taken place at Babylon! Paulinus says: " And Rome herself, powerful through her sacred monuments of the heavenly chiefs,—through Paul and Peter's (Paulin. Natal. iii.) To omit the other facts already mentioned, I only remind the reader that St. Peter's monument at Constantinople had not even a single relic connected with it; and that St. Augustine admits that it was not in his day an ascertained fact that Peter's body was at Rome,—that there was nothing more than a rumour ("dicunt homines") of its being there. But whoever has leisure to look through these poems of Paulinus will receive convincing proof that the place of a martyr's death was not considered by this bishop to be indicated either by the city in which he had a monument, or by the monument which could boast of his remains. For in the eleventh of these poems he says, that the bodies of martyrs were like physicians to the soul, and therefore placed by Providence where they were most wanted; that it was Providence that put it into the head of Constantine to bring the body of Andrew, St. Peter's brother, from Achaia to the new capital, as well as that of Timothy from Asia; and that, although Peter was not fixedly stationed either at Babylon or any other city before his martyrdom, yet that, after that event, his body was supposed to be placed fixedly at Rome, in addition to Paul's, because it was most wanted as a physician in the Gentile city.

XVI.

CYRIL ALEXANDRINUS, archbishop of Alexandria, (A.D. 444,) wrote a letter to Celestine, bishop of Rome, about a folio page and a half long, in which no modern Roman Catholic will pretend that he says one word that has the least reference either to the conjecture of Eusebius or to Jerome's mistranslation. In fact, in the whole letter he neither mentions the name of Peter nor alludes to him in any way. The only words of this Alexandrian archbishop that Baronius's imagination could possibly have connected with the subject in question, are these: "Things absurd and irrational, and which are far removed from the apostolical and evangelical faith which the holy Fathers have all along preserved and handed down to us and to our times." (Cyr., Epist. ad Celest.) It is one of thirty-seven letters ascribed to this patriarch, and is in some editions placed as the ninth, in others as the eighteenth of them.

XVII.

SOZOMEN, an ecclesiastical historian, (A.D. 450,) says that the church of Rome was considered to be one of the churches that had Peter's Chair in it, as well as the churches of England and of Antioch, of Babylon and of Alexandria. The passage quoted by Baronius is this: "Felix, the rival bishop of Rome, survived but a short time, and then Liberius was sole bishop—it having been thus ordained, it seems, by Divine Providence, so as not to disgrace Peter's Chair anywhere by having two bishops sitting in it at once; for this is a sign of discord, and inconsistent with the purity of the ecclesiastical law." (Sozom., Hist. iv. 14.) It was hence inferred by Baronius that Sozomen must have entertained the conjecture hazarded by Eusebius, respecting Peter's not having been put to death at Babylon. But there are no grounds for this inference respecting Sozomen. In his day all the churches recognised the authenticity of Peter's Second Epistle (which, in the days of Eusebius, they did not), and this document leaves no doubt as to his martyrdom having taken place at Babylon; and, besides this, the absurdity of inferring that because England, Egypt, and Italy were considered to have Peter's Chair, the apostle must have gone into those countries, has been fully shown in the sections upon Cyprian, Optatus, and Augustine.

XVIII.

OROSIUS was a Spanish priest (about A.D. 450), but it is not known when he finished his history or when he died. "How long he lived," says Möller, his biographer, "is unknown; but what is most certain is, that he died before the end of the fifth century." The Correspondent in the *Times* does not represent Orosius as affording any satisfactory evidence of the famous hypothesis of Baronius about the second year of Claudius; but Father M'Corry does. Father M'Corry considers that although he says nothing about the "Five-and-Twenty Years," yet he may be regarded as affording his sanction to Jerome's alleged interpretation of the Greek preposition ἐπὶ, with the accusative case of a city (in Euseb. ii. 14); that therefore that alleged interpretation must be considered as correct, and that this writer thence deduced the supposition, not only that there had been no church at Rome until the second year of Claudius—twelve years after the Ascension—but also that the apostle then came into Europe after he went to Babylon. That Orosius supposed this, in the fifth century, is not improbable. But even the Roman clergy do not consider that he was a good judge as to the accuracy or inaccuracy of Jerome's alleged interpretation, nor any authority whatever for the fact in question. He writes thus:—"In the beginning of Claudius's reign, Peter, the apostle of our Lord Jesus Christ, came to Rome, and faithfully taught that faith so salutary to believers, and proved what he taught by powerful miracles; and from that time there began to be Christians at Rome. Rome felt that the following benefit resulted from her faith. For when, after Caligula's death, &c. &c. And will any one therefore deny that it was in consequence of the apostle Peter's coming, and the tender seeds of Christianity which had not yet shot forth into profession, that the tyranny and civil war which had almost begun, were by the Divine Power repressed?" (Oros. vii. 6.) When the Roman clergy, therefore, rejected the alleged interpretation of St. Jerome, it is clear that they also rejected the sanction here afforded to it by Orosius, and that they threw his authority upon the subject wholly overboard. But we cannot be surprised at this, when we reflect that he is represented by writers of all persuasions to be an extremely bad Greek scholar, constantly mistaking the authors in that language, in fact, having little read them, and that he was a very inaccurate historian, as may be seen by consulting the General Index of Baronius, where he has numerous errors, as well as an extreme credulity, attached to his name.

Father Ceillier says: "We find chronological errors in this writer, because, as he did not understand Greek much, he had not read the Greek authors in their own language." (Ceill. vol. xiv. p. 7.)

Father Dupin says of his History: "It is not ill-written, but it is inaccurate. It has many faults, both historical and chronological. He had not read the Greek historians, and easily credited whatsoever might help his subject, without examining whether it was well attested or not." (Dupin, vol. i. p. 368.)

Charles Weiss, in the "Bibliothèque Universelle," a work sanctioned by the Roman clergy, and contributed to by many of them, says: "Orosius, little instructed in the literature of the Greek language, was utterly without critical knowledge, and his work ought not to be consulted without distrust." (Biblioth. Univer., *art*. Orose.)

Fathers Richard and Giraud, in their "Bibliothèque Sacrée," say: "This History of Orosius is useful, but far from accurate." (Peu exacte, Biblioth. Sacrée, *art*. Orose.)

Müller, his biographer, remarks: "Even Baronius himself, on more than one occasion, calls in question the veracity of Orosius, upon the ground of his being extremely credulous."

Casaubon says: "I say nothing of his ignorance of Roman affairs, which is sometimes quite astonishing, as Baronius himself frequently acknowledges."

"His ignorance of the Greek language," says Dr. Rees, in his Encyclopædia, "involved him in many mistakes."

Thus we see that Father M'Corry is quite mistaken in supposing that the Roman clergy were not warranted in rejecting the authority of Orosius as they have done, both as a Greek scholar and as an accurate historian; and thus we see that, even if they had not, centuries ago, acknowledged the error supposed to have been made by Jerome, in his translation from Eusebius, and the utter absence that there is of the least room or evidence for supposing that Peter left the East in the reign of Claudius, yet no sincere inquirer after truth could possibly have regarded this Spaniard as a competent judge of Jerome's translation from the Greek writings of Eusebius.

XIX.

PALLADIUS, bishop of Helenopolis, in Bithynia (A.D. 450), is supposed to have written an obscure work about the Brahmins, in which the fate of the apostle of Babylon is alluded to, as having been brought about during Nero's persecution of the Christians in the East, although not exactly within his eastern jurisdiction there. Speaking of some other things which happened in the East in the reign of Nero, the writer has this clause: "In the reign of Nero—who imposed the penalty of piety upon Peter and Paul, who were, as we know, the leaders of the apostles." (Lib. de Bragmanibus.) This is produced as very fair proof that Palladius adopted the conjecture of Eusebius, and thought Peter had not been put to death at Babylon, but in some part of the Roman empire, and most probably in Italy! It is not known whether this work on the Brahmins was really written by Palladius, but the evidence of this doubt is not laid before the reader, as the words so evidently do not even suggest what they are cited to prove.

XX.

PETRUS CHRYSOLOGUS, bishop of Ravenna, (A.D. 452,) is stated by Baronius to have said, in a sermon "Upon the Nativity of the Apostles," that Peter's martyrdom did not take place at Babylon, but no such sermon was ever by any editor attributed to this bishop. We have only 176 of his sermons at the most, and this is not published as one of them in any edition of his works. No less than five sermons on this subject have been, at different times, attributed by Roman-catholic editors to different writers of this period, and, by Roman-catholic editors, again withdrawn from them; but I do not find that any one of the five has ever been attributed in any edition to this writer.

XXI.

THEODORET, (A.D. 457,) bishop of a town called Cyrus, on the Euphrates, not very far from Babylon, alludes to its being supposed in his day, as it had been in St. Augustine's, that Peter's relics were in his tomb at Rome; and it is hence inferred, that Theodoret must have adopted the conjecture of Eusebius, that the apostle had not been put to death at Babylon, but it will be seen that he gives grounds for no such inference. His words occur in a complimentary and rather inflated address to Leo, bishop of Rome, where he says that there came a light to the nations from Peter's tomb—that the apostle had passed across the meridian of the church like a star, but that, unlike other stars, he continues to give light after he has gone down, and now from the West as he had before from the East. After alluding to Paul's having said that the fame of that church had been noised abroad throughout all the world, Theodoret thus writes: "But if such was the faith of Rome when it first received the seeds of Christianity, how shall we speak of the piety which exists there now? Moreover, at Rome there are the tombs of Peter and Paul, the general founders of all the churches, and the universal teachers of the truth in all; those tombs which enlighten the souls of the faithful. The thrice-blessed star (or team) of these apostles arose in the eastern horizon, shooting forth its rays in all directions, and accepted with joy its declination in the western, and even from the western horizon now illuminates the world. It was they who gave the greatest lustre to your throne. This is the climax of all your fortunes. And Providence has given fresh lustre to this Chair of Paul's and to this Chair of Peter's, by placing your Holiness in it, from whom the bright beams of orthodoxy are sent forth." (Theod., Epist. ad Leon, 113th Letter.) To the reader whose mind is not pre-occupied with the modern hypothesis, it will be evident that Theodoret's metaphor only alludes to the transit of the heavenly bodies from the East to the West, and not to any journey of Peter's from the East to the West; for East and West are relative terms, and this bishop, who lived in the East, on the Euphrates, could not possibly have meant to say that Peter passed in his travels from the east of him to the west of him, as we know that Peter did not come from the east of Babylon. As the metaphor, therefore, cannot apply in this sense to the place where his travels began, so neither can we consistently interpret it in this sense of the place in which they terminated; and even if we were to do so, the metaphor would not indicate Europe as that place; for Jerusalem, where many of the Roman clergy thought the apostle perished, (under an impression that Babylon no longer existed,) was quite as truly to the west of Theodoret's meridian as Europe was. The only evidence, therefore, afforded by this passage is, that one of Peter's *martyria* was at Rome, and that it was supposed by Theodoret to enshrine some of his relics. We must not, however, forget that St. Augustine admits the fact to have been unascertained respecting Peter's relics being in Europe, nor that St. Peter had a much more splendid martyr's tomb at Constantinople than any thing of the kind we hear of his having had at Rome, and yet that he had no relics there.

But even if Peter's head, as Father Hardouin thought, or any other portion of his bones, had been sent into Europe, Theodoret was not likely to have inferred from this that Peter had been put to death there. This is proved by the fact, that Theodoret himself admits that he sought to collect the remains of martyrs from all parts of the East into his own diocese upon the Euphrates. "He was not satisfied," says Father Ceillier, "with gathering up the relics of the martyrs, and with having them carried into his own diocese; he also wrote," &c. (Ceill. vol. xiv. p. 36.) Theodoret, therefore, well knew that the place where a martyr's body was deposited afforded no proof of where the martyr died.

Theodoret is also one of the writers who mention the downfal of the Gnostic heresy everywhere throughout the Roman Empire, through the instrumentality of Peter's influence and prayers, either before or very soon after this apostle's departure from Judæa to Babylon; but he is as far as the rest of the Fathers from saying that tho flying equipage was seen in Europe. His allusion to this phenomenon, like that of Cyril of Jerusalem, and each of the other writers that mention it, fully justifies the Roman clergy when they regard it as an allegory, inasmuch as this allusion affords a large supply of fresh evidence that it was never regarded otherwise in ancient times: for Theodoret not only overlooks Paul's presence altogether on the occasion, as unnecessary, but (which is still more remarkable) seems to represent that the real "contest of miracles" in which the prayers of the apostle made the Samaritan fall from a great height in the presence of so many Romans, was what took place (as Arnobius tells us) at some town called Brunda, because he says that the fall he speaks of occurred subsequently to the destruction of the eight wings of fire, called here "the wings of deception," by which the four horses had succeeded in raising the chariot and charioteer to an immense height for a considerable length of time, above the very highest buildings. Nay, Theodoret goes further towards showing that it was an allegory; he represents that what he alludes to took place after the Samaritan's own times, and after the worship of his statue at Rome had begun. Besides which (as I have just said), the reader, who is aware that the Roman legions were constantly in Samaria and the surrounding countries, will see no reason to suppose that Theodoret intended to connect Rome at all, or any other European city, with the allegory. After expressly mentioning Peter's going to attack the Gnostic on two occasions in the East, but with so little success that a statue was ultimately erected to his memory at Rome, this eastern bishop thus writes: "The divine Peter, again coming up, stripped him of the wings of deception; and then, after challenging him to a contest of miracles, and showing the difference between divine grace on the one hand and witchcraft on the other, flung him down by prayers from a great height, in the presence of all the Romans there, thus converting to the faith the spectators of this miracle." (Theodor. Fabularum Heretic. Epitome, chap. i.) I need not repeat moreover that Peter's prayers do not imply Peter's presence.

It is not to be overlooked in Theodoret's passages, that he distinctly speaks of Rome as "Paul's Chair," and even as "Paul's Throne," (θρονος). Also that he denies any peculiar connexion to have subsisted between Peter and Europe, declaring him the "general founder,— the general parent of all the churches," (κοινος πατηρ,) not the peculiar founder of any of them.

XXII.

St. Leo the Great, (A.D. 461,) bishop of Rome, is only cited by Bellarmine, and by him only to show that this Pope had adopted the vague conjecture of Eusebius, that as Peter's relics were supposed to be in Europe, his martyrdom also may be assumed not to have taken place at Babylon. It is far from certain that Leo means to say so much; but I shall not here raise any question as to whether the words "ubi exitus glorificatus est" mean "where the apostle's martyrdom obtained the most glorious results," or simply, "where it took place;" I only mention it as a remarkable fact, that even St. Leo the Great, late as he flourished, and zealous as he was, had nothing more to go upon for Peter's not having died at Babylon than this unsatisfactory conjecture, if he means even that. His words are: "Besides the reverence with which this day's festival deserves to be regarded everywhere, it is entitled to a peculiar veneration in this city, in order that where the death of the apostolic leaders has been invested with glory, the com-

memoration of their death should have the greatest joy."
(Leo Serm. i. de Natal. Apostolorum.)

There are other passages in the same sermon which would make it appear that Leo, a Latin writer and unaware of the error, wished people to adopt Jerome's erroneous translation of Eusebius (Script. Eccl. *art.* Peter) about Peter's having left the East in the second year of Claudius; but as the Cardinal does not seem to consider him authority upon that point, I shall only remark, that Leo's exertions were not attended with success, as it is a century and a half from his time that we first hear again of this erroneous translation.

XXIII.

St. Prosper, (a.d. 463,) a writer of Aquitania, (the south-west part of France,) but of whom so little is known that we do not know whether he was a layman or a bishop, is supposed by Baronius to say, that Peter and Paul were witnesses against Nero, as Enoch and Elias were against Antichrist, because words to this effect are found in a work called "Promises and Predictions," said to have been written by St. Prosper; and Baronius thence infers that Peter must have been in some European portion of the Roman empire! The words are: "Against Nero were sent two witnesses, Peter and Paul, the apostles, on one hand, and Simon Magus on the other, who destroyed himself, and deceived Nero; and against Antichrist two witnesses, the prophets Enoch and Elias," &c. (De Promiss. et de Predic.) To say nothing of the unreasonableness of Baronius's inference, it is to be observed, that all the modern Roman clergy acknowledge that this work was not written by St. Prosper, nor by any other authority of the church.

Father Dupin says: "The work on 'Promises and Predictions' is not by Prosper, for the author is an African, and the style of the work is very different from St. Prosper's works. . . . . . But however that be, it cannot be St. Prosper's."

Father Richard says: "The unascertained works (attributed to St. Prosper) are that on 'Predictions and Promises,'" &c. &c.

Father Tillemont says, after alluding to the uncertainty that exists as to whether this work is to be supposed written by any one of that name at all or not, "what is quite certain is, that it is not written by St. Prosper."

Father Ceillier (vol. xiv.) says: "It seems that Cassiodorus had no doubt as to its being the work of Prosper. Notker also attributes it to him, and this was the general opinion for many centuries; but, on closer examination, it was clear that whoever wrote it was an African," &c.

XXIV.

St. Maximus Taurinensis, (a.d. 465,) bishop of Turin, is supposed by Baronius to have adopted the conjecture of Eusebius, respecting the rumoured existence at Rome of Peter's relics. The reason—the only reason that the cardinal assigns for supposing this bishop to have joined Eusebius in drawing this unusual inference, is because passages to this effect occur in two sermons, sometimes attributed to this bishop by the Roman Catholics since the present controversy respecting Peter began. The passages are: "Peter and Paul, although they were made by divine dispensation the princes and presidents of all the churches, went to deposit their most sacred remains in the city which had obtained the dominion of all mankind. For our Lord, to show his power, placed the princes of his kingdom in the metropolis of the world." (First Sermon on the Nativity of the Apostles.) Whoever wrote this passage does not say very clearly whether St. Peter ever was at Rome alive. (See Part III. section 15.) The writer of the next passage is more explicit: "And where did they suffer martyrdom? In the city of Rome." (Fifth Sermon on the Nativity of the Apostles.) The sincere and attentive reader will see at once that we have not the least reason to think that Maximus wrote these sermons,—that great numbers of the Roman clergy considered he did not; and that the only reason for now supposing that he did, is because there is no other learned saint of the Roman church so ancient as Maximus to whom they could so well be attributed; and, to give authority to these passages, they must be (according to Bellarmine) attributed to " some one who is ancient, a saint, and learned."

The points to be attended to here, are these:—

1. That these two sermons, now for the first time attributed to this bishop of Turin, were considered by all the Roman clergy for several centuries not to have been written by him.

2. That several writers well versed in the literature of the Fathers, are mentioned by the Roman-catholic writers as affirming in the most positive manner, that these sermons could not possibly have been written by any one so early as this bishop Maximus.

3. That Gennadius, a priest of Marseilles (A.D. 492), who made a list of this bishop's sermons about thirty years after his death, does not specify these two sermons among those he mentions.

4. That the only reasons now discovered for supposing them to be the sermons of Maximus, and the only causes assigned for their being now published with his works, are these three:—1. That they are *so manifestly* not the composition of Leo, Ambrose, or Augustine, that it is *easier* to suppose them to have been written by Maximus than by these Fathers; which is one of the reasons Bellarmine assigns,—but who is there that does not see the utter emptiness of such a reason as this? 2. That some of the Vatican MSS. ascribe them to him as well as to Leo, Ambrose, and Augustine; but every one will see that so far is this from being a reason for supposing them to be his, that it is, on the contrary, a reason for not doing so. For if these Vatican MSS. were guilty of such egregious inaccuracies as attributing them to Leo, Ambrose, and Augustine, why should we think them right when they attribute them to Maximus? Why may they not—ignorant and careless, as Bellar-

mine says they were—why may they not be as egregiously wrong in the one case as in the other? Is it not most probable that they were so? 3. That there are no means now-a-days of ascertaining exactly when or by whom they really were written; and that as Maximus is ancient, a saint, and learned, that is sufficient,—he will answer as well for the reputed author of them as any one else.

The highest Roman-catholic authority upon these points is the elaborate edition of the Sermons of Maximus Taurinensis, published at Rome by the orders of Pius VI., through the College of the Propaganda, in 1784. Of the first of the two sermons now under consideration, this edition says,—" We do not pretend to deny that some of those who wrote the Mediæval MSS. attributed this sermon to St. Leo the Great, as we find done in some of the MSS. of the Vatican."

Philip Labbe, a Jesuit of Bourges, (A.D. 1667,) in his Dissertation on Ecclesiastical Writers, as quoted in this edition of the works of Maximus, says of this first sermon,—" It is published as one of Augustine's upon the saints."

On the other sermon, here attributed to Maximus, called in his works No. V., the edition of Pius VI. says: " It has been attributed to different writers. Some of the older MSS. of the Vatican Library assigned it to St. Ambrose. Other parties have thought that it must be the work of St. Augustine, as is clear from its being so inscribed in other MSS. of the Vatican. But the Benedictine monks, who have thoroughly examined the sermons of Ambrose and Augustine, do not consider that it is the work of either of them. Some of the Vatican MSS. likewise represent it as the production of Leo the Great; but rather more of these mediæval documents give the sermon under the name of St. Maximus. Who then will take upon him to say that it is not the production of St. Maximus?"

Of this same sermon (No. V.) Philip Labbe also says, after remarking that several learned men, not in communion with the church of Rome, and some of whose names he mentions, considered it the production of a subsequent age: "This and some other sermons are to be disowned as forgeries, upon which little or no reliance can be placed,—and why so? Is it because they are found inserted among the sermons of St. Ambrose and St. Augustine, through the UNSKILFULNESS of those who wrote the MSS. in the middle ages, and through the IGNORANCE of those who collected what was written? Those who talk in this way, know very little about examining MSS. How much more rational it would be in them to say, with Bellarmine, that although they were ascribed to St. Augustine and St. Ambrose, this did not much signify; as both of these writers are ancient, canonized, and learned, as well as the person to whom they are now attributed?"

Of both these sermons, Father Tillemont says: "Several of the sermons now published under the name of Maximus have been attributed to Ambrose and Augustine, which is, however, no reason for supposing that they were not written by St. Maximus. (Ce qui n'empêche pas qu'elles appartiennent à St. Maxime.) For people are pretty well agreed that they belong neither to Ambrose nor Augustine."

And Cardinal Bellarmine, in his Ecclesiastical Writers, remarks: "Whose ever they are, they are the composition of an ancient writer and a saint." Again, he says: "So that it is clearly impossible to say whether we ought to attribute them to Maximus or not." And again, "We have said that there were several sermons passing at the same time under the names of St. Ambrose and St. Maximus; but there is more reason to suppose (credibilius est) that they were written by Maximus than by Ambrose. There can, however, be no very great error in attributing them to either, as they are both of them learned, and saints, and fathers."

It is evident, therefore, that until some better reason can be found for supposing Maximus to be the author of these two sermons, no sincere inquirer after truth will pretend to say that this Father adopted the conjecture of Eusebius.

XXV.

ELPIS of Messina, (about A.D. 520,) the first testimony that we have of this sex or of this century, was the wife of Boetius, a Roman consul, who died A.D. 526, and is thought by Bellarmine (but by him only) to afford the required evidence in one of two hymns ascribed to her, and still sung in the Roman church. The hymn is called "De Apostolis," and the passage refers to the first great persecution in Nero's reign, when Rome became stained with the blood of martyrs who perished, "not in Italy only," as Baronius justly remarks, "but in other states and in other provinces." "Oh happy Rome!" exclaims this lady—

> "Oh happy Rome! dyed in the hallowed blood
> Of many chiefs!—not by thy light, but theirs
> Dost thou transcend the charms of all the world!"

Strange testimony this, it must be conceded, of St. Peter's not having been put to death at Babylon! Of course Rome and the Roman Government were responsible for all the blood that was shed in that persecution.

XXVI.

ARATOR, (A.D. 556,) an Italian poet and sub-deacon of the Roman church, is the next and last authority adduced by Baronius, who thus admits that he could not find what even he could call an allusion to the supposed tradition about Peter's having been put to death in Europe for a whole century after Theodoret; and then, only in a few almost unintelligible words in the verses of this obscure ecclesiastical poet, which were dedicated to one of the bishops of Rome, and which even Baronius himself is obliged to condemn as an inaccurate (he goes so far as to say "heretical") account of Peter's martyrdom. This, also, is strange proof of the fact in question. After shadowing forth that Peter being in the "holy body of the church," went about with it from shore to shore,—that Paul at Rome, "though supreme chief of all the Gentile world, resigned the reins when 'Peter's Chair' appeared," the poet thus proceeds in the words referred to by Bellarmine and Baronius:

> "And it was well worth Paul's and Peter's crown,
> Thus to o'ertop the glory of the Cæsars,
> And to proclaim in Nero's tyrant halls,
> The world's great law—ay, and to overcome
> In martyrdom his power; lest, weak and poor,
> As Nero was, the church should give him greatness."

In these verses there is evidently nothing contrary to the Scriptural intimation of Peter's martyrdom having taken place at Babylon, nor more than the generally received notion that it was in some way or other during Nero's persecution of the Christians that the Jews were led, as our Lord predicted they would, to carry this into effect, and that it was in consequence of the great moral code propounded from "Peter's Chair" at Rome, that Nero acted with the more severity in this persecution against "Peter's Chair" in the cities of the East. Arator does not deny that Peter was put to death at Babylon.

XXVII.

GREGORY TURONICUS, (A.D. 595,) bishop of Tours, is the only other writer of the sixth century cited on this subject. He repeats that Peter's martyrdom at Babylon was brought about by Nero's agency, as well as that of Paul's at Rome, whether we are to suppose that it was through Vespasian, the general Nero then had in the East, or not. This French bishop's words, as quoted by Bellarmine, who alone cites him, are: "Nero gave the orders by which Peter was crucified, as well as those by which Paul was decapitated," (i. 25,) where we find not the slightest reference to Europe as the scene of either martyrdom. What evidence, I ask, does this afford of this Gregory's having even heard of the conjecture of Eusebius?

XXVIII.

St. Gregory the Great, (a.d. 604,) bishop of Rome, from whom we might naturally expect to hear all that it was possible to allege upon this subject of Peter's being supposed to have left the East, does not even allude to the superficial inference of Eusebius, that as the apostle had trophies or martyria at Rome, it may be supposed that he was transferred there from Babylon to be put to death. This Father merely contradicts the old Roman Calendar as to the duration of Peter's general episcopate with regard to Rome, by saying that it did not terminate at Rome until his death at Babylon, (although it terminated sooner both at Alexandria and Antioch,) for this Calendar had said that when Peter died at Babylon, he was not bishop of Rome, (or, in the Chair of Rome,) but that his general episcopate terminated, with regard to Rome, ten years before his death and twenty-five years after the Ascension. The passage cited from Gregory is that celebrated one in a letter to the archbishop of Alexandria, in which the bishop of Rome acknowledges how unorthodox it was to deny that Alexandria was Peter's Chair quite as much as Rome ever was, and therefore acknowledges also, that Rome's being called "Peter's Chair," or Peter's being said to have lived or died in this Chair, had nothing whatever to do with the supposition of Eusebius. His words occur where he speaks of Alexandria, Antioch, and Rome as three of Peter's Chairs: "Although, therefore, there were many apostles, yet as far as the supremacy was concerned, Peter's Chair alone had it; which in these three cities is still only the Chair of one apostle; for by his own act he dignified his chair when in it he condescended to remain always and to die; by his own act he adorned his Chair when to it he sent his disciple the Evangelist; and by his own act he consolidated his Chair when he sat in it seven years, although he did not mean to occupy it always. As, therefore, this See (or

Chair) of Peter, belongs to one apostle, and is one, although by divine authority the three bishops of these cities now sit in it, whatever merits I hear ascribed to you I attribute to myself, and if you can credit anything good you hear of me, set this down to your own deserts, for we are one," &c. (Greg. Letters, book vi. No. 40, to Eulogius, archbishop of Alexandria.) On which passage the Benedictine Fathers, in their edition, say that Peter's Chair at Rome (or his Roman See) was one and the same thing as Peter's Chair (or See) at Alexandria, and as Peter's Chair (or See) at Antioch (unius sedem esse atque unam.) The utmost then that we gather from the words of St. Gregory the Great is, that he was one of those who considered that of the Roman church Peter never gave up his presidency till his death at Babylon, (*i. e.* during thirty-five years,) and that Rome was the only one of the three churches now in question of which this could be said. Of these opinions the first, as has been said, is contradicted by the old Roman Calendar, a century before Gregory's time, and the second by the writers of the Greek church, who all considered that the apostle retained the presidency or chair, or see of every local church, and of Antioch among the rest, until his martyrdom at Babylon. (ὁ δι αυτος μετα της εν Αντιοχεια εκκλησιας και της εν Ρωμη πρωτος προεστη εως της τελειωσεως αυτου. Syncellus apud Scaligeri Thesaur. Temporum.) But (without discussing these opinions) we see that Gregory's words do not imply his concurrence in the conjecture of Eusebius; Peter's chair anywhere implying only (as all the Fathers who use that expression are agreed) his being considered bishop there; and his dying in it, therefore, his dying bishop of that place wherever it might be,—although his death took place at Babylon.

XXIX.

St. Isidore, (A.D. 636,) bishop of Seville, the last of the alleged testimonies on this subject, has written a work, called "Illustrious Writers," in imitation of St. Jerome.

and in his memoir of Peter in this work, he mentions as a fact the supposition of Eusebius, that as some of Peter's relics were in his Roman martyria, Peter is not to be supposed to have been put to death at Babylon, where he lived when he was writing his Epistles, but to have been transferred for that purpose to Italy, as Ignatius was from Antioch. The only passage quoted by Cardinal Bellarmine, who alone cites this Father, is as follows: "In the 37th year after our Lord's death, Peter was crucified by Nero at Rome, in an inversed position, as he himself desired." Granting the accuracy of Isidore's MSS. with regard to the words "*at Rome,*" I do not think that any sincere and conscientious inquirer will for a moment regard Isidore's sanction as the slightest justification of an inference so contrary to all early ecclesiastical usage, as to suppose that because some of Peter's relics were merely "SAID," as St. Augustine justly remarks, to be deposited within his Roman tombs, our Lord's prediction of this apostle's martyrdom, by the Jews of the Dispersion, could not have been fulfilled, although St. Peter himself tells us that he was among the Jews of Babylon when this very martyrdom was impending.

No other Roman-catholic writer but Cardinal Bellarmine cites St. Isidore, and he only cites the words given; because, though Isidore wrote other words, as did also Gregory of Tours, they are so exactly the words of Jerome's translation, from the 14th chapter of the 2nd book of the History by Eusebius, that they only prove this translation to have been all that existed in those times, to go upon for the hypothesis of Baronius, about the second year of Claudius. It is not to be wondered at, therefore, that none of the Roman clergy, not even Baronius, cite either this Gregory or Isidore upon this point, and still less is it to be wondered at that the cautious and discerning Bellarmine does not do so.

Thus the conjecture in Eusebius was formed nearly 300 years after Peter's time, and the first allusion in the Fathers to this conjecture does not occur until nearly

300 years after it was formed. The next four writers mentioned as adopting either the conjecture of Eusebius, or the alleged misinterpretation of St. Jerome, are Bede in the eighth century, Ado and Freculphus in the ninth, and Bernardus in the twelfth. Then follows the Golden Legend of the thirteenth century, which it will be seen was founded upon the patristic allegory of the Fiery Chariot.

XXX.

THE GOLDEN LEGEND, of the 13th century, in which Italy is mentioned as the scene of the Fiery Chariot, is supposed by Father M'Corry and the Correspondent in the *Times* to afford the clearest evidence of Peter's having been there. The incidents of this story are cautiously spoken of, in general terms only, by the former, as "THE DIABOLICAL ARTIFICES" of the Samaritan, and by the latter, as "THE IMPORTANT TRANSACTIONS" of St. Peter in Europe, for the truth of which they refer us to the Pseudo-Hegesippus and to "several others." I have already mentioned, in the progress of this Analysis, that all the Fathers who advert to the Fiery Chariot of Samaria, speak of it as an allegory, and leave us to suppose the East as the scene of it; and that the more enlightened of the Roman clergy have also regarded the story as an allegory, while the rest have rejected altogether the authority of those writers of the 13th and 14th centuries, who alone place the scene of the events in Italy. And this will seem to most readers sufficient upon this subject. As, however, the two writers just mentioned, and, according to their accounts, a great many other Roman Catholics in Scotland and England as well as Ireland, regard this Golden Legend as a series of historical facts, and the mediæval writers in question as really believing in the reality of what they told, and in Peter's having abandoned his mission to the Jews, it will not be inappropriate to give a detailed account here of the alleged facts, first mentioning the works in which they are to be found.

The original author of the "Legenda Aurea," or "Golden Legends," is admitted, on all hands, to have been Jacobus de Voragine, a Roman-catholic archbishop at Genoa, (A.D. 1298,) portions of whose story about Peter were immediately caught up by various writers, both in the Greek and Latin churches. "The 'Golden Legends' circulated extensively," says Father Tillemont, "and it was one of the books most frequently printed in the fifteenth century." Some of the copyists and editors seem however to have suppressed portions of the original, and to have interpolated a few marginal notes, mentioning, as corroborative testimonies, some of the spurious writings in which extracts of the story were given as soon as it appeared. The French version, Paris, 1843, is the last edition of it.

The greater part of the story about Peter in these Golden Legends is copied into a work called the "Historia Apostolica," supposed by Baronius to have been written in the following century, and for some time attributed to Abdias, first archbishop of Babylon after the martyrdom of Peter.

Baronius also attaches importance to the following, as corroborative authorities upon some parts of the story:—

1. Nicephorus Callistus, in his "Ecclesiastical History," written in the fourteenth century.
2. The Pseudo-Marcellus, in the "Acts of Nereus and Achilles." Date unknown, but supposed to be the fourteenth or fifteenth century.
3. The Pseudo-Hegesippus, in the work on "The Destruction of Jerusalem." Date unknown. This writer transcribed his statements, as any one can immediately perceive, clause by clause, but in better Latin, from the Pseudo-Abdias.
4. Metaphrastes. Fourteenth century.
5. Cedrenus. Date unknown, but supposed to be the thirteenth or fourteenth century.
6. Glycas. Fourteenth century.

To which we may add, the "Historia D. Petri," by Hieronymus Xavierus, originally written in the Persian language by this learned priest, near relative to St. Xavier, and appointed to an archbishopric by Philip III. of Spain. The annotations to the Protestant edition of this work were unfriendly to the See of Rome, which was the reason that that edition (the only one, I believe, yet published) was placed in the "Index Expurgatorius." Father Xavier died A.D. 1617.

The story is as follows:—

The Golden Legend
ABOUT
THE LEARNED DOGS AND THE FIERY CHARIOT
OF THE
SAMARITAN IMPOSTOR AT ROME.

Which is supposed by some moderns to place it beyond all doubt that St. Peter and his daughter, St. Petronilla, came from Babylon to Europe in the reign of Nero.

The Samaritan lived at Rome in great prosperity and comfort for nearly five-and-twenty years; that is, from the commencement of the reign of Claudius until near the end of that of Nero, and acquired an immense reputation by his witchcrafts, among which it may be mentioned, as we are assured by Nicephorus, Cedrenus, Cardinal Baronius, and other writers approved of by the Roman church, that "he was in the constant habit of making statues walk, of changing everything into gold, of making the household utensils transfer themselves without being touched to wherever they were wanted; of assuming the appearance of a dragon, a sheep, or anything else he chose, and of transforming other people into all kinds of animals," (Nicephorus, ii. 297.) Nothing was more usual, it appears, than to send for him in the case of death, to restore the animation of deceased relatives; and he was, as we may imagine, in the greatest possible favour,—nay, on the closest terms of intimacy and affection with the Emperor, who was at this time, as Baronius informs us, a liberal patron of everything like witchcraft.

Towards the close of Nero's reign, when established at Rome under these favourable circumstances, the Samaritan was one day sitting in his study, with the far-

famed Helen and some visitors, when he was surprised
to see rush furiously into the room his immense dog—
something, it would seem, between the Mont St. Bernard breed and the mastiff, but very savage,—which
was usually kept chained in the porch of his house to
keep off the crowds of people that, as may be supposed,
were constantly flocking to his door. As this dog was
known to have killed several people, it is easy to understand that Helen and her visitors felt uncomfortable at
its rushing into the room in this manner. But what
was their consternation when it stopped short in the
middle of the room, and began to speak with the human
voice,—not improbably in the Samaritan dialect, announcing the apostle Peter from Babylon. It would
seem that Helen and her visitors ran off in the utmost
alarm, exclaiming, "What is this?—who is this?"—
although her more philosophical partner conjured them
not to be alarmed, and told Helen that, as she might have
known, he could make the dog speak that way himself.
Seeing, however, that it was no use, and that they were
irrevocably off,—"Go, tell Peter to walk in," said he to
the dog; "and, I say,—be sure to speak to him like a man,
as you have done to me. I'll not be outdone by the old
fellow." Whereupon the dog went out, and almost immediately afterwards, the great apostle of the Jews,
then nearly in his eightieth year (as Baronius tells us),
entered the room, leaning on his staff, and with his grey
hairs falling over his shoulders. A very amicable
conversation ensued upon the omniscience of the angels,
which will be found detailed in Glycas, (Ann. ii.,)
who, as well as Cedrenus, Nicephorus, and others, gives
the full account of this speaking dog. (Cedrenus writes
thus:—Του μεγαλου Αποστολου Πετρου την Ρωμην καταλαβοντος και προς τον Μαγον απελθοντος, ιυρε κυνα παμμεγεθη
διδεμενον αλυσει εν τω πυλωνι ον ο Σιμων δεσμησας δι' αυτου
εκωλυε παντας ους ουκ ηθελε προς αυτον εισιεναι· και τουτο ην
πρωτον θαυμα τω μελλοντι προς Σιμωνα εισερχεσθαι. Ο δε
Πετρος ιδων τον κυνα ουτω μεγαν και απηγριωμενον, και μαθων
οτι πολλους απειλει επιχειρησαντας εισελθειν προ της επιτροπης

Σιμωνος, κρατησας ιλυσιν αυτον λιγων "εισελθε προς Σιμωνα και ειπε αυτω ανθρωπινη φωνη, Πετρος εισελθειν προς σε θελει." Και του κυνος ευθυς δρομω εισελθοντος και ουτω λαλησαντος κατεπλαγησαν οι μετα Σιμωνος, λεγοντες, "τις εστι Πετρος και τις η τοσαυτη δυναμις αυτου;" προς ους φησιν ο Σιμων, "τουτο υμας μη ξενιζετω, οπερ καγω ποιησω." Και προσεταξε τω κυνι ανθρωπινη φωνη ειπειν τω Πετρω εισελθειν. Και τουτο ποιησαντος παλιν του κυνος, εισηλθε Πετρος προς Σιμωνα, και συμβαλων μετα του Σιμωνος, εις θαυματουργιαν, &c.—Cedrenus. Hist. Comp.)

But although the conversation had been amicable, the impostor soon proceeded to business with the apostle—soon proceeded to those "diabolical artifices," as Father M'Corry calls them, which were the great business of his life, and which called forth the "important transactions" of St. Peter. He sent for an immense bull, which was of course immediately brought to his hall door; and Peter, before he had time to look about him, was challenged by the Wizard to a contest of miracles in the presence of a great crowd of people, who had collected to see what was going forward at that well-known door. The Impostor whispered something into the bull's ear. The huge animal instantly dropped dead upon the pavement. The apostle said something, and the animal as instantly resumed its legs, looking as healthy and vigorous as before. The people shouted. "Life is a greater miracle than death," cried they, "to do, than to undo;" and from that hour we hear of no more amicable conversations. From that hour the wizard looked upon the venerable apostle as his mortal foe. They, nevertheless, had frequent encounters subsequently of the same supernatural character. All this is thus also attested by Cedrenus. (Προσταξαντος του Σιμωνος αχθηναι αυτω ταυρον παμμιγεθη ιλαλησιν εις το ους αυτου, και παρευθυ τεθνηκεν ο ταυρος. Ο δε Πετρος ευξαμενος ηγειρεν αυτον. Οι δε λαοι ιδοντες εθαυμασαν λεγοντες, "αληθως το ζωογονησαι υπερ το θανατωσαι μειζον θαυμα εστι." Και μεν τοι και αλλα σημεια επραξαν πολλα ου μονον εν Ρωμη αλλα και εν Συρια.—Cedrenus. Ibid.)

It was not long afterwards that the Samaritan was sent for to revive a young Roman nobleman who had just died, a relative of the Emperor's. On entering the room, he, to his vexation, found Peter already there before him, who, on this occasion, assumed the initiative, and at once challenged the wizard to a contest of their powers in the resuscitation of the deceased,—a challenge which the other as promptly accepted. It was agreed that the Samaritan should begin. But exasperated apparently by the presence and challenge of the apostle, he insisted at the same time upon the condition that, if he succeeded the apostle should be put to death; adding that he was quite willing himself to be put to death, if, upon his failure, the apostle could succeed. This condition being agreed to in the presence of the countess (the deceased's mother) and a large assembly of afflicted relatives, all heathens, the Samaritan began. He advanced to the bed. He stooped close over the corpse. He repeated awful incantations into its ear; and the head began to move, no one perceiving the impostor's hand behind it. "See!—see!" cried every one—"He lives!—he lives! they are talking to one another!" The countess could hardly be kept back. The rest of those present began to attack Peter. But the diabolical artifice was frustrated. This outburst of indignation did not terminate, as the Wizard expected, in the instant destruction of the defenceless old man from Babylon. "Be just," said the apostle, with firmness, "be just, and be silent. If he is alive, why does he not get up?" Misgivings arose. A pause ensued. The head continued nodding, and the impostor stooping over it. Impatience succeeded. "Take the Samaritan from the bed," said Peter, "and you will see that he deceives you." They did so. The head dropped back inanimate. The countess was in despair. The impostor was arrested in his endeavour to run down stairs. The whole room was in confusion. Amidst it all, the placid tones of the Galilæan were again heard, enjoining silence and forbearance. A breathless expectation followed. All eyes were fixed on him. The apostle, at a considerable distance from the bed, uttered a few words, and instantly afterwards the scion of the house of Nero rushed into his mother's arms. To stone the diabolical impostor was then what was uppermost in everybody's mind. But, "No," said Peter, "do not hurt him. Let him go. The exposure—the disgrace—is sufficient punishment." These occurrences are detailed, with many further particulars, out of Jacques de Voragine, by the Pseudo-Abdias, from whom they are transcribed, with very slight verbal alterations, into the Pseudo-Hegesippus. They are also fully recorded in Father Xavier, and are mentioned, as well as the rest of this legend, by Cardinal Baronius as incontestable facts.

It would appear that either from conversion or from curiosity, some of the witnesses of this contest, among whom seem to have been Titus, the son of Vespasian, Nero's general near Babylon, and another young Roman nobleman named Flaccus, walked home with Peter to his house, where several of the Roman Christians used to lodge. It was the hour of the afternoon meal, and as a large party of them were enjoying themselves together, Titus, who sat near the apostle, inquired for his daughter, St. Petronilla. He had heard she was with him at Rome, he said, and was surprised not to see her doing the honours of her father's table. He had also heard, no doubt, though he did not say so, that she was very beautiful and accomplished. (Præstanti formâ corporis. *Marcellus.* Juvenis et pulchræ formæ—de præstantiâ formæ et vitæ celebris. *Father Xavier.*) "She is ill," said the apostle, "confined to her bed—has been a long time. She has had a paralytic stroke, with many feverish symptoms." "Dear me!" exclaimed the future conqueror of Jerusalem, "I am surprised to hear that. How is it that you who can, as we have just seen, do so much good for others, allow your amiable daughter, in the midst of her youth and beauty, to be so long an invalid?" The question seemed to annoy the old man; for it is not improbable that it was exactly on account of that very youth and great beauty that he kept her aloof from all the strangers who were constantly temporary inmates of his house. He therefore answered rather short, "She is very well where she is." (C'est que cela convient. *Jacques de Voragine. French version.* Sic enim ei expedit. *Marcellus.*) But seeing that Titus was evidently dissatisfied with this account of the matter, and not wishing to do anything to disturb the faith of so influential a person, he added, after an uncomfortable pause of a few minutes: "It is a useful religious exercise, Titus, for my daughter to be in that condition; but lest you should suppose it to result from inability on my part to effect her cure, you shall see her." Peter rose from the table, and going into an adjoining room, desired St. Petronilla to come in to dessert, or, as some of the writers express it, to come and wait upon them. (Ministrare. *Marcellus.*) Peter had not long returned to his chair, when Titus had the pleasure of seeing this fair child of the Euphrates enter the apartment. She appeared to be in her eighteenth year; was rather tall, and in the full bloom of health and extreme loveliness. She first ascertained that every one present was helped to what he wished for, and then seated herself quietly and gracefully in a vacant chair that had been placed by Titus for her near her father. It was now for the first time that this young Roman and his friend Flaccus were able to contemplate undisturbed those magnificent Jewish features, with their engaging Eastern expression, and all that profusion of beautiful smooth black hair. What occurred while she was present, or what remarks, if any, passed between her and the company, we are not told. But she had not been sitting long when the apostle said to her, "Go back, my love, to your bed and your afflictions." (Abi; in statu tuo mane. *Father Xavier.* Jussit eam Apostolus redire ad lectum suum. *Marcellus.*) She rose with a look which, although not a smile, seemed one for very sweetness—kissed her father, and bowing graciously to his friends, left the room. Whatever the Christians present might have thought of this, the two young heathen courtiers began each to ask himself if it might not possibly have been a dream. She went, we are told, immediately to bed, and the paralytic afflictions of all kinds returned as bad as ever. This account is given out of Jacobus de Voragine by the Pseudo-Abdias, the Pseudo-Hegesippus, and the Pseudo-Marcellus. It is also given in Father Xavier and others; all which accounts agree as to the lady's youth and extraordinary beauty. For what reason Cardinal Baronius should be so ungallant as to maintain, in opposition to them all, that she was both old and ugly—that she must have been at least sixty, and that a person of that age, constantly suffering from illness, as she was, could have had very little beauty left, it is not easy to see nor worth while here to examine. Suffice it to say, that he has not one single authority upon his side. The reader will do well to refer to Baronius upon this point; as he even insinuates that if she were so very beautiful, she might not have been the apostle's daughter at all.

This ecclesiastical miracle had scarcely passed off—the bright apparition that it brought has scarcely vanished—when the meditations of the assembly were disturbed by the arrival of an Imperial Messenger. The apostle was summoned to the presence of the Emperor. Titus, Flaccus, and all present, except the undaunted Peter, stood aghast; for no one trusted Nero. To explain matters, however, we must go back a little.

As soon as the Samaritan escaped from the scene of the morning's tumult, he ran as fast as he could run to the palace, demanded an audience of his imperial friend, and implored him to send at once for that insolent Galilæan,—that, if he did not, they would have Rome again in flames. Nero had, we are told, a very great affection for this wicked fellow-heathen; and, partly to soothe the agitation of a friend, whom we are told he looked upon as the greatest safeguard of the state, partly, however, it may be presumed, to gratify his own curiosity as to the sort of person this was, that was said to have that very day revived a near relative of the imperial family, he did send for Peter. The messenger just mentioned was despatched, and, after a very short interval, during which the Enchanter stalked impatiently about the Presence-chamber, the venerable apostle of Babylon entered, and stood for the first time in the dreaded presence of the Chief of Rome. "I cannot tolerate this enemy any longer, Cæsar," said the Samaritan, under much excitement, as Peter entered; "and I wonder very much that one so discerning as you are should save from the general persecution this stupid and treacherous old fisherman, (miror te Cæsar hunc alicujus momenti hominem existimare imperitum piscatorem mendacissimum, &c.,) who possesses no power, either in word or deed, and who this very morning pretended to revive your relative, when it was, as I have told you, by my science alone that this was done. Let me order my angels to come at once and deliver me from him." "I do not fear your angels," said Peter, quietly; "on the contrary, it is they fear me."—"What!" said Nero to the apostle, unaccustomed to hear his friend thus set at defiance, "do you not fear one who proves to us by his actions that he is one of our gods?" and the impostor strutted about the room as before, full of indignation. "If there is anything divine about him," said Peter, "let him tell what I am thinking of, or what I am going to do; and I shall first whisper to you, most excellent Cæsar, what it is, so that this time at least he will not be able to impose upon you."—"Come close to me, then," said the Emperor, nothing startled at this overture; "come close, and tell me what your thought is," (qu'il me dise ce que je pense, et je vais confier à ton oreille la pensée que j'ai en mon esprit, et il ne pourra nous tromper. Neron dit: approche-toi et dis-moi ce que tu penses. *Jacques de Voragine.—French translation Paris.* 1843.) "Tell them to bring me some barley bread," said Peter, in a very low whisper to the Emperor's ear, "and to give it to me without his seeing it." Nero had become interested in the singularity of the proceedings. The servant received the orders outside the door, at Nero's desire, from the apostle; who, waiting

outside the door until the bread was brought to him, put it in his pocket (sous sa tunique), except a little of it that he hid in his two fists, (in dextrâ atque sinistrâ manicâ suâ collocaverat.) He then re-entered the room, carefully closing the door after him, and presenting his fists to the Samaritan, said, " Now, then, tell me what I have here, and what I have been doing and saying."—
" Well, my good friend," said the Emperor, seeing that his protégé did nothing but stare at the two fists, " what do you say to that? What Peter says seems fair enough."
—" Let Peter tell me what I have been thinking of and doing," said the wily impostor, somewhat embarrassed.
—" So I will," said Peter, addressing Nero; " but let him tell me first."—" You must know, my dear Emperor," (bone Imperator), said the Samaritan, seeing that Nero expected him to say something, " you must know that no creature can tell that.—Peter is a liar."—
" But you consider yourself more than a mere creature," said Peter; " so tell, even in a whisper to the Emperor, what it is I have here." The impostor had the good luck to avoid this trap, and turned away. As to what the Emperor thought of all this hesitation on his friend's part, our story leaves us a good deal in the dark; but the end of the matter was, that the testy impostor became furious at having the apostle's two fists thrust into his face at every turn, as he strutted about the room, with the everlasting question, " Come, tell me my thought?" So, forgetting the respect that was due to the Emperor, he roared out at last, in a voice like thunder, " Let my big dogs come and eat him up." Whereupon, the doors and windows being all at the time closed, two enormous dogs suddenly tumbled down the chimney and rushed at the apostle. Peter stretched out his hands open towards them, showing them the barley bread in his palms, and backing them in this manner about the room, as he had just before done with clenched hands to the infuriated Samaritan. The effect of this upon the animals was to make them rush off again by the same way they came, to the great astonishment and

disappointment of their wicked master. Some doubt has been raised as to whether the apostle's gesture is sufficient to account for the abrupt exit of the dogs on this occasion; but there appears no good reason to doubt it. It certainly is not impossible that the rest of the loaf which Peter had in his tunic fell out, unobserved by the Samaritan, and was caught up by one of the dogs, which, naturally running off with his prize, was immediately pursued by the other. This, indeed, is not impossible; but there is no excuse for the impious explanation which some have given of this matter. "Thus, Emperor," said Peter, "I have shown you, not in word but in deed, what it was that the Samaritan was thinking of. He was thinking of these dogs when he talked of calling down his angels to destroy me, showing that his angels are only dogs." Nero does not seem to have much appreciated any portion of this performance. He ordered them both to quit his presence, calling them several hard names, one of which seems to have been "teratologoi," (ὡς τερατολογους και αμφοτερους εκ προσωπου αυτου θαττον εξελασειν. Cedrenus. Hist. Comp.,) and requested them not to annoy him with any more of their ecclesiastical miracles; that he would not have it. Many further particulars of this part of the story are given by Jacques de Voragine in the Golden Legend, as well as by the Pseudo-Abdias, Father Xavier, and various others.

The disgrace into which his dogs brought him on this occasion was a severe blow to the Samaritan, and he resolved to have revenge on the apostle. It happened that there was a priest at Rome named Marcellus, a very intimate friend of Peter's, whom the apostle was in the habit of visiting at a stated hour every day,—a little after one o'clock, (post horam unam. *Marcellus.*) The Samaritan took the largest and most savage of the four dogs he had—one that had not yet seen Peter, and tied it in the porch of this priest's house, just before the hour for Peter to make his visit, in the hope that it would tear him to pieces when he attempted to go in. The apostle soon came up. Of course the dog flew at him, barking and howling in the most terrific manner. Peter saw at once what had been done. He succeeded in tranquillizing the brute, and having untied him, told him to go tell his master that he had better give up his diabolical artifices,—unfortunately adding that he was to be sure not to hurt any one until he reached him. The dog, it seems, misunderstood this part of what the apostle said, and thought it meant he was to attack him as soon as he found him. So the moment he came up to where his wicked master was watching the success of this manœuvre, he rushed at him, knocked him down, and was so intent upon tearing his garments, that he would certainly have choked him, but that Peter, perceiving in some way or other what was happening, hastened to the spot, and told the dog on no account to hurt his master. The dog obeyed the letter of the apostle's mandate, but tore the Samaritan's clothes in such an unaccountable manner that not one single shred of anything remained upon him. (Corpus quidem non attigit sed vestes adeo laceravit ut nulla pars corporis tecta maneret. *Marcellus*.) In this deplorable state he got up a very Adam, from the pavement; and seeing the condition in which he was, ran off at the top of his speed towards the nearest of the gates of Rome, with a great crowd of little boys hallooing after him; and what was still worse, his own terrible dog not very far behind. (Populus vero et imprimis pueri una cum cane cum insectantes extra urbis mœnia seu lupum expulerunt. *Marcellus*.) It is most probable that Helen heard of what had happened to him and sent him clothes immediately, but he did not make his appearance again for some time (some accounts say for nearly a year) within the walls of Rome.

During this interval an event of sad domestic interest occurred to the apostle. St. Petronilla regained her health, and was now often to be seen engaged in the domestic duties that devolved upon her in her father's house, but it had been long manifest to the Christian community at Rome, that both her father and herself were averse to her forming a matrimonial alliance. Nothing of the kind therefore was proposed from any quarter of the Christian world. She was, nevertheless, seen by many of the Roman court; and in her case, as in that of so many others, to be seen was to be loved. Among her heathen admirers, the most importunate was Count Flaccus, who, after frequent fruitless efforts to obtain her consent to marry him, surrounded the apostle's house one day with an escort of dragoons, and alighting from his horse, entered unannounced and impetuously, into the lady's presence. Her friend Felicola was with her. "This day, my beloved Petronilla, must be the term of my wretchedness. This day you become my wife. There is a carriage and an escort at the door. The Emperor consents—nay, commands, (added he, with the appropriate look and emphasis.) Your father will not have the madness to oppose the Emperor."—The poor girl was terrified at all this, but most of all at those last words. If she feared anything on earth, it was that her father should incur the displeasure of the dreadful Nero.—"What! my Lord," said she, promptly, and with admirable firmness, "do you come in this manner, with an armed force, against an unarmed girl?—For shame, my Lord!—Allow me at least to form the acquaintance of those Roman ladies by whom, according to the customs of your country, I am to be conducted to my new home. Allow me at least three whole days, and send me my twelve bridesmaids to visit me and to be my friends. You cannot treat me thus;"—and Petronilla here shed a flood of large bright tears, without seeking to arrest, to dry, or to conceal them. There are cases in which it is said that the lion will "turn and flee," and this seems to have been one of them. The armed soldier trembled. He felt—those convincing tears had taught him—that he had been wanting in consideration to her he loved. He promised to do what she desired,—to wait—to hope— to do anything but cause those tears. He withdrew his troops. He bade her an affectionate adieu;—for three long days he was not now to see her. Upon his departure, however, St. Petronilla instantly renounced this world and everything by which we hold on to it. All the entreaties—all the tears of Felicola could not induce her to take food; and on no account was her father to be apprized of anything. One after another the twelve fair Patricians called and had their interviews with Petronilla; and such was the winning power of grief, and gentleness, and truth, that every one of them successively, before leaving the house, requested the apostle to baptize her. On the third morning, they all arrived together. The beautiful orphan of the East was at her prayers by her bedside. They saw her—they stood around her—they disturbed her not. "The Christians make long prayers" thought these bright-eyed converts of the Capitol. "Why do you weep?" said one of them, to Felicola; "your friend is not going far."—"She is gone far—she has left me for ever," said the disconsolate girl, bursting into an agony of tears. "She has been at those prayers since the day dawned." It was but too true. They raised the face. Petronilla was no more! It is unnecessary to say that the usual amount of consternation and bewilderment upon these occasions ensued,—that Flaccus was sent for and duly ushered into his despair; but to the discredit of human nature, it must be told that he immediately transferred his affections to Felicola, and that upon her refusal to take her dear friend's place in his heart and home, he compassed both her death, and even that of her dear friend, the priest who gave her absolution. This affecting portion of Jacques de Voragine's narrative, is also given in the Acts of Nereus and Achilles, by Marcellus, as quoted by Baronius. It is likewise to be found in Father Xavier, and several others.

But the venerable apostle had little time for sorrow. His daughter's relics were scarcely deposited upon the Ostian Road, in the catacombs there, before the Samaritan was again in the field against him, with fresh projects, and the accumulated resentment of many brooding hours. This bad man's first step on re-entering Rome was to solicit a private audience of the Emperor, which he seems to have obtained with the usual facility. "I know," said he, as he entered the Presence-chamber, "I know, most excellent Cæsar, how much right you have to question my supernatural powers, and to disbelieve my pretensions, but I have not come to you this time without my proofs. Order them to cut off my head." After a pause, during which the two stared at one another, the impostor proceeded,— "Yes,—I am in earnest. Order them to cut off my head; and you shall see that the power of life and death is in my hands. In a few days afterwards I shall call on you again. Nero, tired of the farce which had been so long played at his expense, and which seemed to be now beginning again as bad as ever, took him at his word. The chief executioner of the palace was ordered to decapitate the Samaritan after the most approved manner, in one of the out-buildings of the court-yard. Baronius and other writers inform us, as has been already mentioned, that the impostor was constantly in the habit of transforming himself into various kinds of animals; and was always expected to do something of the kind by those in whose society he was. We must not, therefore, wonder to find that the executioner, who seems to have detested this pest of man as much as any one, believed himself subjected to some diabolical artifice of the kind on this occasion. The Samaritan was before him with his head held down. The executioner merely turned round an instant to whet his scimitar, and on again looking round, he saw a great ram with its head held down by the attendants. "But where is the Samaritan?" said he, fiercely.—"Behold him, sir," said the attendants. "We have never let this head go."— "That is not a man," said the executioner, getting angry.—"What else is it, sir?" said the attendants. "It seems to us to be a man."—He shall not escape then, this time," said the executioner, who considered that his master had been sadly humbugged by these transformations before; and without another word, the head was instantly severed from the body. "It is to be hoped that we shall hear no more of this confounded Samaritan," said he, wiping his scimitar, and restoring it to its scabbard. As was usual on these occasions, the executioner had an audience to apprize Nero in person that the deed was duly done, which seemed to afford great satisfaction to both these bloodthirsty creatures. Within four or five days, however, the inexhaustible Samaritan again entered the presence-chamber of the astounded Nero. "Why," said he, coolly, on going into the room, "what is this for, Nero? You have not yet given them orders to wipe up my blood. I have just been looking at the place where they cut off my head the other day, and it is quite disgusting to see it. Do send them to wipe it up." Nothing could exceed the amazement of the Emperor. He held out his hand to him. He assured him that he should never doubt him any more, but it was too late. The Samaritan was offended—nay, worse —he was hurt. "Adieu, my dear friend," said he to Nero, as he turned to depart. "A long—long adieu. I shall leave Rome to-morrow, in my fiery chariot, and you shall never see me any more."—"Impossible," exclaimed Nero. "No my dear fellow, this cannot be, we cannot spare you. I cannot, in this manner, lose the greatest safeguard of the state. You must not leave me;" and the Emperor became deeply affected.—"Well," said the Samaritan, relenting, "since you wish it so much, I shall return,—I shall return with good things for Rome; but my four-in-hand is ordered for to-morrow, and I have many reasons for wishing to make a short visit to the skies."—"Let it be as short as possible," said Nero; "farewell, until to-morrow. I shall go to see you off; and when you return, I promise you that you shall not be any more tormented by these Babylonians and Galilæans."

The morrow came. A magnificent chariot and four, in an atmosphere of unconsuming fire (quadrigæ igneæ) very much, the Romans thought, like Phaeton's chariot and four of old, awaited the Samaritan at a tower on the top of the Capitoline Hill. The sparkling wings of the impatient steeds produced a beautiful effect. The day was fine, and the people flocked in dense crowds from all parts of Rome to the foot of the Hill. Conspicuous, however, amidst that immense assembly, was to be seen the luxurious, though more ponderous, equipage of the Emperor, in which he was sitting, with one or two of his friends, surrounded by the various carriages of the Court; and at a humble distance behind it, yet within hail, might be seen the apostle Peter, and with him St. Paul, who, some accounts tell us, had returned a day or two before from Spain. At length the Wizard of Samaria appeared upon the tower, arrayed in a garment of light, with a crown of laurel on his head. "Farewell, Romans," said he, never much celebrated for his eloquence; "farewell. I am sorry you make such fools of yourselves about those contemptible Galilæans, and allow yourselves to be humbugged by them. But since you do, I am determined not to stay here to witness it. Whenever you act differently I shall return, and bring you some good things from the regions of the sky. My only request is, that you take care of my beloved Helen, who, wherever I go, is always, as I have often told you, *my first thought.*" (It is supposed that this last expression had some mysterious meaning in it, on which see Baronius.) He mounted the chariot (conscensis quadrigis igneis), the wings of the impatient horses, streaming with fire, waved gently but powerfully through the unyielding air; and, like an enormous but radiant bird, such as we read of in fairy stories, the Samaritan and his flying chariot gained the upper strata of our atmosphere, (ab illâ turri excelsâ avolans, in modum volucrium, sublime petiit.) The people shouted loud *vivats* for the Samaritan. "There," exclaimed Nero, rising up in his carriage, and turning round to Peter and Paul, "look at that. I told you that what that man said was true, and you—you are but impostors," (vous—vous n'êtes que des imposteurs,) added he, impatiently, as he re-adjusted himself in his carriage to watch the flight of his aerial friend. The apostles looked at each other. "What shall we do?" said Paul.—"See where he is now," said Peter. (Lève la tête et vois—oculos tuos attolle et vide.) "I see well enough," said Paul. "He will soon be out of sight if you don't make haste. What on earth are you ing for?" (pourquoi t'arrêtes-tu? Achève;) we are told that Peter became here nervous and agitated, (εν αγωνια μαλλον ην. Nicephorus.) Some of the writers defend his hesitation, by suggesting that it was very probably intentional, in order that the flight being the higher, the fall might be the greater, and Peter's share of the ecclesiastical miracle (viz. the Samaritan's not being killed by the fall), the more striking. At length the Emperor and the crowd, which was very great in the neighbourhood of his carriage, heard Peter's well-known voice: "Angels of Satan," said the apostle, "you may let him fall now. The flight has lasted long enough. Let him fall, angels of Satan, but let him live." The chariot and horses were never seen again. They vanished into thin air (quadrigas igneas Petri ore difflatas evanuisse), and the impostor dropped from the very clouds like a stone; yet, wonderful to relate, (and this we must not forget was Peter's principal share in the so-called miracle,) according to the best accounts, he only sustained a simple fracture of both his legs; though some indicate other portions of him as injured by the fall; and it was not until some time afterwards that he died, when, distracted by mental and bodily sufferings, he managed, in some equally miraculous manner, to drag himself to the window of his room, at the top of a house in some other town, and throwing himself out, was killed on the spot. When Nero heard of this, he had Peter arrested, and kept him some time in prison, to see whether the Samaritan would re-appear; for Nero, naturally enough, fully expected that he would, he had been so used to his re-appearing. The hope, however, was at length abandoned. He considered he had been robbed of his best friend; and thus even after death

this diabolical impostor persecuted the apostle; for
Nero was vindictive, and Peter was put to death upon
an inversed cross. On which occasion, we are told, that
the apostle made a long speech, notwithstanding the in-
convenience of the posture in which he was fastened;
and that among the aerial forms that hovered round
him, one was seen handing him a book; but how he
took it, or what he did with it, we are not told. It is
not, however, improbable, that it may now be in the
library of the Vatican. Nor are we told what became
of Helen or of the dogs after this; but we may reason-
ably conclude that Nero did not leave these sole de-
pendants of his lost friend unprovided for. Indeed, it
is but too probable that he appropriated the dogs, for he
was fond, we are informed, of everything that was savage.
Several minor matters occur while Peter was in prison,
for which we have not room here, but which the curious
will find in the original work by Jacques de Voragine.

Upon the evidence of Peter's being believed to have
left the East which the foregoing story is supposed to
afford, it is unnecessary to raise any discussion. The
Legend shows that the archbishop of Genoa had read
the conjecture of Eusebius in some of the translations,
if not in the original; but it affords not the slightest
reason for thinking that he acquiesced in it, or that he
supposed any one else did. A statement made in that
Legend is not only no sign of the statement's being true,
but no sign even of its being a tradition. The work is
too late and too manifestly a mere fiction. Nicephorus
Callistus, in his Ecclesiastical History, Metaphrastes, and
various other writers of the same period, as Jacobus de
Voragine, state, in works of much higher credit, that
Peter came to England, and that, while he lived among
us, he founded several churches here; yet what Roman
Catholic will pretend to regard this as a sign that there
must have been a tradition of Peter's having been in
England? I need not, however, enlarge upon a point
so obvious. I have no doubt that Father M'Corry and
the Correspondent in the *Times* are utterly mistaken as

to the state of education in Great Britain and Ireland; and utterly mistaken when they suppose that any class of the community—Protestant or anti-Protestant—in these Islands, will, in the 19th century, accept such a frivolous guarantee as this story of the Fiery Chariot for the apostolic authenticity of the chains which they now seek to cast around us, or will even easily excuse the imputation of so much credulity and so much ignorance as are attributed to us in the promulgation of such an argument.

APPENDIX.

THE EIGHT
PRINCIPAL COLLECTIONS
OF THE
ALLEGED TESTIMONIES,
WITH SHORT NOTES.

I.—BARONIUS.
(From the Annals, A.D. 44, paragraph 25.)

"To ascertain into what countries each of the apostles went, we shall cite all that we can find in the Fathers or elsewhere. And above all we must speak of Peter, who, according to the general opinion, (communis sententia,) came to Rome in the second year of Claudius; for that is attested, first of all by Eusebius (A.D. 340) in his Chronicon; that is attested also by St. Jerome (A.D. 420), and afterwards, by all who have written the history of that event. (*See* Latin Translation of the 'Chronicon,' by Jerome, and the 'Ecclesiastical Writers,' translated from Eusebius by Jerome, *art.* Peter.) All other historians have written the same thing of the peculiar time of his going, so that there is no more room left for doubt or contradiction upon these points; and, in the same manner, all the ecclesiastical writers have confirmed this same Peter's journey to Rome, and have adorned it with everlasting records, viz.—

Sixteen Latin writers:

Tertullian,	Arnobius,
Cyprian,	Lactantius,

Optatus,	Philastrius,
Jerome,	Orosius,
Ambrose,	Prosper,
Augustine,	Maximus,
Sulpitius,	Chrysologus,
Prudentius,	Arator.

Eleven Greek writers:

Papias,	Eusebius,
Caius,	Chrysostom,
Dionysius of Corinth,	Cyril of Alexandria,
Irenæus,	Theodoret,
Hippolytus,	Sozomen.
Petrus of Alexandria,	

"In short, not to lose time in a thing so evident, all the general councils have confirmed this great fact,—all the bishops of Rome in their letters, and all the emperors in their edicts, have confirmed it; (to dismiss the matter with a single word), the event was of such vast importance, that it was most deservedly recorded in writings of every description; so that no brazen faced heretic or schismatic until now has dared to raise even the least doubt about this journey."

Note.—1. No one could be expected to contradict what no one had asserted. Not one Bishop of Rome has even alluded to the alleged tradition in his letters;— not one Emperor mentions it in his edicts. 2. The two writers he puts forward as highest authority, are both of too late a period to be any authority at all, even if they had made the statement. 3. Neither of the statements attributed to them, however, belong to either of them; that attributed to Jerome being merely a translation from another writer, and that attributed to Eusebius not being in any of his works. 4. Saying that a certain matter was attested by all who wrote of it, is not saying that anybody did so. 5. Baronius was deceived about several books in his time, since discovered to be spurious; and, 6, as to the Fathers having made Europe the scene of the allegory about the Fiery Chariot, not one of them does so.

II.—BELLARMINE.

(De Summ. Pontif., lib. ii. c. 1, 2, and 3.)

"WE have four questions here to consider. 1. Was Peter at Rome at all? 2. Did he die there? 3. Was he bishop there? 4. Was he never translated from that See to any other? Of these four, it is the last only that is either absolutely necessary for the papal supremacy, or sufficient to establish it. For as to the *first*, it is clearly neither necessary nor sufficient for the purpose we have in view, as many people come to Rome without being bishops of that city, and many bishops of Rome have never been in that city at all, as Clemens V., &c. As to the *second*, that also is neither necessary nor sufficient, as is proved by the facts that many bishops of Rome did not die at Rome, and that many other people who never were bishops of the city, die daily within its walls, &c. But, as the four points above mentioned can be proved, I shall here indicate the peculiar arguments of each.

"1. To begin, then, from the beginning. Peter's having been at Rome is proved, *first*, by Peter's own testimony in 1 Pet. v. 13; for that this Epistle was written from Rome, and that Rome is here called Babylon, we have the assurance of Papias, as is mentioned by Eusebius, (ii. 15,) and of Jerome, as is mentioned in the 'List of Ecclesiastical Writers,' *art.* Mark; in which way it is also explained by Bede and Œcumenius, and all who have written commentaries on this Epistle. Besides, St. John calls Rome 'Babylon' everywhere in his Apocalypse.

"2. Our second argument is, that the point in question is proved from the last chapter of the Acts of the Apostles, and from the Epistle to the Romans. For from these it is evident that there were several Christians—in short, a large and flourishing church at Rome before

Paul came there. I should like to know, therefore, who made these converts, if Peter had not been at Rome to do so? For many of the ancients tell us, that Peter was the first of all who proclaimed the gospel to the Romans, and that he had founded that church before Paul went to Rome; and it cannot be proved by any satisfactory evidence, that any one else did so.

"3. Our third argument is founded upon the history that we possess respecting Mark's gospel. For authors of the highest authority agree in relating, that Mark wrote the gospel at Rome, as he had heard Peter proclaim it there." (Here follow the names of the same writers as are cited by Baronius, Papias, Irenæus, Clement of Alexandria, &c.)

"4. Our fourth proof of Peter's having been at Rome is, the history of the Samaritan impostor, the reality of which has been already demonstrated from the writings of many of the ancients. (The proofs given by Baronius that this was not an allegory, are mentioned by Bellarmine in another part of his work.)

"5. Our fifth argument consists of all the clear proofs that we have of Peter's having died at Rome; for he could not have died there if he had never been there. And the *first* of these is his tomb being there. For if Peter did not die at Rome, who carried his body there? From whence, and when, and in whose presence, was it carried there? But if it be answered that there is no reason for supposing that the apostle's body is at Rome at all, where, then, I should like to know, is it? We do not hear of its being anywhere else; nor is it at all probable that the body of one of the principal apostles should have been neglected, when the bodies of so many other saints have been so carefully preserved. Eusebius, ii. 25, looked upon this argument as so complete and final a proof of Peter's having been put to death at Rome, that he did not produce any other. (Hoc argumentum tanti fecit Eusebius ut superfluum putaverit alia quærere.) And that Peter's body was really at Rome, is proved by its being thought by all mankind to be there; as we may see from the pilgrimages that were made to that part of St. Peter's which is called the 'Limina Apostolorum,' (viz., the vault beneath the chief altar.)

"But further; our adversaries do not deny that it was always believed, till the fourteenth century, that Peter had been at Rome. Now, it is utterly incredible that there should have been no one in all that time to expose the error, if it was an error; especially as it was nothing that was done in a corner, or in an instant of time, or without witnesses, so as to be either easy to feign, or difficult to disprove. How is it to be believed that this event, which was, as we maintain, so universally known, should have been false, and no one found during fourteen centuries to show that it was a mistaken supposition?" (Here follows a list of supposed testimonies, in which he thought it better to omit the nine following that Baronius gave—viz., Hippolytus, Cyprian, Optatus, Prudentius (in Peristeph.), Prosper, Chrysologus, Petrus of Alexandria, Cyrillus of Alexandria, and Sozomen; and in which he added the ten following, chiefly very late writers, that Baronius thought it wiser to leave out—viz., Ignatius, Hegesippus, Athanasius, Eutropius, Paulinus, Isidore, Leo, Gregory of Tours, Pope St. Gregory the Great, and a Roman lady whose name was Elpis.)

Note.—1. This cardinal does not think it necessary that Peter should have been in Europe, in order that a Roman-catholic church should subsist anywhere. 2. He (like Baronius) does not seem to have read the Greek Fathers, except in modern translations, which led to his making many mistakes about them. 3. Neither Papias nor Jerome says, as he supposes, that we are to understand the city of Rome by the city of Babylon in 1 Peter. Not one of the Greek or Latin Fathers, even in their commentaries on this Epistle, says so, and he tacitly admits that even Eusebius does not. 4. When he asks, who made the first Roman converts if Peter was not in Europe to do so? he forgets Acts ii. 5. He is mistaken in supposing that any one of the Fathers says Mark's Gospel was written in Italy. Not one does so. 6. Also in supposing that any of them assert the reality of the story about the Fiery Chariot. Even the writers of the thirteenth, fourteenth and fifteenth centuries (though they wrote the story out more fully), never intended their words to be understood as of a reality. 7. As to what he says of Eusebius's celebrated conjecture, and Peter's tomb at Rome, the cardinal is hardly as candid as usual. He acknowledges, indeed, that this was the great argument of Eusebius, THE ONLY ARGUMENT THAT WRITER EMPLOYED; but when he asks, would there have been so many pilgrimages to Peter's tomb, if his body was not in it? and, if it was not there, where was it? and, again, if Peter did not die at Rome, can any one tell us who carried his relics there? these are questions which every honest Roman Catholic can easily answer. 8. In his conclusion he incautiously adverts to the main prop by which the story of a tradition has been upheld. OUR ADVERSARIES DO NOT DENY THAT THE TRADITION EXISTED. To this the answer is plain. There was so much else connected with the alleged tradition, and upon the face of it, that was untrue and preposterous, that the comparatively little question, whether it ever existed, was passed over as unimportant.

III.—FATHER FRANCIS FEUARDENT.
(Notes on Irenæus, b. iii., c. 3.)

"IRENÆUS distinctly asserts in the first chapter of this book, that Peter proclaimed the gospel at Rome, and laid the foundations of that church, which is confirmed with wonderful unanimity, before his time, by Hegesippus, Caius, Linus, Clemens, Anacletus, and Papias, and also by all the orthodox and illustrious writers that came after him, whether in the East or in the West, in the North or in the South. And this being the case, I cannot but wonder at the abandoned effrontery with which Velanus, Illyricus, Funccius, and other French Protestants, have the impudence to jabber about Peter's having never been at Rome."

Note.—1. He candidly confesses, that the most convincing argument for Peter's having left the East was Irenæus's statement (supported as it was by other writers), viz., that Peter proclaimed the tidings of salvation at Rome, and that he founded the church there. The answer is in Acts ii. 2. He was mistaken in supposing that we have a single word of the writings of Hegesippus, Linus, or Anacletus; and the reader has seen in what way the names of Clemens Romanus, Papias, and Caius have been brought into this discussion.

IV. — HENRY DE VALOIS.
(Notes on Eusebius, b. ii. c. 15.)

"NOTHING within the whole range of ecclesiastical history is better known (illustrius), nothing more certain or better proved, than that Peter went to Rome. For, besides Papias and Clement of Alexandria, whose testimony is here adduced by Eusebius, the same thing is stated by Dionysius of Corinth, Irenæus, Caius, and Origen. The attentive reader will find the passages from all these writers proving what I have said, introduced by Eusebius in different portions of his history."

Note.—1. He seems to have laid it down as a principle, that facts in ecclesiastical history do not require the same amount of proof as other facts; a doctrine which no one will, I think, concede to him. 2. He admits that we shall find nothing more satisfactory in the present case than the six passages of writers cited on other points by Eusebius. The reader will, therefore, do well to direct his minutest attention to these six passages, for the authority of Valesius in his church is deservedly very great. 3. He considers that Eusebius himself is too late a writer to have any weight in the controversy.

V.—BISHOP PEARSON.
(On the succession of the earliest Bishops of Rome. Dissert. i. c. 7.)

"PETER's journey to Rome is proved by Ignatius Papias, the Κηρυγμα Πετρου, Dionysius of Corinth, Irenæus, Caius, Clement of Alexandria, Tertullian, Origen,

Cyprian, Lactantius, Eusebius, Athanasius, Epiphanius, Julian the Apostate, Augustine and Palladius. So that it is strange that persons should have been found to deny that Peter ever was at Rome."

On the words of Ignatius he says:—" For what can be more manifest than it is from these words to the Romans, that Ignatius must have had an idea that Peter proclaimed the gospel (in person) at Rome, and was put to death there, as well as Paul?"

On Papias, he says:—" Papias appears (videtur) to attest the same thing in Eusebius, ii. 15, for his testimony is there added to that of Clemens Alexandrinus, about Mark's Gospel having been written at Rome, and approved of by Peter there. (De Evangelio Marci Romæ Scripto, et a Petro Romæ approbato.) Papias also mentions that Peter's First Epistle was written at Rome, and that Babylon in that epistle means Rome. . . . . These points seem to me to establish in the clearest manner possible that Peter was at Rome. (Mihi videntur validissime stabilire.)"

On the Κηρυγμα Πετρου, he says:—" Clemens Alexandrinus frequently mentions this book as an ancient document; and in his Stromata (lib. 6) he transcribes and explains several of its statements. Now in this Κηρυγμα Πετρου it was distinctly asserted that Peter and Paul proclaimed the Gospel at Rome. For it is so I understand (its interpretor) what Lactantius says in his Institutions, iv. 21."

On Dionysius of Corinth, he remarks:—" This is signal evidence of the point in question, and free from the least objection. (Omni exceptione majus.) Some of the learned, however, have attempted to show its inaccuracy."

He thus concludes:—" As Peter's having proclaimed and died at Rome, is stated with so much unanimity almost from the first, and as no one ever said that his martyrdom took place elsewhere, and as our Lord himself clearly intimates that it was to be by crucifixion, I think that we may SAFELY ENOUGH attach credit to this story, (tuto satis huic historiæ fidem adhiberi posse existimo.) For who can believe that so eminent an apostle could have died in such obscurity that no one should have ever remembered where he died? Who can believe that, while other countries claimed their apostles, there was no city, no country, no church, to say that it had been ennobled by Peter's blood? .... During the last two centuries, however, learned men (viri docti) seeing that the advocates of the Papacy attached too much importance to this portion of its pretensions, began at first to have misgivings respecting it, and afterwards positively asserted that there was no reason for thinking that Peter had ever been at Rome at all."

Note.—1. He unconsciously betrays how little evidence satisfied him on the point in question, when he says that it is as " manifest" from what Ignatius says as from anything else; for but few thought the words of Ignatius any sign of the thing at all. 2. He was one of those who had been led by the papal writers to suppose that the city of Babylon did not exist in Peter's day. 3. He also makes the usual mistakes about Papias and Mark's Gospel 4. As a reason for his being satisfied with the evidences he adduces, he mentions the circumstance, that if we do not infer from them that Peter was put to death in Italy, we have no record of where he was put to death at all; and how could it have happened that there should have been this absence of all record on the subject? The answer is, that this is exactly what would have happened if Peter had adhered to the Jewish mission intrusted to him by our Lord, and had undergone his martyrdom at Babylon, as he himself tells us he expected soon to do. For it is admitted on all hands, that the early records of the church at Babylon have been lost, as well as those of almost all the eastern churches.

VI.—BARATIER.

(On the succession of the Bishops of Rome, c. i.)

This writer considered the thing proved as much as anything was capable of being proved at all, by the writers who preceded Eusebius. He therefore omits the last six of Bishop Pearson's references. He adds, however, thirteen Antenicene testimonies, which Pearson did not think available, and of which there are no less than ten that are not mentioned by any previous writers. These thirteen are as follows:—Clemens Romanus, the Apostolic Constitutions, Heracleon, the Recognitions, the Clementina or Actus Petri, Hegesippus, Lucius Charinus, Victor, an anonymous writer (in Euseb.), Hippolytus, Sextus Julius Africanus, Firmilian, and Stephen.

On the absence of any supposed allusion to Peter's having been in Europe in the first century, Baratier says,—" I confess that we have not any contemporaneous statement in express terms, of Peter's having been at Rome. But it is quite unnecessary that we should have been able to produce anything of the kind."

He also remarks: "How is it that no one contradicted the person that first set the story going? (Qui factum ut nemo eum refutaret?)"

On Ignatius, he says:—" Why does this writer mention Peter and Paul in this way together, if it were not that they were both at Rome? Why is Peter mentioned at all if he stood in no relation to the church of Rome? For as he did not write to the Romans if he did not live in their city, he had no more to do with them—he no more 'instructed' them than James, or John, or Judas did. It is evident, therefore, that Ignatius believed that Peter had been at Rome."

On the apostle Peter's Κηρυγμα, called in Latin the " Prædicatio Petri," he makes the same remark as Bishop Pearson, and adds, " For there can be no doubt that this is the work to which Lactantius alludes, (iv. 21,) for there was none other of that name in the time of Lactantius,—to say nothing of there being no other then generally known or considered as being genuine."

After mentioning Papias, and all the rest up to the times of Papias, Baratier says: "Look at all these testimonies (en multos testes), all flourishing in the very commencement of the second century—all living in the first age after the apostles! Who will have the hardihood to contradict all these? To them no objection can be raised; for they were neither able to deceive nor to be deceived. It is therefore absurd to say, as many have done, (quod dicere aggressi sunt multi,) that all the subsequent writers drew from Papias alone whatever errors they have adopted on this subject."

Of Victor, whose writings were then known to be lost, he says, that the testimony he had to produce from him was some of the most satisfactory that was to be met with anywhere, and introduces it with the words, "Propero itaque ad gravissimum testimonium," (I go on, therefore, at once to that which is among the most important proofs of all.) After he cites it, he adds: "Manifestum itaque est Petrum Romæ fuisse," (there can therefore be no doubt that Peter was at Rome.) The reader will see from the section of this work upon Victor, what Baratier calls most satisfactory testimony.

Baratier concludes thus: "Peter's Roman journey, therefore, is a public event which could not be feigned, and which it was in nobody's interest to feign; which squares in perfectly with the statements of contemporaneous writers, and is even indicated by some of them; which, after the first century, is mentioned by all who require to mention it, (quibus de eo loquendi occasio fuit,) which, in the subsequent centuries, was admitted by all writers, and was never questioned in ancient days by anybody. If this is not sufficient for historical certainty, I do not see what there is that we can now call certain."

This writer has a section (sec. vi.) on what he calls the "Fable, or Fiction about Peter's Five-and-Twenty years, and the origin of it," (Fabula de xxv. annis Petri, ejusque origo.)

Note.—The extreme confidence with which young Barntier draws his inferences, and cites nearly a dozen works, known by the Roman Catholics to be interpolated, spurious, or lost, and therefore not even mentioned by any of them, might lead a reader versed in such matters to fancy that he was making a jest of the whole business, and caricaturing the arguments of the Roman clergy. This, however, there is every reason to think, is not the case; although it is difficult to see how the thing could have been more effectually or cleverly done.

VII.—CORRESPONDENT IN THE "TIMES."

(*Times* for January 16, 1851.)

To the Editor of the Times. "Sir,—In reply to your several correspondents upon this subject, I beg to refer them to the following authorities:—

"That St. Peter before he went to Rome founded the See of Antioch is attested by Eusebius, Chron. and Hist. l. 3 c. 30; Origen, Hom. 6 in Luc.; St. Jerome, in Catal. c. 1; St. Innocent, Ep. 18 t. 2 conc. p. 1269; Pope Galasius, in his Roman Council, conc. t. 4, p. 1262; St. Chrysostom, and others.

"That St. Peter founded the church at Rome is expressly asserted by Caius, apud Eus. lib. 2 c. 24 *alias* 25, a priest of Rome under Pope Zephyrinus, A.D. 202 *ad* 218, who relates that his BODY was then (buried) on the Vatican Hill, and that of St. Paul on the Ostian Road. That Saints Peter and Paul were crowned with martyrdom at Rome is affirmed by Dionysius, Bishop of Corinth, in the second age. St. Irenæus, who lived in the same age, calls the church at Rome "the greatest and most ancient church, founded by the two glorious apostles, St. Peter and St. Paul. Eusebius IN SEVERAL PLACES, l. 2, c. 13 and 15, &c., mentions St. Peter being at Rome and THE SEVERAL IMPORTANT TRANSACTIONS of this apostle in that city. The fact is also mentioned by Origen, Hegesippus, Arnobius, St. Ambrose, St. Austin, St. Jerome, and several others. St. Cyprian, Ep. 55, *ad* Cornel. pap., calls Rome the Chair of St. Peter. Theodoret, lib. 2, c. 17, calls it his Throne, which the general councils and ecclesiastical writers through every age, and on every occasion, repeat.

"Eusebius, Euseb. in Chron., St. Jerome, and the old Roman Calendar published by Bucherius, say that St. Peter held the See of Rome twenty-five years, though he was often absent upon his apostolic functions in other countries. According to this chronology, St. Peter arrived in Rome in the second year of the reign of Claudius; of Christ, forty-two. Lactantius mentions only his last coming to Rome, under Nero, a few years before his martyrdom. (Lactant. de Mort. Persec.) See Baluze and Ceillier, t. 1. To come down to later times, Whiston, in the Memoirs of his own Life (p. 599), writes as follows:—' Mr. Bower, with some weak Protestants before him, almost pretends to deny that St. Peter ever was at Rome, concerning which matter take my own former words out of my three tracts (p. 53). Mr. Baratier proves most thoroughly, as Bishop Pearson has done before him, that St. Peter was at Rome. This is so clear in Christian antiquity, that it is a shame for a Protestant to confess that any Protestant ever denied it.' Mr. Baratier, a Protestant divine, printed at Utrecht, in 1740, his Chronological Inquiry about the Most Ancient Bishops of Rome, from Peter to Victor, in which he demonstrates that St. Peter was at Rome, as Bishop Pearson had done before by a learned dissertation in his posthumous works. Apologizing for the length of this letter, "I am, Sir, yours obediently,

"London, Jan. 15." "TRUTH."

Note.—1. The first paragraph only regards Antioch. Baronius informs us, that Peter founded that church while he was at Jerusalem, in the same way as he founded so many other churches. The Correspondent is mistaken, therefore, in thinking that we have any means of learning from the writers he quotes whether Peter was or was not at Antioch. It is from the New Testament alone that we learn this. Yet, strange to say, this is not mentioned as one of the credible sources of information cited upon this subject by the Correspondent in the *Times*. 2. As this writer does not agree with Cardinal Baronius and the rest of the Roman clergy, that a church might have been founded by Peter without Peter's presence, and by Paul without Paul's presence, he of course draws the usual erroneous inference from the words of Caius and Irenæus. 3. This is the only writer who ever fancied that it was IN SEVERAL PLACES that Eusebius supposed Peter to have left the East, which Eusebius does in only one; or that Eusebius alludes anywhere to what this writer so unaccountably calls "THE IMPORTANT TRANSACTIONS" of that apostle. 4. For the supposed martyrdom in Europe, he considers the passage from Dionysius as the best testimony that his church possesses, and gives no other. 5. Origen, it will be remembered, is only cited by Eusebius as mentioning Paul. 6. Hegesippus, as has been seen, has not left one word either about Paul or Peter. 7. Arnobius, St. Ambrose, St. Austin (Augustine), and St. Jerome, are likewise supposed by this writer to allude to the "important transactions;" but none of these Fathers make Europe the scene of the allegory with which they are connected. 8. St. Gildas, calling Canterbury Peter's Chair in the sixth century; Optatus, calling Carthage Peter's Chair in the fourth century; and Cyprian, calling Rome so in the third, do not prove Peter to have been in any of these places. It may be asked, therefore, why the Correspondent in the *Times* mentions this as a proof of Peter's having been at Rome. We cannot suppose that he meant to deceive. Will he inform us what he did mean by the quotation? 9. "Throne," in the Greek Fathers, has the same sense attached to it as "Chair." It does not imply presence, although Rome, by the same Theodoret here quoted, was called "Paul's Throne,"

"Paul's Chair," and the "See of St. Paul." This expression is so used in all such cases, without any reference to Paul's presence in that city, nor does it imply his being local bishop of that church. 10. The passage here, about the hypothesis of the Five-and-Twenty years is copied *verbatim* out of Butler's "Lives of the Saints," which proves that the writer made no researches of his own upon the subject of it. Not one word of it, however, is correct. Eusebius nowhere makes the statement imputed to him, and his Chronicon is lost. Jerome nowhere makes it in his own works, and his translations from Eusebius are admitted by the Roman clergy to be full of errors of all kinds. The old Roman Calendar does not say Peter ever on any occasion left the East, but the reverse. The Roman clergy themselves admit that this story of the five-and-twenty years was an invention or mistake; and not, perhaps, more than three or four writers (of course very modern) pretend to say that it was OFTEN that Peter went into Italy. 11. Father Palma, of the Propaganda at Rome, could have informed this writer that the work "De Mortibus Persecutorum" was *not* written by Lactantius, has not been even supposed for centuries to have been written by him, and was *never* known, or even heard of, by name until the seventeenth century; all which is fully admitted by the Father Ceillier, whom this writer, under some infatuation or misconception, cites to prove the contrary. 12. As far as a modern opinion on the general question can be of any use to him, this writer is entitled to Whiston's support, such as it is. But as to Peter's mission to the Jews of the East, and as to his having been crucified with his head downwards at Babylon, as he expected, we accept Whiston's words: "This is so clear in Christian antiquity, that it is a shame for a Protestant to confess that any Protestant (or for a Roman Catholic to confess that any Roman Catholic, for, *à fortiori*, he must have meant this also) ever denied it." 13. The church of Rome does not hold that Peter's "body" was ever buried on the Vatican Hill. One half of it, as well as the head, was always thought to be on the Ostian Road, by those Roman Catholics who thought it was at Rome at all. 14. Caius says that Peter had a tomb on the Ostian Road as well as on the Vatican Hill, but does not say what relics were in it, nor whether there were any in either of his tombs.

VIII.—Father J. S. M'Corry.

(In his Tract, "Was St. Peter ever at Rome?" Dolman, London, 1851.)

"The first witness that we shall bring forward is Clement the Roman, a disciple of St. Peter. After the persecution of Dioclesian had subsided, he wrote an Epistle to the Corinthians, in which he speaks of those who had suffered martyrdom AT ROME, and makes DISTINCT MENTION of St. Peter AS THE GREAT BISHOP WHO HAD FOUNDED AND GOVERNED THE ROMAN CHURCH. He says: 'Let us always have before our eyes those good apostles; Peter, who endured so many labours, and who, dying a martyr, departed to glory; and Paul, who obtained the reward of patience, and suffered martyrdom under the emperors. To these men who led so angelic a life, a vast multitude of the elect were added, who, rivalling one another in suffering, reproaches, and torments, have left behind them, for our sake, the most beautiful example.' Now here is a declaration from a contemporary writer, bearing evidence to the fact that the prince of the apostles died a martyr at Rome. Surely such a testimony must SPEAK VOLUMES.

"Our second witness is Ignatius. When led to martyrdom, about the year 105, he wrote a letter to the Romans, entreating them not to prevent, by their prayers, the fulfilment of his desire, (to suffer martyrdom.) He begins thus: 'Ignatius to the sanctified church that presides in the country of the Romans,—I do not command you, as Peter and Paul; they were apostles; I am an insignificant person.' Now this proves that the Romans had been taught by St. Peter and St. Paul, and had received their 'commands,' and OF COURSE shows that both apostles had been at Rome.

"Our third witness is Papias. Papias TELLS US (in Eusebius) that Mark records in his Gospel what he had HEARD FROM ST. PETER AT ROME; and, HE, moreover, TELLS US, that St. Peter wrote his Epistle from Rome, calling it by the mystic appellation of Babylon. THE WORDS of Papias are: ' Which Epistle of Peter was written at Rome, although he calls that city by the name of Babylon.'

"The fourth witness is Irenæus. He says:—' As it would be very tedious to enumerate in this volume the successions of all the churches, we shall confound our adversaries by referring to that church which is the greatest, the most venerable, and universally known,— that church founded and established by the two most glorious apostles, Peter and Paul.' Again, he adds,— ' St. Matthew wrote his Gospel among the Jews, in the Hebrew tongue. Peter and Paul PREACHED at Rome and founded the church there.'

"The fifth witness is Dionysius of Corinth. He says,—' Peter and Paul having both COME INTO our city of Corinth, and having instructed us in the doctrine of Christianity, WENT FORTH TO Italy, and instructed you also, Romans, and suffered martyrdom at the same time.'

"The sixth witness is Caius—a Roman—whose words are peculiarly TOUCHING. He declares:—' I can point out to you the trophies of the apostles PETER AND PAUL. For whether you direct your footsteps to the Vatican, or to the Ostian Way, the trophies of those who founded the Roman church present themselves to your view.'

"The seventh witness is Tertullian. His testimony is exceedingly telling. 'ISTA quam felix Ecclesia!—O church, peculiarly happy, into which the apostles poured forth their whole doctrine with their blood. WHERE Peter was crucified, like HIS DIVINE MASTER; and Paul, like THE BAPTIST, was beheaded; WHERE John the Apostle (after having been thrown into a caldron of seething oil) came forth unhurt, and was banished to the island.'

"The eighth witness is Origen:—'Peter is thought to have preached to the Jews who were dispersed through Pontus, Galatia, Bithynia, Cappadocia and Asia. He afterwards came to Rome, and was nailed to a cross with his head towards the ground.'

"The ninth witness is Optatus of Milevi. Arguing with a Donatist adversary he says:—'You cannot deny that you know that the Chair of Peter, first of all was fixed in the city of Rome, in which Peter, the head of all the apostles, sat. . . . . Peter first sat in that Chair, and was succeeded by Linus.'

"The tenth witness is Eusebius, who says:—'During the reign of Claudius, Peter CAME TO Rome, by the providence of God.' Again, HE SAYS IN HIS CHRONICON, 'Peter having founded the church at Antioch, came to Rome, where he preached the gospel, and was bishop of that city for twenty-five years.'

"The eleventh witness is Orosius, who writes:— 'Claudius governed fourteen years; at the beginning of his reign Peter came to Rome.'

"Our twelfth witness is St. Jerome, who in his Catalogue of Ecclesiastical Writers, thus speaks:—'Simon Peter, after having governed the church at Antioch, came to Rome in the second year of Claudius. He put to shame Simon Magus there, and governed the Roman church for twenty-five years; when in the fourteenth year of Nero he was crowned with martyrdom.' In the same work he tells us: 'His BODY was buried at Rome in the Vatican, near the Triumphal Way; and his feast is celebrated by the veneration of the whole city.' Appropriately to this subject, we may remark that the illustrious orator of Constantinople, St. John Chrysostom, while discoursing on the Last Judgment, bursts out into a most eloquent apostrophe, alluding to St. Peter's tomb at Rome.

"We may finally refer to Arnobius, who distinctly tells us that Simon Peter exposed THE DIABOLICAL ARTIFICES of Simon Magus at Rome, to Hegesippus, to Cyril of Jerusalem, to St. Ambrose, to St. Augustine, and to many other writers of unexceptionable character. It would seem, however, an idle parade of research to bring forward any more testimonies from the ancient writers, whether from the first, second, third, or fourth centuries, corroborative of our position, and altogether superfluous to indulge in any lengthened comments on those already adduced."

On 1 Peter v. 13, he says, page 5:—"The word Babylon, used in that epistle, ALL THE ANCIENT FATHERS understand to be Rome." And again, page 29: "All the old writers understand the word 'Babylon,' here used by St. Peter, to mean Rome; and they assign various reasons why he gave the ancient city of Rome that designation. The historians to whom I refer are Papias, Clement of Alexandria, Eusebius, and others whom IT IS NOT NECESSARY to mention. The great ecclesiastical historian, Eusebius, DISTINCTLY TELLS US that St. Peter called Rome by the name Babylon, BECAUSE IT WAS THEN THE CENTRE OF PAGAN IDOLATRY! Dollinger writes: 'ALL THE FATHERS understand the word Babylon, used in St. Peter's Epistle, to signify Rome. The Jews had been driven from Babylon and Seleucia a short time previous to the writing of this Epistle; AND WE CANNOT SUPPOSE THAT ST. PETER, THE APOSTLE OF THE CIRCUMCISION, SHOULD TRAVEL TO SO DISTANT A CITY, IN WHICH HE COULD FIND NONE OF HIS NATION.' We, moreover, contend that . . . Babylon of the Assyrians had long since fallen."

Note.—1. The *translations* of this writer are invaluable, as showing to what lengths a few of the Roman clergy now among us go, and are obliged to go, upon this subject and these passages. Some of the more remarkable words and clauses are here indicated by capitals. 2. He is one of those who are so much misled as to what the Fathers have said of Mark's Gospel. He thinks they said it was composed in Europe, under Peter's *surveillance*, and that even Papias tells us this. 3. He makes great use of the word "preached" instead of "promulgated" or "proclaimed," as a translation of κηρυξας: and makes the usual inferences from this expression; and from the apostles founding a church in one city while they were stationed in another. 4. He is mistaken in supposing that Caius, in the only passage that we have of his, mentions the name of either Peter or Paul. There is nothing of the kind in the text. 5. The Latin word quoted by Father M'Corry, to assist the construction he places upon Tertullian's passage, is not in any MS., and no Roman-catholic editor pretends it is. 6. He states, as if casually, that St. Jerome said a portion (from other sources we learn one-half) of Peter's relics were, in Jerome's day, supposed to be on the Vatican Hill. He does not, however, say that relics in a city make it probable that a saint was put to death there. All the Roman clergy know that no such inference could be drawn, however likely the uninitiated are to fall into this mistake. 7. He says that Hegesippus and the rest of the Fathers mention the DIABOLICAL ARTIFICES of the Samaritan as having occurred in Europe. In this he is quite mistaken. Not one of them mentions even the Fiery Chariot as having occurred there. The pseudo-Hegesippus, who took it from Jacobus de Voragine, and from the pseudo-Abdias, appears to have deceived him. 8. He is also mistaken in thinking that all the Fathers, or a few of the Fathers, or even one of the Fathers, thought that when Peter wrote "the city of Babylon" he meant the city of Rome. This writer seems to have taken too many things upon trust from other authors; and yet, about Peter's being supposed to have gone to Rome, we cordially accept the principle that he quotes from Father Dollinger—"WE CANNOT SUPPOSE THAT ST. PETER, THE APOSTLE OF THE CIRCUMCISION, SHOULD TRAVEL TO SO DISTANT A CITY, IN WHICH HE COULD FIND NONE OF HIS NATION." Rome was four times as far from Jerusalem as Babylon was, and frequently had no Jews at all in it.

ADDENDA.

Notes on Jerome's two alleged Misinterpretations of Eusebius, 2, 14.
[See pp. 243—5, of this work.]

ALTHOUGH those who are conversant with the early writers of the church, will see at once that the "*pergit*" and "*mittitur*" of these passages do not speak of a journey at all, but only of ecclesiastical action; yet as some writers of influence have inadvertently given countenance to the other interpretation, and as there may therefore be some less experienced readers who will continue to think it probable that Jerome, from his ignorance of Greek, intended to translate Euseb. 2, 14, of a journey rather than of a book, and intended to impute to Eusebius the notion that Peter had come in person from Babylon into Europe for a short time " to storm the fiery chariot" after he had written his First Epistle to his Christian neighbours (παρεπιδημοις,) in Pontus, Galatia, Cappadocia, Asia, and Bithynia, I have thought it advisable to exhibit here at one view such facts and principles as will help us to a just appreciation of the inaccuracies and inconsistencies which such an interpretation of Jerome's language would involve, and some of which would have apprised Jerome (even if his partial knowledge of Greek had not done so) that such a translation of Euseb. 2, 14, as that which these readers here impute to him, could not be the correct one.

1. The whole passage from Nicephorus (xiv. 39) is as follows:—Και γαρ πρωτος Ο των Αποστολων κορυφαιος Πετρος της Ρωμαιων καθηγησατο πολεως · ειτα και επι την Αλεξανδρου πολιν πρωτος κληρω μεταβαινει. Εν αις Λινον

και Μαρκον χειροτονησας, εφ' ετερας πολεις αντριχιν; thus translated in the Roman editions: Nam primus apostolorum ille princeps Petrus Romanæ urbis gubernavit ecclesiam; deinde primus etiam Alexandriam sorte TRANSIT;—such expressions alluding probably to the deputations sent up to Jerusalem from the different synagogues or Christian Jews of Europe, Asia, and Africa, all located in different parts of that central city, and to each of which, as occasion required, the Apostles could address themselves, going as it were, in each case, to the very city from which the deputation came. From the foregoing quotation, we see that there is no grammatical necessity for our understanding the "pergit" and the "mittitur" of a real journey.

2. There is no room whatever to doubt that the words in Euseb. 2, 14, here translated by Jerome, are not about a journey, but about a book (p. 158), &c. The Greek preposition as well as the context proves that. Why, then, should we suppose that Jerome's ignorance of Greek misled him where it is not necessary to suppose this?

3. All the Fathers as well as Eusebius speak of Peter's relation with the Fiery Chariot of Simon Magus in figurative terms, and Jerome's own expression "expugnandum" shows in the clearest manner that he is himself doing the same thing as the rest of them. Why, then, seek to force a literal interpretation upon any of his words here, merely to make it appear that he was mistranslating Euseb. 2, 14?

4. No ancient writer of any kind has said one word about a journey of Peter's into Europe in the reign of Claudius. Let us, then, consider well what pretext we have for supposing that Jerome's words might possibly (as is supposed) advert to such an event.

5. If there had been such a journey to speak of on the occasion of the Fiery Chariot, is it not quite certain that Eusebius would have mentioned it?

6. From the Acts of the Apostles we learn, as all Roman-catholic scholars are agreed (p. 164), that Peter remained constantly in Syria and Palestine, until after the fourth year of Claudius. Why, then, should we seek

to interpret Jerome's translation so as to make it contradict the very Scriptures themselves? This would not be treating that Father's words with fairness.

7. No ancient writer of any kind after Jerome's time has alluded to those passages as being about a real journey, which it is incredible that all should have omitted doing if that were the purport of the passages.

8. No writer after Jerome's time alludes to those passages, even in their figurative sense, for nearly a century, and they are then only mentioned by a French Bishop and a Spanish one. (p. 269.)

9. The proceedings against Rome and the Gnostic heresy are here distinctly described as having been taken *after* Peter had written his first Epistle at Babylon, and not, as some imagine, *before* he went to Babylon; for Jerome everywhere recognises the fact, that it was at Babylon that that " prædicatio" was written to Peter's Jewish "neighbours" (παρεπιδήμοις), as Peter himself calls those to whom he wrote it. (p. 67, 168, 170)

10. But further: the whole purport of these passages seems to have been to transfer Peter's twenty-five years' episcopate of the Gentile Church, mentioned in the old Roman Calendar, from the commencement to the end of Peter's apostleship. Whether Jerome did this through mistake, or whether he had a reason for doing so, and if so, what his reason was, it is not now either easy or important to determine. The confusion, however, which results from his having done so is so great, that although this point is not immediately connected with the signification of the "pergit" or the "mittitur," it will not be out of place to point some of it out here to those who think that this transfer was not a blunder on Jerome's part, or that the passage which contains it can have any ecclesiastical authority.

11. The old Roman Calendar, published by Bucherius and Henschenius, had already appeared some twenty years before Jerome died, and is evidently the source from which he drew the twenty-five years' episcopate which he has embodied in a confused manner in these two so-called translations (p. 229, &c.), as until that time there is no

trace of the expression in patristic literature. Eusebius, to whom some attribute this expression, never speaks of Peter as a Bishop at all, much less Bishop of Rome. The Roman-catholic commentators admit that he does not (p. 206), nor was he called a Bishop by any writer until Jerome's time.

12. This old Roman Calendar distinctly says that Peter was Bishop of Rome only until the second year of Nero,—*i. e.*, until about twelve years before his martyrdom, at Babylon,—and that his episcopate at Rome began under Tiberius, immediately after the Ascension; whereas Jerome says that Peter did not begin to be Bishop of Rome for twelve years after the Ascension (viz., until the second year of Claudius), and that he did not cease to be so until Nero's persecution reached him at Babylon, —*i. e.*, for twelve years after Linus had been established local Bishop of Rome, as mentioned in Eusebius and the old Roman Calendar (p. 231), thus making it appear that at first there was no bishop of Rome at all for twelve years, and that at last there were two bishops of Rome together for twelve years.

13. The Church of Rome had been already in existence and even flourishing for twelve whole years in the second year of the reign of Claudius. (p. 63, 73, 230.)

14. Linus, the first local bishop of Rome, was appointed, according to Eusebius and the old Roman Calendar, exactly 25 years after the Church of Rome was first founded, about 12 years before Peter's martyrdom on the Euphrates, and in the 2nd year of Nero's reign when Paul was sent as a prisoner to Rome. (p. 231.) This Linus, (the Roman-catholic authorities further inform us) was ordained on that occasion by Paul. (p. 56.)

15. As the old Roman Calendar exhibits Peter as general Bishop for thirty-five years of all the Christian churches that had not local bishops from A.D. 30 to A.D. 65, and as Bishop of Rome in no other sense than as he was Bishop of England, of Alexandria, and of every other place in the world where there was a Christian church (231, 165-6), Jerome clearly did not consider that to have been Bishop of Rome for 25 of those years, implied the having left the East at all. We cannot,

with anything like fairness, impose such a sense upon the words which he employs to express this relation of the apostle to the Church of Rome.

16. As Peter's general episcopate lasted thirty-five years, *i.e.* from the Ascension to his death at Babylon, (as Father Henschenius and the old Roman Calendar explain,) and as his episcopate in any given place was spoken of as terminating on the appointment of the first local bishop in that place (p. 230-1), so Evodius, the first local Bishop of Antioch (p. 56), is described in one of these passages as having been installed at Antioch eighteen years before Linus, St. Paul's Bishop, was installed at Rome, and about the same time as the church of Christ is said to have first assailed the Gnostic heresy in this latter city.

17. To say that "Peter was bishop of Rome for five-and-twenty years and made a journey into Europe in the reign of Claudius" (if Jerome had written about a journey) would be precisely the same thing as to say that "he made this journey into Europe in the reign of Claudius, and was Bishop of Rome five-and-twenty years," notwithstanding all the efforts that have been made to make it appear that these two expressions are different, and that a residence at Rome of five-and-twenty years is implied in the latter phrase although not in the former one. To pretend this is merely seeking to turn the ignorance or inadvertence of one's readers to account. In Peter's case the old Roman Calendar clearly shows us that no residence was ever implied in his episcopate anywhere, or at any time, whether under Nero, or under Claudius, or under Caligula, or under Tiberius; for in the fifth century he was said to be Bishop of Rome under all these Emperors.

18. Nor does his having been put to death by Nero imply his not having been put to death among the Lost Sheep of the House of Israel on the Euphrates, it being admitted that Nero's persecution extended to Babylon (p. 42—4), as Peter himself tells us.

19. Nor does his having heralded or proclaimed or preached the gospel anywhere imply (as our English word "preach" would now do,) his having been in that

place, but merely that he did so by letters or messengers, or even by words addressed to the natives of that place at Jerusalem. (p. 73-4.) We know, for instance, that it was by letters from Babylon that he " preached " to his " neighbours," (παρεπιδημοις) in the five Asiatic Provinces mentioned in the first of these two passages in nearly the same order in which he names them in that " Prædicatio" (1 Peter i.), and that it was by the book called "The Preaching," that he did so at Rome when "storming" the Fiery Chariot. (p. 160.)

20. Even if, notwithstanding all the contradictions such a conclusion involves, we nevertheless conclude, as some learned men have done, that Jerome's imperfect knowledge of Greek led him to suppose that the words επι την Ρωμην χειραγωγεισθαι, signified " Romam proficisci," and that Eusebius intended there to speak of a journey, yet we see clearly that what Jerome would thus have attributed to Eusebius is not, as Cardinal Wiseman and Father McCorry imagine, Baronius's absurd hypothesis about Peter's having lived five-and-twenty years at a distance from "the Lost Sheep of the House of Israel," which no ancient writer says, and which Baronius only inferred from Peter's being called Bishop of Rome for that length of time from the Ascension. All that Jerome can in any case be supposed to attribute here to Eusebius, is merely a statement (taken from 2, 14) to the effect that Peter left the East for a short time and a definite purpose, the year after Caligula's death, immediately after the events described in the 8th Chapter of the Acts of the Apostles. But that such terms as those here used by Jerome do not necessarily imply a journey, in Ecclesiastical writers, is well known to all who are conversant with the ancient literature of the church, and manifest in the passage already given from Nicephorus. It is at all events most certain that, even if Jerome did mean to impute the alleged statement to Eusebius, he was mistaken about what Eusebius said, and that Eusebius was as far from any such idea as Jerome himself was.

FINIS.

www.ingramcontent.com/pod-product-compliance
Lightning Source LLC
Chambersburg PA
CBHW030008240426
43672CB00007B/869